Please return/renew this item by the last date shown.
Items may also be renewed by the internet*

https://library.eastriding.gc

* Please note a PIN will be
- this can be obtained from

D1464958

THE GUV'NOR

LEE WORTLEY AND ANTHONY THOMAS

REVEALED

THE UNTOLD STORY OF LENNY McLEAN

JOHN BLAKE

Published by John Blake Publishing Ltd,
3 Bramber Court, 2 Bramber Road,
London W14 9PB, England

www.johnblakebooks.com

www.facebook.com/johnblakebooks 🅵
twitter.com/jblakebooks 🅵

This edition published in 2017

ISBN: 978 1 78606 449 3

British Library Cataloguing-in-Publication Data:

A catalogue record for this book is available from the British Library.

Design by www.envydesign.co.uk

Printed in Great Britain by CPI Group (UK) Ltd

1 3 5 7 9 10 8 6 4 2

Papers used by John Blake Publishing are natural, recyclable products made
from wood grown in sustainable forests. The manufacturing processes
conform to the environmental regulations of the country of origin.

Every attempt has been made to contact the relevant copyright-holders, but
some were unobtainable. We would be grateful if the appropriate people
could contact us.

John Blake Publishing is an imprint of Bonnier Publishing
www.bonnierpublishing.com

This book is dedicated to Billy Wortley,
greatly missed 'Uncle Bilbo', who sadly passed away
during the writing of this book. With love from
Lee and the entire Wortley family.

CONTENTS

FOREWORD BY
KELLY McLEAN

It will have been nineteen years on 28 July of this year, 2017, since my dad passed away, and I have to say, it still feels like only yesterday that we said goodbye to him. It has also been almost a year now since I joined forces with one of the authors of this book, Lee Wortley, to set up a site named 'Dedicated to my Dad The Guv'nor' in honour of my father and his memorable legacy. Over the past nineteen years my dad's book has brought so much joy and sanctuary to a great number of people from the four corners of the world.

Our site, along with Anthony Thomas's 'The Lenny Mclean' Facebook page, fills me with a fantastic sense of achievement, accepted with immense pride on behalf of my late father. Now believe me when I say this, my dad would have been so proud of the support from his increasing number of fans – an amazing wealth of loyal fans brought together by the fine work of my dear friends, Lee Wortley and Anthony Thomas. These boys have never given up on promoting Dad, and for that he would have been so proud.

As I read through this book and the stories that many of my dad's friends and colleagues have taken the time to share it greatly accentuates with detail a mark left upon these people by the sheer power and influence exuded from Dad's larger-than-life character. Lee and Ant have worked very hard to bring it all to life, in this, their fantastic tribute to my dear father, Leonard John McLean.

I have on so many occasions tried my best to let the boys know just how proud my dad would have been of the two of them, and I hope that in my words written here, they will finally realise it. I can just see him now, Dad sat in his pants in his favourite chair, roll-up in one hand, and a cup of my mum's fine tea in the other, laughing hysterically at the stories written here for all the world to see. He would have revelled in it. As you all know, my dad was also one of the finest storytellers around – 'The Gangster Keats', as Lee calls him.

Dad was a charismatic showman and let's be honest, a proper fucking show-off too. He loved nothing more than to play to a crowd, so if he was here now, holding this book in his hands, and you just happened to be in his company, then let me tell you this, you would not have been leaving until he had read you every last fucking word! Oh, and then of course, you would have had to read it back to him too.

Joking apart, and to get a little serious for a moment, Dad was more than just a street fighter, cobble fighter, bare-knuckle fighter or whatever else people have him down as. My dad was a thinker; he was sharp and witty, with a hidden ability to create something from nothing, and as the boys have accented so well in this book, answer me this, how many 'bouncers' do you know of that have gone on to build a life as diverse as my father's, from fighting bare-knuckles on a gypsy camp to acting in a blockbuster movie with the likes of Bruce Willis? Make no mistake, my dad had it all, and this is fantastically documented for your eyes to feast upon in this book, a fabulous UNTOLD insight into not just the well-known fearsome fighter, but the life behind the man, the man that I am truly honoured to have called my father, Lenny McLean.

In closing, from myself, Kelly McLean, and the rest of the McLean family, past and present, I would just like to take a moment to say a very well done to my dear friends, Lee and Anthony. I am positive that in your hands you have a book to be very proud of, and I wish you all the luck in the world, not that I think you need it one bit.

Good luck, God Bless, and thank you from the bottom of my heart.

Kelly McLean,
January 2017

INTRODUCTION
BY LEE WORTLEY AND
ANTHONY THOMAS

As a few of you know, we have both been massive Lenny McLean fans for over twenty years and have run websites, blogs and Facebook pages for a similar amount of time. Over the many years we have managed to keep Lenny's name alive and growing in popularity as every day passes, and now today, between us, we have accumulated over 12,000 loyal members and also a network of over 100,000 too. We are convinced Lenny would at least be ultimately proud of what we have achieved. The first seeds for this book were planted over six years ago when Anthony started collecting stories for a follow-up to a book he had already written on Lenny called *The Guv'nor Through the Eyes of Others* (John Blake Publishing , 2007). Lee had also contemplated writing a book on Lenny himself after speaking to Peter Gerrard (co-author of *The Guv'nor*, who Lenny referred to as his 'book man') and after we both got back in touch in our fight to keep Lenny's name alive, we started speaking regularly, which we've done for the past two years. It was about a year ago that we decided to join forces. Since that day, we have been flat out, writing this book. We have made so many new friends, and we have enjoyed the experience and the ride so much.

Seeing our words finally in print makes us feel very proud indeed. Proud of the fact that all of our hard work over the years has finally and unequivocally paid off. We have been told on numerous occasions by so many people that Lenny too would be proud in the knowledge that all of these people have taken the time to recall and relive his many stories. So with this in mind, we truly hope that those of you who have bought this book will enjoy reading it as much as we have enjoyed researching and writing it.

Visit us at our dedicated sites...

The Lenny McLean – Facebook Page
https://www.facebook.com/groups/617629598252635/

Dedicated to My Dad The Guv'nor
https://www.facebook.com/groups/LENNYMCLEAN/

CHAPTER 1

THE HAYESY DAYS OF GODWIN HOUSE

As a great many of you will already be aware by now, the Hayes family played a major part in Lenny McLean's life, growing up in Hoxton, East London – Lenny being the second-eldest of six, Linda being the eldest, then Barry, Lorraine, Raymond ('Kruger') and the youngest, Sherry. As for most people growing up between the fifties and as far up as the nineties, if you're anything like we were as kids, there was always one family that stood out on your block, probably because the children were of a similar age.

Well, the McLean family, consisting of Lenny's father, Leonard, Len's mother, Rosie, and of course the five kids I mentioned a few lines back, all lived in Godwin House and the Hayes family moved in right above the McLeans, into flat number forty-two. Alfie Hayes' and Lenny's friendship has been documented on numerous occasions, most notably by Lenny himself in his best-selling book, *The*

Guv'nor, and in Anthony's first book, *The Guv'nor: Through the Eyes of Others*, but we never really got to hear from any of the other Hayes family members, until now that is. In June 2016, myself and Anthony managed to track them down with the very kind help and assistance of the late Alfie Hayes' son, Robert. In a short but very sweet informal chat I had with two of the remaining sisters, Patsy and Hilda, I clicked 'record' on my little Dictaphone machine, and those two sweet ladies, still sharp as a tac, reminisced back to the days spent in Godwin House, and this is what they had to say...

'The McLeans' parents were sort of different to my mum and dad,' recalls Patsy Hayes. 'My mum and dad were very strict. I mean, Rosie and Leonard McLean were strict as well, of course, back in those days, it's just that my father was a lot more military in our upbringing, I think. Leonard, who was Lenny's dad, was a lovely man, very handsome he was, and sharply dressed all of the time. My father also knew Lenny's great-uncle, Jimmy Spinks, very well – another great fighting man from Hoxton. Lenny, by all accounts, was an out-and-out Spinks, this fact ultimately proven by his Lenny's amazing fighting prowess, owed undeniably to his Spinks' family DNA make-up. Jimmy was a fearless man of Hoxton, and also highly regarded by the Kray family.

'Also, Jimmy's wife was big pals with my mum – she still visited Mum, I think the last time I saw her was at my mum's eightieth birthday. Of course her husband, Jimmy, had long since passed away, the men in that family all seemed to die young. I think

Lenny's dad, Leonard, was only around for a couple of years of us moving into Godwin House, and it was very strange in that day and age, believe it or not, for him to die of tuberculosis because it wasn't really heard of by the fifties.

'Lenny's mum, Rosie, was quite close to my elder sister of the same name, but me, I never really knew her all that well. I do know one thing, though; she was a real "Hoxtonite" as we referred to them, a thoroughbred Hoxton girl – her personality sort of borne out of the area. She was very house-proud, almost to the point of obsessive, if I'm to be brutally honest. It's funny really because she would sling all of the children outside, Lenny included, while she did the washing and cleaning. This one time, my older sister, Rose, was over at their house and she went into the bathroom and Rosie the mum was bathing Lenny and Kruger using a box of Tide washing powder – there was suds and bubbles all over the place. She was very different to us, Lenny's mum, Rosie. I remember coming home from work one day on my lunch break – you see, I worked quite local and so I would come home for my lunch – anyway, I only got half an hour back in those days, just shows you how times have changed. So, as I'm coming down the stairs to go back to work, I bumps into Rose and she said to me, "Could you go down to the shops and get me some cigarettes?" I said, "No, I can't – I've got to be back at work at one." I thought to myself, what a bloody cheek! She was just very forward and up-front like that, was Lenny's mum – I suppose that's where he got his confidence from. Like I said, different to his dad, because his dad wouldn't have asked you to do such a thing as that.'

Patsy also remembered the time when she borrowed Lenny's bike:

'Lenny said to me, "You can go on it for a penny an hour, but don't have it all day." Anyway, I took no notice and kept it for hours on end. I don't think Lenny was very happy and I do remember being very frightened to eventually take it back!'

Lenny's reaction to Patsy keeping his bike all day will come to light at the end of this piece on the Hayes family.

Patsy continued:

'Another funny little thing happened one day while we were walking along past the school with Lenny and his mum. As we're walking along I said, "Rose, Lenny's got his shoes on the wrong feet," and Rose said, "Do you know, I thought there was something wrong with his feet!" She hadn't realised Lenny must have been walking along like that all day, with two left feet. It's funny, I suppose, really.'

Talking at length to Patsy and her sister Hilda, both agreed that Lenny was definitely from Spinks' stock. Lenny and his mum, Rosie, were definitely from that fighting Spinks' background as Rosie McLean wasn't one to suffer fools lightly, not for one minute. They went on to say that not many of them really went into the McLean household. It

4

was different to their house: all of the kids, especially the McLeans, came into their house. They were the first ones on the block to have a TV, so it was almost like a cinema in their house on certain days. Also, when Jim Irwin moved in after Lenny's dad had passed away, you could feel the tension with the kids, especially Lenny. And as Patsy says, being very good pals with Lorraine McLean ('Boo'), she remembers that Boo seemed very on edge and scared of Jim Irwin. The sisters also added that if everyone had been privy to just what was going on with him and how he was treating those children, something would have been done about it. Hilda takes up the story...

'The last time most of our family saw Lenny was at his Guv'ner's Pub. We were invited to the opening, must have been around 1994. Lenny welcomed us into his new world as if we had never been apart, and Alfie [Hayes] and Lenny looked like the two little urchins that they were forty or more years previous. One thing he did say with regard to the earlier story of Patsy borrowing his bike, though: Lenny shouted her over at the pub and said, "Eh, Patsy, I think you owe me a few bob still for the loan of my bike. Come on, let's have it, sweetheart," to which Patsy replied, "OK, Len, you got me! Must be at least three pence by now, eh, Lenny?" and they laughed as they all reminisced over those days in Hoxton and Godwin House.'

ALFIE FISHER

'When I was younger, we moved into Geffrye Court on the top floor. Len's cousin, Johnny Wall, was also living on the same landing and Lenny was on the ground floor. When I went to Daneford School on my first day I met up with Lenny, who was with Tommy Webb, who also lived in Haggerston, and both of them were two years older than me so I knew I was in good company. After a few weeks Lenny and Tommy had a row with a teacher named Mr Baron – Lenny threatened to poleaxe him and Mr Baron disappeared. Lenny and Tommy then wrecked the class. Instead of leaving, I hung around and was then taken to the headmaster's office and I ended up getting expelled. I was then moved to another school and by the time I came back, Lenny and Tommy had left.'

CHRIS REID

'I grew up in Hoxton and Lenny lived the other end of Hoxton to me, and as you all know, at that age, it seems like the other side of the world. But when your name is Lenny McLean distance means nothing. I was two years younger, but would watch him do some good stuff. He was very cool and calm and never threatened anyone; he just did it and walked away. He would hop over small fences and stuff that we would have to climb.

'I recall once when the Cypriots came to the UK and they were right nutters. One was called Mustapha and he had a sharpened screwdriver and threatened to use it on us. We were only kids and were on a bomb site in Wilmer Gardens. Lenny must have been about thirteen and wore an army belt. Well, without a word he unclipped it, swung it over his head and caught him square on the chops, then Lenny casually walked away, muttering, "Fuckin' wanker!" We never had any trouble off Mustapha again.

'In Hoxton, during the very early seventies, a young Jewish girl named Carol sang in the local pubs professionally with the likes of Ricky Stevens in, amongst other places, The Horns in Shoreditch. She wanted her own flat so she asked the local mini-cab company if she could do a bit of driving for them. They laughed at her as there were no girl cabbies at that time. She insisted and asked for night shifts to get the best money. They finally gave her a job and she started doing pub trips. One evening shortly after, Lenny got in her cab and he heard her story but to her surprise he refused to pay her, but he said, "Girl, I don't pay for cabs round here but I tell you what, I will let it be known I look after you and you won't have any punters take the piss!" From then on she got the prime jobs with the faces – Lenny always kept his word.

'One mad memory I have of Lenny was him riding on top of any car through Hoxton to "save his legs" – obviously, not a soul ever complained. He would jump on the bonnet of any passing car and ride through the Hoxton streets on the bonnets, even strangers' cars.'

TERRY JAMES CONWAY

'I grew up with Lenny in Hoxton. My father was a well-known hardman named Jimmy Conway, who even Lenny respected. Lenny was a great mate and a good laugh, considering his tough upbringing. He was a bit of a loner when he was younger, though, was Lenny, and everyone knew you didn't mess with him. We were at a party around the end of the sixties in Geffrye Court and we were all on those Purple Heart tablets that were all a go at the time. Lenny had crashed out and one of our mates had nicked a bag with all of Johnny Walls' gear in. Johnny's woke up and gone mad, and then shook Lenny to wake him up to find out who nicked it. Lenny pinned me up against the wall by the neck – I will always remember that. I had an apology later, when Lenny and Johnny found out who had taken it. I'll leave it to your imagination with regard to just what happened to him…'

TONY STARBROOK

'Lenny's brother Kruger was my best mate at school, so obviously I knew Lenny very well too. Lenny was a top bloke – he was a fierce man mountain, but if you knew the man he had a heart of gold.

'He once told me to fear no one but fear everyone. Sounds strange but I know exactly what he meant.'

Tony went on to say that the majority of people never realised just how kind and generous Lenny was, and of course, as remarked upon by many in our book, this was simply the way he would always remain. Tony tells us that when he was about fifteen years old, he and his mum, who was wheelchair-bound because of arthritis, were in a pie'n'mash shop in the area:

'Now Len at this time would be about twenty-one and so he was only young himself but his reputation was such that you did as he said or else. So anyway, Tony says that three guys who were not from the manor [area] had fucked around with the salt pot and as he went to salt his mum's food, it went all over the place, like a fucking big white mound all over his mum's grub. Anyway, Tony kicked off a bit with these lads, but remembers that he was only a young boy. Now this bunch of fellas weren't just young boys of his age, Tony says, they were all in their twenties – much the same as our boy, Lenny. Anyway, Lenny just happened to be sitting in there at the time. With that, and Len being Len, he gets up from his table and comes over to this bunch of fellas and makes them apologise to my mum and also made them buy us another lot of pie'n'mash. Lenny then took them outside and educated them in his own special way – he did love his own people.

'I remember once we were in Brooksie's pub in Hoxton, sitting at a table. Lenny told my dad, Jack Starbrook, who was a bit of a lad himself back in the day, 'Everyone can fight, Jack – I'm just better at it,' and he laughed to himself.

'Also, his paper shop was once robbed and within thirty-six hours he knew who did it. Rumour has it they lost parts of their anatomy. What's more, no police investigation was involved – you dealt with things yourself in them days.'

Tony went on to talk about Len's reputation:

'The thing is, Lenny was impossible to hurt. We used to fuck about, sort of sparring with Len. He was just way too powerful for any of us boys, and fast – fuck me, you'd have to have your wits about you when Len was flinging his fists around! I'm telling you, Lee, not a man alive could knock Lenny down when he's coming at you on the cobbles. Lenny had a fucking head of steel – I mean, his fingers were like a bunch of bananas, for fuck's sake!'

Tony says the fact is, Lenny was an awesome fighter – 'I'm sure the man was a fucking freak, in the nicest possible sense!' He added that he was so sad to hear of Lenny's passing, just at a time when he was starting to live a quiet and mostly untroubled life. Lenny Boy will always be remembered fondly in Hoxton and of course in many a Starbrook household.

ALAN REES

'I knew Lenny McLean when I was a teenager and he used to regularly visit my local pub, The Lion & Lamb, in Hoxton. Anyway, the pub at that time was frequented by a lot of local villains and was a meeting point for most of them before moving on elsewhere. There were always rows with something firing off on a regular basis. It was also frequented by Len's brother, Kruger, and his cousin, Tony, who was a very funny bloke.

'When Lenny entered the pub, everybody knew it immediately because of his stature and presence. Now I must be honest and say that at that time he was not everybody's flavour of the month, but he was always fine with me and my brother, Dennis, who sometimes used to run the pub with my Uncle

George and friends. Unfortunately, because of his volatile character he did put some locals on edge and any small incident could spark him off, but generally he was fine with the regulars.

'At that time there were two shove ha'penny boards in the pub because of its popularity with the villains who believe it or not were all competent players and on some Sunday mornings there could be up to thirty players. Lenny used to play sometimes, although he was only a low-average player and on a particular Sunday morning a doubles tournament was arranged for fifty pence each, with the winning pair taking all.

'Now my dad, Les, was East London Champion at the time and was paired with Lenny. There were better partnerships, but they paired Lenny with my dad because Dad was old-school East End and Lenny had a lot of respect for him. Lenny raised his game to win the competition, which was against the odds. I can tell you he was pretty chuffed about that at the time. Lenny also knew my cousin, Billy Rees, who was also a bouncer mentioned in his book. Lenny has always been a fascination to me and I have followed his career over the years, particularly as he came from the same area as me. It was a great shame when he died just at a time when his acting career was set for take-off. He was no angel but most certainly was a one-off and a mountain of a man.'

LEESA LITCHFIELD

'I was roughly ten years old when I and my family knew the McLean family. The year must have been around 1978 or 1979, and we lived a few doors down from them in Allen Road, near the Roman Road market. There was me, my two sisters and my mum and dad. I used to be friends with Lenny's kids, Jamie and Kelly. Growing up, we had a hard life as my dad used to beat my mum and us kids a lot, a fact of which I was soon to read in Lenny's book – that he was beaten at a young age too.

'Anyway, this one day while my dad was beating me, my mum got involved, trying to save me from another beating, and my dad ended up throwing my mum down a whole flight of stairs. Mum finally managed to drag herself away, which saved us because the street door was downstairs and she managed to open it. Lenny was outside knocking at our door because he could hear us screaming inside from his own house and had run down to see what was happening. He saved us that day – my dad was made to get out and Len cared for my mum and us kids, made sure we were all OK and safe. I will never forget the help he gave us that day; he always had a kind word for us every time he saw us after that, bless him. I was invited in to Len's house to play with his kids a lot – their house was a place where I felt really safe.

'In the end, we moved out of Allen Road and lost contact with the McLean family. I never forgot about Lenny, nor will I ever forget him in the future for what he done for us.'

THE HAYESY DAYS OF GODWIN HOUSE

METIN HASSAN

Anthony says: I met up with Metin on the film set of *My Name is Lenny*, where he was sitting with Lenny's nephew, Warren McLean. I had heard him in conversation mentioning Lenny's name and then messaged him on Facebook, asking if he would be interested in contributing at a later stage. Following this, I managed to chat with him in between his busy schedule, where he was filming for weeks on end, and this is what he had to say.

'I've known the McLean family and grew up by them since the sixties. I have had a few past experiences with Lenny as a kid growing up in Hoxton. Growing up in the sixties in London was hard enough in itself, but growing up in East and North London was even harder as a lot of the Jewish community had moved away from East London towards North London, Stamford Hill and beyond.

'Being a Turkish boy, I always stood out from the crowd in 1961 as there was not many of us about then so whenever we used to play down Hoxton, Lenny would at times shout out, "Hassan, come here and go and get you and Kruger some chips and a loaf of bread and cut it in half and have half each." For those of you who don't know, "Kruger" was the nickname for Lenny's younger brother, Raymond. Anyway, Len would then give us the money out of his own pocket. At the time of us growing up in Hoxton House School, we had these Jewish kids who thought they were hard boys. They had never heard of Lenny McLean and to be honest, I didn't know he

13

was anyone either, other than one of the older boys and my friend at the time.

'Lenny had a tear up [violent fight] one day in Hoxton and his name spread very quickly. All of a sudden the Jewish kids were eager to hang out with him and were very quick to exploit Len's reputation by saying, "Don't mess with us, Lenny McLean is our best mate". For this reason I also then got on with the Jewish kids simply because of my friendship with Lenny.

'Another time Lenny told me that his brother, Raymond, liked this girl called Cheryl. Raymond ended up marrying her and having a boy along the way called Warren and I have stood by him for the last fifteen years through thick and thin.

'When I was a DJ in the Green Man pub in Hoxton Lenny loved the song 'When Will I See You Again' by The Three Degrees. He must have made me play that song seven times this one night. It did the other punters' heads in.

'When I was about twelve years of age I asked every stallholder for work on their stalls but had no luck whatsoever. One day I was in the pie'n'mash shop and Lenny said to me, "Why the long face, Hassan?" I told him I'd tried getting work on the stalls but no joy. Lenny then said, "Come with me" and he called over to the vegetable stall and said, "Burt, have you got any work for this lad?" He then replied, "Of course, Lenny, he can start now." I was over the moon and said to Lenny, "I won't let you down, Lenny." He then replied, "You better not, boy, you better not."

'There's not much in the way of me telling you of

his reputation. To be honest, I only ever saw Lenny in action the once in a pub in the Old Kent Road. I'm not sure if he was minding the pub or collecting from there. It was the late eighties and I was chatting to him when three lads walked in. They were being loud so Lenny said, "Not tonight, boys, you'll have to leave." I think they were looking for trouble and they said to Lenny, "You don't know who you're messing with." The landlord then told Lenny that they had been in before causing trouble. It then kicks off and one of the lads tried to punch Lenny, but within a minute or less he had ironed them all out. He then screamed at them, "Now you know who you're messing with, I'm Lenny McLean!" The pub landlord told me the pub never had any trouble again.

'This one time my cousin was in Victoria Park with Lenny, jogging around. Suddenly three lads in a car went past them – this was the time when you could drive in the park before they banned cars. As the lads drove past, they shouted at Lenny, "You wanker, you fat git!" Well, as they got to the gate to pull out of the park the car stalled because there was loads of people crossing. Lenny managed to catch up with them but they fled from the car. Then he went over to the car with his jogging partner, picked the car up and turned it over onto its roof. He walked off with my cousin, pissing themselves laughing. My cousin then said, laughing, "Nice one, Lenny!" and Lenny replied, laughing, "It's a long walk of shame." I believe it was in the papers the following week.

'Another time I was in Kingsland Road and I was looking at cars in this car lot and the guy who owned the lot was also from Hoxton. I was on the bridge by the canal and at that moment, Lenny was going past. He shouted out to me, "Oh Hassan, those cars are fucking shit, I wouldn't bother!" Anyway, I left it and a week later, I seen Lenny driving a car from that same car lot, and he pulled up to talk to me. I then said, "Oh Len, how come you've got a car from that lot?" He said, "I got a good deal on sale and return" and then starting laughing.

'Looking back, growing up in a time when you had to make your own opportunities, having the likes of Lenny McLean about, opening doors for so many people in his full yet relatively short life, was amicable to say the least. Everyone can say that they knew Lenny, but how many people can step forward and say "I am who I am because of Lenny"? I'm very grateful to him for being a small part of my life, and his memory is more than just a fighting machine. I will remember him as the Hercules of Hoxton – a Hoxton that was safe, all thanks to a true legend and a giant.'

CHAPTER 2

STREET FIGHTING MEN

Anthony: I first heard of the name Paddy Monaghan just after the release of my first book, *The Guv'nor Through The Eyes of Others* (John Blake Publishing, 2007). Paddy also had a book out at the time called *Street Fighting Man* and he had one hell of a story to tell. He had an unbeaten bare-knuckle boxing record of 114 fights, unrivalled to this day. I managed to track him down and we spoke a few times. A few years ago, Paddy agreed to meet with me again and next thing I know, I'm on my way on a 170-mile three-hour journey to him. Once there, I'm welcomed in to Paddy's house and I raise my hand to shake his and he says to me, "Don't squeeze my hand too hard, Ant" – his hand's hurt from all the years of fighting bare-knuckle. I could see he was now fighting the greatest battle of his life with illness, but he still sat me down and made me feel welcome, like I'd known him for years. Paddy's wife,

Sandra, also sat in on the interview, saying little stories as well. Here's what they had to say about their experiences with Lenny McLean.

PADDY MONAGHAN

'I was born in Northern Ireland and then moved to England when I was five years old with my family to look for work. I got bullied by a lot of older kids and then I started to learn to fight by picking it up myself. I then met this ex-fighter named Ernie, who worked in the boiler room in school, and he took an interest in me and he started showing me some moves and it went from there.

'I first met Lenny after he had just seen me fight – I think it was in my trainer Tommy Heard's barn, which used to hold bare-knuckle boxing and was always full of the Underworld, including the Krays. We just started talking to each other. I knew who he was and he knew who I was, so it was a bit of mutual respect. He was five years younger than me, but he was such a hard fucker – he was a hard son of a bitch, I'll tell you. I then went on to see Lenny fight quite a few times bare-knuckle. He would go into the ring with hate, but first he had to build himself up to get it – Lenny had the adrenaline flowing before he got in to do the business.

'Lenny then approached me one day to come up to Newmarket horse traders' fair to fight bare-knuckle. So, I went with him, not knowing that my trainer, Tommy Heard, would have the hump. Now Lenny was only about twenty at the time and like I said, I was five years older, but he was a bit worldlier than I was. Don't forget I was living out in the sticks and not used to seeing the stuff he did.

That day Lenny beat Phil McCaffrey, the Irish Heavyweight champion. Now Lenny was a big powerful lad, but McCaffrey was even fucking bigger, he was enormous! Lenny put him out in the first round. Now coming up to the fight, Lenny kept onto me every night, saying, "Paddy, are you training? Make sure you're training." Every fucking night I'd tell him I'd been training. This went on most nights and it started playing on my mind why he was so interested in me winning my fight.

'Anyway, I had my fight and I knocked Lafferty out and Lenny comes up to me and wraps this big arm around me and says, "Well done, my son, you have just won me a monkey." Knowing that my purse or [prize] money was only a hundred and fifty quid for winning, I turned to Lenny and said, "What, you got five hundred fucking quid and all I got is hundred and fifty? That's why you were ringing me all a time before the fight." He turned to me with this big laugh and said, "Fucking right I did!" He turned around and tried giving me half, but I told him I didn't want his money.

'Lenny came to my house this other time – I'd been off for a good few months with broken hands and he asked me, was I alright for a bit of scratch? I told him I was OK and thanks for the offer. I could've been broke but I wouldn't have told him, that was just the way I was and for that matter, the way I am to this day.

'Lenny was a good boxer, but he wasn't a long-distance fighter as he'd always tried to take them out quick. I'd be training my bollocks off and I'd think, "Where's Lenny?" and I knew he'd be in the changing room, rolling a fag.

'He used to get me mad, though – he used to sing this song called 'Carolina Moon' all the time. Now when I'd go to the ring for a fight he would get in front of me and start singing it out of tune as he knew it would get me fucking mad. He'd be there, "Carolina Moon, keep shining," I'd get in the ring and he'd still be singing his heart out and laughing at me.

'My kids used to love him; he was a gentle giant, a big bear of a man with his bull neck on him. My kids were only little and he would be there, saying, "Cutchi, cutchi cu" – it was quite funny to see. Lenny used to come to my house in Abingdon and he would have a little blue car. My kids would run at him when he got out of the car and start kissing him. With that, he'd pick three or four of them up at the same time. They really took to him and it's not everyone a child will take to like that. When he used to leave, the kids would go outside and watch the car go down the road and Lenny would be laughing with them.

'He was always on the phone, trying to get me to go London to work on the doors for years, but my wife hated the thought of me working the doors even though I'd be in Lenny's company. He loved his tea, that's all he fucking drank. Lenny would go to a pub with me and he'd have a cup of tea the same as myself. This pub landlord said to me and Lenny one day, laughing, "I'd swear this was a café, and not a fucking pub!"

'I started to work on my own book while Lenny was writing his. Me and Lenny made a pact not to mention each other because we didn't know what the other was saying and that's why I wasn't in his book, *The Guv'nor*.

'Lenny used to ring me when he was making *Lock, Stock and Two Smoking Barrels* [1998] and offer me a part. "It's money for old rope, Paddy," he'd say. "I've got to get you in it, you can do it easy!" I told him I didn't want to be in it. He would then phone me all the time and he'd ask me to go to Pinewood Studios with him.

'Lenny was a proper character. It was a shame how he died, and it broke my fucking heart when he went. Val and I and a few others were the last ones to see the casket in the English & Son funeral parlour in Bethnal Green Road. The two of us were close and were good pals, and I'd never, ever hear a bad word said about my good friend, Lenny McLean.'

TYRONE MONAGHAN

Lee: A few years after Anthony interviewed Paddy, I came across Paddy's son, Tyrone, on social media and managed to catch him in his busy schedule for an interview – he was working on his dad's new book, and a film script of his dad's life. A lot of the stories Tyrone mentioned to me, which had been passed down to him from his dad, had already been written by Anthony, but here's a few other little snippets Paddy must have forgotten to mention...

'The thing is, Lee, I was only young when Lenny came to my house quite a few times and he was always good to us kids, giving us money and stuff. It was the late seventies and he would give us fifty pence each, but in those days to kids like us it was a lot of money. We were living in Abington at the time. He was great with us kids and I didn't know Lenny any other way. He spoilt us, he always made a fuss, and then when he and my dad needed to chat, Mam would make us go out of the room. Like I've mentioned, and as my dad has told Anthony, Lenny had about four or five fights at the Barn, which was in the countryside in the Northwest of London, and Lenny won them all.

'Lenny came to the Barn with Ginger Roy, who was a friend of Tommy's, and Charlie Shawrey, who had a car showroom in South London. When my dad was down there at Charlie's training, Lenny would pop in and chat with him – Dad was a few years older. Lenny was only a young kid of about seventeen, but he was fucking vicious and a very dangerous man, my dad told me.

'Lenny and Dad then lost touch for a bit and Lenny started boxing unlicensed. He then rung my dad up one day and said, "Paddy, I'm unlicensed, boxing in Croydon, if you want to come down?" My dad said, laughing, "You're a turncoat bastard; you're getting all soft now fighting with the gloves on!" – they were roaring with laughter. Dad would call him a cissy and Lenny would always come back with some funny stuff. My dad once said to Lenny, "I'm glad I'm no heavyweight, Len," and Lenny replied, "I'm glad I'm no middleweight either." That was, of course, the mutual respect they had for each other. In 1997, my dad was on the banned *Bare Fist* documentary with Lenny and I was in the film with Dad when they filmed his scenes.

'The last time I saw Lenny was at Ronnie Kray's funeral in 1995. I went with my dad and we were across the road by the Chapel of Rest in Bethnal Green and this big fucking hand came down on my left shoulder and this voice went, "Hello, my old son." I said, "Alright, Len?", he shook my hand and swallowed it up in those big shovels of his. We exchanged a bit of small talk and then he says, "Where's your father?" I pointed to where my dad was and Lenny said, laughing, "I'm going to fucking tear him up!" He then started shouting, "Paddy, Paddy!" They wrapped their arms around one another, they were proper old school like that, because obviously they had a history together that spanned over many years – it was a lovely sight. Later, we all went to Lenny's Guv'ner pub and had a cracking night. Rest in peace Lenny, with love and the utmost respect from the Monaghans.'

CHAPTER 3

RETURN OF THE MAC

Kenny, Kenny, Kenny, Kenny, Kenny... Now where do we start with our main man 'Mac'? Oh, this is going to be interesting! Right so in true Lenny McLean style, jump in the motor, people, and let's go to work.

Now we are presuming at this point that anyone reading this book has of course read Lenny and Peter Gerrard's book, *The Guv'nor* and for that matter will remember Len going over to a lorry yard: it was Ridgway Motors, Groves Road, in Dunstan. Anyway, Len walks in and buys a little motor off a fella for forty-seven pounds and fifty pence – it was all the dough he had in his pocket.

So, Len leaves the yard and according to Len in his book, *The Guv'nor*, he says that he put up with that motor for about two days and then got his pal to tow it back to Mac's yard. So, Lenny gets back to the Kingsland Road to have it out with said car yard owner. This is of course the one and only Kenny Mac, and let me tell you, by this time Lenny 'Boy' has a right raving hump.

Now listen up, readers, here's a little insight into the kind of fella that our man Mac is. So, I have spoken to Mac on a number of meets and let me tell you, this fella is a right funny fucker, and at seventy-five he's still as sharp as a tack and also has more front than a Page Three model from the eighties.

'Mac', as he is known to a close few of us, is about the size of Dustin Hoffman, with a mouth and heart easily as big as our boy Lenny's. Right, so you can well imagine how that little conversation they had back at Mac's car yard over the motor went. Len has just handed over his last forty-odd notes so let's just say I imagine that it didn't end too well, or did it? Yes, it did because, thank fuck for us as fans and of course for the history of the Lenny McLean legacy, Kenny being Kenny turned it around to both of their favours with, 'I've heard that you're pretty tasty with your fists, boy. Stick with me and I'll get you some bare-knuckle fights, and we'll sort you a better motor than that piece of junk I sold you the other day.' For fuck's sake, that fella must have had some arsehole, delivering a line like that to a temper-filled Lenny McLean! So, can I now say that I've built up a solid gold character reference for you of the man that is Kenny Mac? OK, right, so let us move on to the Lenny and Mac tenure.

So, I talked to Mac with regard to Lenny as an orthodox boxer – his actual ability in the ring, etc. Mac had this to say:

'When McLean came to me to train him up, he was a young man of just twenty-eight years old. He was a scrapper, a street brawler. His boxing prowess was virtually nondescript. Yeah, Len had moved around a bit inside of a boxing ring, but as for technique, he had hardly any to talk of. Now listen, Lee, Lenny was an out-and-out cobble fighter and a fucking fantastic one at that. It's as you undoubtedly know, a totally different game so over the coming months I made it my goal to get McLean ultra-fit and into a training programme, ready for the ring, and very quickly, the signs started to show.

'Lenny under my wing had by now at least acquired a certain amount of technique and discipline, and overall was looking a lot more focused. Oh yeah, he was still a fucking loose cannon and could go off in a split second, make no mistake about that, boy.

'So, let's move over to Mac's car yard. Kenny had turned the shed bit of the yard into a gym of sorts – well, a few punch bags filled with sand hanging on chains set to a canvas of fucking hay, that was about the size of it. With, I must add, the best flycatcher known to man, placed covertly in one corner – yes, that's it, a big fucking pile of horse shit. "Keeps the fucking flies out of the gym though, doesn't it, fellas?" Kenny would say to an audience of whomever was hanging around the yard on any given day. So, now, to elaborate on that and make things even more interesting, here are a few names to add to the mix, like for instance, chirpy chappie Georgie Warrington (Deceased), Leslie Groom Senior, Guggy Lane (Deceased), Mickey and Dave, just to name a few. Oh, and on to the makeshift boxing ring, designed and put together by Leslie Groom's son, Les Junior. Anyway, the ring consisted of three tall gas bottles, a pile of tyres and a bunch of rubber rope, ripped from a flatbed truck, acting as the makeshift ropes. It was pure class, a fighter's playground, or as many would come to realise, simply a place to have a fucking granny bashed out of you.

'This one day Len's cousin, John Wall, or 'Bootnose' as he was more popularly known, had brought a video camera in with him to the scrapyard and he was filming everyone. I'd go in first and smash the bags to make sure they were OK for the boys. "Yes, they're fantastic, these bags, fellas," I'd say, all the while thinking to myself, you'll break your knuckles on those fuckers – they were like a couple of bags of concrete hanging from the rafters.

'So, John then set the camera up to film the training session. Lenny had been drinking the night before so how serious he was taking the fight, I don't know. Minutes before he and Bootnose are about to train, Lenny would be smoking, and Mac heard him shout to the boys in the yard, "Here, hold up, fellas, gotta fill the lungs up first," as he's searching around for a light for his roll-up. Now Johnny was another practical joker like Lenny, always full of energy and dancing about. Numerous times, he and Lenny would just grab hold of one another and start ballroom dancing; they would have everyone in stitches. Kenny would then glove Lenny up and get him smashing the heavy bags – after a few rounds you could see the sweat coming out of him.

'So, in preparation for fights, Kenny as Lenny's trainer-cum-manager would have a strict regime mapped out for Len and Johnny to go at. They always started with a chat in the office and a big mug of tea and a smoke to 'fill up the lungs', as Lenny would often put it – a phrase that with hindsight would add to the demise of our man in the not so distant future. Anyway, I'm straying off the tracks although it's quite an apt turn of phrase with regard to a little story I'm coming up to. So, as I said, Len and John started with a chat in Mac's office and then it was out to the 'gym' for some bag work, this under the instruction of Mac and his Casio wristwatch for use as a timekeeper. They would do ten minutes on each bag and then rest for twenty to thirty seconds depending on Mac's mood that day and then Bootnose and Lenny would switch with one another.

'Bootnose was a lot lighter than Len, probably like a light middleweight. He was a very agile fella with a fantastic reach. Now Lenny on the other hand was like a bull, very powerful and headstrong, although he did have some style and finesse for a "big c***" as Bootnose would call him. While on the bag or sparring, Lenny was always moving forward and tapping his forehead and grunting – yes, come to think about it, he was every bit like an actual fucking bull. A fact I'm sure 'Bootnose' would tell you if he was alive today, God bless him.'

Lee: Lenny and Johnny had numerous sparring sessions in Mac's yard, a handful of which we have on film. This priceless footage that I talk about will be shared with you one day, myself and Anthony have waited some seventeen years to have it in our possession.

Now when you watch the footage, it is very clear to see that Lenny is way too powerful and heavy for Bootnose, a fact of which is true, according to Mac's analysis. Mac informed me that Len was, as we always knew, a solid-hitting heavyweight, while Bootnose was more of a light middleweight and floated about the ring away from an oncoming Len. Bootnose ducked and dived, and eased his way out of Lenny's massive bombs. He never let up, though, giving Len many a flurry of punches, all landing on his face, right on the button. But Len was never phased by this, of which Bootnose was immediately aware. In one of the many bouts, Bootnose is smashing Len with everything in his locker – well, almost – and Len is just swallowing each blow up like a knife through butter. Then all of a sudden Len lets loose with a quick combination and Bootnose is winded. Bootnose shouts over to Mac, "Kenny, tell him to ease up!", Lenny's saying, "I *was*, I fucking was," and Bootnose is like, "Was you, fuck! You're a big c***, a big powerful c***!" Everyone there is just laughing. Bootnose takes over at the camera and you hear him say, "Right, I want that on camera! He's a big c***, a big fucking powerful c***!" It's all in jest, Len and John were like brothers – Lenny wouldn't want to hurt John for the world and that's a fact.

As part of the daily training regime, Mac would drive them in his little white Morris Minor over to Victoria Park (or 'Vicky Park' as they referred to it locally). Here, he had them doing jogs, sprints, press-ups, squats, etc. This one time Mac was on a pushbike, shouting orders at them, and both men started pissing about, throwing combinations at Mac. So with that he put his foot down and starts pedalling faster and they both sprinted after him, like something out of a *Rocky* movie. Then after about an hour they would head back to Mac's yard for more bag work and sparring.

RETURN OF THE MAC

Mac said they were always pissing around between sessions – Bootnose was a right joker just like Len.

Now prior to all of this in about 1974, Mac had set up a bare-knuckle fight for Len with a well-known bare knuckler of the time from a famous gypsy family. Anyway, the fight was all set and the fighter and his team of three were driving over to East London when in some terrible twist of fate they got stuck on a level crossing and within seconds a passenger train had hit their car, killing all four of them instantly – a sad day for all involved. We would like to send our love and respect out to the family involved, a heart-wrenching and tragic event, which I'm sure the family will never ever forget.

Mac organised a bunch of bare-knuckle fights for Len, a couple of tear ups over Epsom for Derby Day, the first of which was with a gypsy champion known as 'Blonde Simey'. It was over in no time: Len hit him twice and then it was all over. He walked away with a tidy £500 in his bin, not bad for a couple of minutes' work in the late seventies. Len also had a bare-knuckle fight with some gypsies at Mac's car yard – this lot had been causing a bit of grief around the yard so Len challenged them. Mac says Len was up for taking all three of them on, one after another, but the gypsies only had a few quid between them so he challenged their tastiest, a big caveman-looking fucker with half an ear missing. Anyway, Mac says that before he had chance to kick the gas bottle for them to start, Len went into him and smashed him to bits with a thundering left that took the gypsy's breath away, and then finished him off with a right-hander, knocking this Brian fella out cold. So, with that the two other fellas started going off at Lenny, so Len just charged at them, growling, and they had it away on their toes and flew out of Mac's yard.

In the melee the two gypsies had left the big leather money wallet on the set of tyres they'd been sat on, so Mac split the contents with Len, and that was the end of that. Mac said, "Never trust a gypsy where a bit of folding's concerned." They said that they only had two hundred notes between them, and there was well over three hundred and fifty in the wallet.

Len also fought an Irish tinker, Paddy Bury, who was renowned on the bare-knuckle circuit. He was very big and powerful, was Paddy, but Len finished him off in about twenty seconds. Bury steamed over to Lenny, Len immediately dropped his shoulder and done him with a blinding left hook to the side of the head. Bury was out cold and kissing the tarmac. We walked away with two grand for that bit of work. Mac said, "Lenny didn't fuck about, you know what I mean, Lee boy."

Kenny was telling me that around 1982, Lenny was training for a fight in his yard and Cliffy Fields from over Dunstable was training there, also for an upcoming fight. Anyway, what happened was Lenny turned up down Kenny's yard and the pair of them started sparring a little. In the heat of the moment Cliffy caught Len with a left hook with some force. I think Len saw this as a bit of a liberty because they were only fooling around. Suffice to say, he jumped from the ring, picked up a bit of four-by-two timber and smashed Cliffy over the head with it. Kenny informs me there were murders that day, but after a bit of gentle persuasion from Mac and others at the yard, they decide to save it for another time. Lenny had lost twice to Cliffy a few years earlier after it was looking like Lenny was winning both fights, but Cliffy showed his experience and came away with a win. A third fight was lined up for an outdoor show at Mac's yard but never came off. Lenny was right up for the fight and telling everyone, but things just didn't go to plan.

Here's a funny little story off the back of one of Lenny's Waldron losses. Mac said to Cliffy at the end of the fight, "Jump in the ring at the end and challenge the winner." Well, anyway, Len lost, Cliffy jumps in the ring and only fucking puts a challenge out to Lenny. Lenny didn't take kindly to this and started to smash into Fieldsy. Len's fucking stuck the nut on [headbutted] him and he's going off his nut. Mac was sat with Joe Carrington and they're both in fits of laughter. When Cliffy jumped back out of the ring to get away from Lenny, Mac goes to him, "What the fuck are you doing, you big dozy c***? I said challenge the winner, what the fuck are you challenging Lenny for?" Kenny said they couldn't stop laughing for weeks about it.

One afternoon Lenny flared up in Mac's office. Ken said Len just lost it – it was over the cancellation of a proposed upcoming fight, on which he and Mac could not agree. Mac told me that if Cliffy Fields hadn't been in the office to calm Len down, he honestly can't imagine what would've happened. I did say to Mac – sorry to defend him, Kenny but as we all know, Lenny was just like that in the seventies and eighties – when Lenny put his blinkers on, and was working his way towards a certain goal, then anyone silly enough to contest it would be bang in trouble. Unfortunately, the amount of pull that Mac thought he had with regard to Len's fighting career was obviously not quite as strong as he first imagined. Anyway, the disagreement was very quickly ironed out, Len finally got his way and the contested fight was on.

Another time, Mac and Len and a few others are over at the Thomas A Becket Gym in the Old Kent Road and a well-known local debt collector, enforcer and self-claimed nutter called Barry Dalton is also there. Anyway, he and Len get in the ring for a bit of a spar up. Now, for the record, Len and Barry Dalton weren't the biggest of fans of one another. So, anyway, they're having a bit of a fight and Lenny pings Dalton on the chin a bit heavy. Dalton doesn't take kindly to this and goes off at Len, "You c***, McLean! Don't get fucking leery," so they have a bit of a square-off and they all jump in to calm it down. So, that's the end of that, or so they thought.

Later that evening, Dalton takes a diabolical liberty and goes round to Lens with a fucking shooter. Anyway, he bangs on the door, Len shouts down, "Come in," Dalton opens the front door and as Len's at the top of the stairs, he goes, "Right, McLean, you piss-taking c***, that's the last time you have me over!" Len starts running down the stairs to do him again and Dalton lets loose a shot from his sawn-off, which, fortunately for Lenny, ends up in the wall above Lenny's head. Dalton has it away on his toes double-lively. Now I'm sure you can well imagine just what's about to erupt on the East End manor now, can't you?

So let me tell you... In 1986, Mac put on a show at Snakes Lane, Woodford, at Woodford Town's football ground. Myself and my co-author, Anthony, often pondered long hours over any reasoning there could possibly be for the organiser of said event to put Barry Dalton on the same bill with Lenny. Now, in recent talks with Mac, this was one of the questions obviously I couldn't wait to have answered.

RETURN OF THE MAC

Let's just say, now I think about it there can be only one answer and it was, of course, none other than the simple honest pound note and the will thereof to earn it. After the shooting escapade at Len's front door Mac ordered Dalton to a meet at his yard. You see, between Lenny and Dalton, the feud that was building as every day passed would never come to an end until someone was in a box. Now in a fist fight there could only ever be one winner, that of course being McLean. But Dalton was a bit of a psycho, at this time very trigger-happy and wouldn't think twice about blowing Len's head off down a dark alley one evening. So, Mac steps in and sorts this row out amicably. Here's what went down.

'Dalton comes to Mac's yard. He tells Mac that he's skint, Mac gives him a few bob to tide him over, and says, "Look, son, let's have this fucking ruck between you and Len put to bed. Len's on my books and he's a very lucrative asset to me and my business." He then adds, "I will put you on the bill at my next event that Lenny McLean is headlining, and mark my words; you'll walk away with a tidy bit of dough in your back bin." Of course Dalton agreed, and everything is now settled.

'Now listen, Lenny and I ain't soft in the head, and I'd already marked his card about this eventuality. You see this Dalton fella is a proper notorious character on the manor, and his name sells hundreds of tickets, so we were all on to a winner and nobody's got murdered in the process although due to Barry's antics in the ring, he did manage to cause a bit of aggravation in the crowd that day. But like I said previous, that's why we did it, and the event was a fantastic success. After Snakes Lane, Lenny decided to hang his gloves up – he'd already mentioned this to Mac – but actually announced it after he'd beaten "Man Mountain" Dave York that day. As Len steps out of the ring, he shouts to the announcer, "I've retired," the announcer then puts it out over the loudspeaker. Of course there's a little bit of positive and negative feedback shouted back from the crowd.'

There was a bit of villainy that day. Mac says that the West Ham footy lot, the 'Inter City Firm', kicked off for one reason or another – probably someone looked at someone else's pint funny. Kenny says it was mayhem for a while, but it all simmered down as these things always do. Anyway, as Mac says they all done well from that event and it was a fantastic little pay day for Lenny's retirement fund.

There was a little more villainy going on behind the scenes that day at Snakes Lane. You see, Kenny had set on a retired pro boxer and his wife to take care of all the charity events that day, but as it turned out, this fella wasn't quite the trustworthy kind of geezer that Mac had first believed. This boxer fella had it away on his toes with the majority of the charity dough. Now Mac informs me that news of this travelled fast around the East End and of course half of London's Underworld was out in force to retrieve it, and probably retrieve the no-good boxing tea-leaf for that matter too. Anyway, the two'n'half grand or so was never returned, and Mac being the honourable fella that I have come to know, put his hand in his own pocket and paid the balance himself – he's a solid fella like that is Mac.

Mac told me that although he and Len stayed friends

and kept in touch until the very end, their relationship was undoubtedly a little fractured by the dark days of Lenny the boozer. As I'm sure you all know by now, Len was on the wagon from the early eighties, but in the years leading up to this, he had given people a bit of a hard time. Kenny was certainly not exempt from Len's aggressive attitude. Listen, they'd had their falling-outs and made up on numerous occasions – the apologies all came from Len, though, he knew when he'd taken a liberty. This by no means casts a shadow over Lenny and Mac's tenure because as Mac said, they had some fantastic times together, made a good few bob here and there, and shot Len's name to the stars in one way or another. Make no mistake; if not for the union of Mac and Len, I do not think I'd be sat here writing this book as I am today. That for me is an unequivocal fact.

Along with many of their mutual associates Ken paid his respects to Lenny at his funeral. He told me, "Here, Lee boy, listen mate. I do miss Lenny, you know – he gave me a step up too, son – don't you worry about that, boy."

CHAPTER 4

THE GLOVES ARE ON

After fighting night after night in the roughest and toughest pubs, clubs and gambling houses, and also travelling the many towns and cities dotted around the UK, taking on challengers in the bare-knuckle fighting arena, Lenny was very quickly introduced to a world of 'Unlicensed Boxing'. A world where the winner's purse grew increasingly healthier, and reputations would echo between the ropes of each and every torrid and blood-drenched battle. It was here that he would finally make some serious dough. Below are some of the people we have spoken to that Lenny met on his way to the top and the once notorious yet now iconic title of 'The Guv'nor'.

GINGER TED ONSLOE

'I first became involved with the unlicensed boxing scene through taking photos and selling tickets, and also I had been good mates with Roy 'Pretty Boy' Shaw since he was sixteen. I knew Roy from borstal, and also from prison; you see, the pair of us were Dagenham boys. Roy had been in Broadmoor for ten years and when he was released, he came to my car site. I first heard of Lenny McLean through my uncle telling me stories about this McLean fella from Hoxton.

'In 1976 Roy had started the unlicensed scene after his fight with Donny "The Bull" Adams. I then refereed his second fight against Mad Paddy Mullins at the Blueberry Hotel. I did go once with Lenny in the early days up to Cambridge for a bare-knuckle fight. Lenny came and seen me and said, "I heard you went there with Roy, do you fancy coming with me, Ted?" So I went with Lenny and it was supposed to be a five-grand bet, but Lenny only had four on him. I said, "That's a bit dangerous, Len" and he said, "Fuck them, Ted, don't worry about that." So as we're stood there before the fight Lenny's arguing with this pikey about the money and this big pikey c*** came up to me and said, "Me and you, we have a fucking fight, what you reckon?" I replied, "You fucking what?" With that Lenny heard it and came steaming over, pushed me out of the way and said, "Oi, hold up son! When I've done my c***, I'll fucking do you as well." The pikey's face was a fucking picture and he said, "Nah, that's alright." Lenny then said, "You talk to him like you fucking talk to me, it's as simple as that, now fuck off!" Anyway, Lenny sparked his opponent in under a minute and took their four grand. Shortly after that, he got in the ring and challenged Roy at Cinatra's nightclub in Croydon.

'A fight was then lined up between Shaw and McLean

at Cinatra's. I remember Roy saying to me, "You know that McLean, Ted?", I said, "Len's alright, Roy, he's a big bastard and he's a lot younger than you." But Roy didn't care. The night of the fight came and Lenny got in the ring and the gloves wouldn't fit him, he was shouting, "My hands are too big" to everyone. The fight was really good. Roy was steaming in and Lenny would throw him about. Lenny was blowing at the end of the first round and breathing heavy. In the second, it was another hard-fought round, but by now Lenny was worse and could hardly breathe. In the middle of the third round Lenny was cuddling him and whispering. Roy looked up and said, "Do what?", Lenny then said, "I've had enough!" Roy just turned away and the ref came in and Shaw was the winner. Lenny then admitted he wasn't trained up, and really was knackered, but said that he wouldn't be next time they got it on in a rematch.

'In the second fight, again at Cinatra's, Lenny bashed him up and knocked him down in the first round after about a minute. All of a sudden the bell went very fast for the end of the round. It started again and Lenny knocked him spark out.

'It was now one apiece by both men. Then one day I was with Roy and he said, "We're going down the pub to see McLean." I said, laughing, "Don't start eating the glasses, Roy, for fuck's sake!" When Roy got a bit pissed, this is the stuff he would do – there would be blood pouring out of his mouth as he's spitting out bits of glass.

'I then went with Roy and we went through the Rotherhithe Tunnel and we picked up Joey Pyle and

Mickey Savage and headed down to the Needle Gun in the Roman Road in Bow, which was one of the pubs Lenny was looking after. When we got down there, Lenny wasn't even there at all, so Roy shouted out to the barman, "You tell that McLean I've been down to see him," but it was just a bit of thuggish PR to play the fight up. It was pointless talking to Roy and telling him to behave as he was off his nut, so to put all of the bullshit to bed, fellas, no, we weren't really looking for him.

'A bit of a wasted journey, but the landlord would get the message back that Shaw wanted McLean for another fight. Then it came to the third and final encounter at the Rainbow Theatre. Frank Warren laid that one on. A camera crew turned up at my car site and asked me who did I think was going to win and I said, "Well, Roy, innit?" The news clips turned up on the television and also featured Lenny running round Victoria Park. My cousin rung me up laughing and says to me, "I was watching the TV last night, Ted, and your fucking big head came on."

'I was asked by Roy to go into Lenny's changing room and make sure they hadn't put anything in his gloves, so when they put his bandages on I had to sign my signature passing it, and one of Lenny's team had to do the same with Roy. Bobby Warren came back in and said to Lenny, "He's sweating like a fuckin' pig in there, Len." Lenny turned round and said, laughing, "'as he seen me then?" Lenny then turned to me and said, "You happy with this Ted or what?" as he showed me his hand, I said, "Yeah it looks good, Len." Lenny then said, "It's about time you come with me, Ted. He's made his money, the old boy's had enough, so you should come with me because I need loyal people like you around me." I then turned to Lenny and said, laughing, "Well, I wouldn't be fuckin' loyal, Len, if I went with you and left Roy, now would I?" Lenny then starts laughing and looks at the others in the changing room and says, "There you are, that's fuckin' loyalty for you, and I'm surrounded by mugs and it's people like Ted I want. Put your hand there. Any time you want to come work with me, you know where I am," and I shook his hand before I left.

'Lenny really bashed him that night; he must have hit Roy about thirty times before he went down. Roy had laid a victory party on at the White Swan near Stepney station, which Lenny looked after, as he thought he was going to knock Lenny out. He was right disheartened after the fight and mentioned he'd taken ginseng. Roy then said, "Fuck the party, let's get home to Dagenham." He mentioned the ginseng again and said, "Even my girlfriend, Dorothy, could have flicked me on the chin and I would have gone over."

'I see Lenny a couple of times bouncing on the door at the White Swan as I was passing through to the West End. I was talking to him in there one night while he was drinking his lemonade. A row then started with some men next door. Lenny then gets up from behind this counter and says, "Excuse me, Ted." He run in and there was fucking murders. I said to him, "Len, they're only youngsters," and he replied, "Fuck them, they don't misbehave in my pub." He then kicked this one man up the arse as he was getting thrown out. Lenny was the type to take no nonsense in his job.

'A few years later after the Shaw-McLean fights, Roy was fighting this bloke named Kevin Paddock from Southampton at the Ilford Palais. I was on the door, doing the tickets and Roy said, "If that McLean turns up, don't let him in." I then said to Roy, "Well, I can't do that, Roy, if he has a ticket." Lenny turned up and said, "Alright, Ted?" I then explained the situation to him and he said, "No worries, Ted, I'll stay in the background, don't worry about it."

'Roy had the fight and took the decision after eight rounds and was in the ring celebrating. Now it might not be true but I think that Roy out of the corner of his eye had seen Lenny and was a bit worried that he was going to challenge him again there and then. Roy walks over to the compère and says, "Tell the crowd I've retired," the compère then says, "Hold on a minute, Roy Shaw has just told me that this is his last fight, he's retiring." Lenny's strolled up to the ring and the compère says, "Hold on a minute, here's Lenny. Come in, Len, shake hands, not the best of friends, not the worst of enemies." They then shook hands and Lenny gave Shaw a hug.

'I don't think Roy wanted to fight him again because Lenny was too heavy and too young for him, also Roy was a middleweight and Lenny was a natural heavyweight, a big man. Lew Yates then comes in the ring and a match was set up between him and Lenny for a future date. Lew was a good boxer when he was younger, but I think Lenny would have done Lew as Lew was overweight.

'It was me that informed Roy that Lenny had passed away with cancer and he said, "I would like to go to the funeral but it will make me look a hypocrite, and I'd hate to see anyone go like that, if I'm honest." Roy seemed genuinely upset about it. He always said, "Anyone who gets in the ring I take my hat off to them, because it takes guts to be a fighter and no two ways about it, Lenny was a fighting man." I personally liked Lenny – he was a character and a very, very funny man.'

NOSHER POWELL

Anthony: Nosher had also been involved in the unlicensed fight scene, MC-ing and refereeing fights. I first met Nosher with Joey Pyle, who introduced me to him at a party for an upcoming fighting documentary in London. At first he began telling me stories, but then gave me his number so that we could chat.

'Being an ex-boxer myself, I had heard the name Lenny McLean on many occasions. Then as I got involved in the unlicensed scene, I met him on various shows. Lenny was a bit of a wild card in those days, a fella out to make a name for himself. I was then told by my good mate, Roy Shaw, that their fight was going ahead. I remember thinking to myself, this is going to be like a box of fireworks going off. Both men had it in their heads that they were unbeatable.

'Now we both knew Lenny was a bouncer and pretty handy on the streets but this was now in the ring and Lenny, I think, had only had one fight prior to this, so obviously, Roy had much more ring experience and at the time was undefeated. I trained with Roy down the Becket [gym] until the day of the fight, and I could sense that he was ready to explode. On the night I was the ring announcer and also the timekeeper for the main event. In the first round, Lenny went at Roy, hitting him with everything, but Roy just soaked it up. Lenny was getting cocky, thinking he was on for a win in round two, but Roy went to work on Len's body. Round three was another hard-fought round for both men, and the pair of them were exhausted at the end of it. The fourth round came and I knew that Roy would win with his experience and Lenny could no longer throw anything. I was right because with that the referee stopped it. Roy knew he'd been in a fight that night and young Lenny had certainly made a resounding impact.

'I bumped into Lenny quite a few times after that as he was now training over [at] the Becket too. He was still this cocky young kid, but by now had the passion and the will to learn. It was here that Len and I became good friends, we would often go for a bite to eat after training. The loss to Roy hadn't really bothered him, and he was still confident he could win in a rematch that had now been signed up, and true to his word, he went and knocked Roy out.'

With one apiece, a third and final fight was set up – 'You've probably seen this fight on video, Ant, the one where Lenny becomes The Guv'nor', 'Yeah, quite a few times, mate!' I say, laughing. Nosher went on to say that he had seen Lenny a few days later and he was still smiling from ear to ear.

'I continued to see Lenny at boxing shows here and there, and always stayed in touch with him. His reputation grew and grew over the coming years, and I always knew I could call on him if I had any trouble and once or twice, I had to. Big Len hardly ever had to use a muscle, and the grievance was sorted.

'In my lifetime I've never met a scarier man. I've seen him on meets and just the faces he would pull without speaking nearly had those men crying. He was so big and powerful, but also very funny. I was gutted when I heard the sad news that he had passed away, I went along and paid my respects at his funeral.'

RAY HILLS

Ray started off by telling us how he had appeared in the eighties documentary about unlicensed boxing, *Box On*, which also featured Lenny fighting Ron Redrup. He went on to say that he had known Lenny for years. This is his story.

'We had words quite a few times, and we had sparred together many times. We trained at a pub called The Ring, which had a boxing gym upstairs. Now Lenny and I wanted to get it on, but we always held back when we sparred because it could have ended in a war. It was strange that he and I never fought each other because most of the guys Lenny fought, I also fought. It would have been a good fight. I always felt I was the better boxer, but Lenny could sell the tickets – he was good at that, he could fill the place.

'We were due to fight on Monday, 10 September 1979 at the Rainbow Theatre in Finsbury Park, where

Cliff Fields was fighting Tshaka in the main event. Posters were put out with it, saying, 'Daddy Cool Continues His Fight Back to the Top'. The poster also mentioned I had two knockout wins in two fights as well. How the fight never came off, I do not know, but it would have been a cracker!'

STEVE 'COLUMBO' RICHARDS

Hungarian-born Steve moved to London at a young age, picking up amateur boxing titles before turning pro and then later in life, entering the unlicensed ring. He also appeared with Lenny in the unlicensed documentary, *Box On*, and fought on the same bills as Lenny quite a few times. When an opponent pulled out of a sell-out show no one would face Lenny at such short notice, but Steve stepped in despite the weight difference and he and Len put on a show which had the crowd in hysterics. We travelled to London to meet Steve and he then took us to a local boxing gym, where he had the following to say about Lenny.

'I knew Lenny McLean really well, he was a giant of a man. He came to our gym and was just coming off a loss to Roy Shaw, a fight he should have never [have] lost. I give him a right bollocking for losing and we trained really hard for the next fight, doing bags, pad work and sparring. I was training as well because I was on the undercard of Lenny's rematch with Shaw. I was once sparring with Lenny and he'd stick his head out and yell, "Come on, Columbo, hit me, hit me harder!" so as he's looking down with his head forward, I thought I'd have him and hit him with a body shot, which put him down on one knee. I shouted to him, "You looking for something, Lenny?" He then laughed it off as we continued for a few more rounds.

'I remember this one Christmas, Reggie Chapman had a boxing dinner show on, and I was speaking to Lenny in the gym a few days before and he asked me to be his cornerman for the night against big Johnny Clark. Lenny's music was playing and he was jumping up and down with his hands on my shoulders as I led him to the ring. Lenny's gone in there and headed straight for his opponent, pushing the MC man out the way. I grabbed Lenny and pushed him back as he rips his boxing gown off and goes at them again. Lenny's showboating and doing muscle poses as I'm trying to get him to his corner.

'Lenny came back after round one and I was screaming at him to start going up the middle with uppercuts as he's dropping his head. Second round starts and not long into it Lenny's actually listening. Next thing I could see was Clark on the floor after a terrific Lenny uppercut. The fight was over and the crowd were loud, chanting for Lenny. It was a good night and even his son and a few others came into the ring to congratulate him. His music started playing again and he was still doing muscle poses leaving the ring. He was a very funny man, I liked the big man Lenny a lot.'

THE GUV'NOR REVEALED

KEVIN PADDOCK

Kevin started boxing from the age of thirteen and within ten years had a hefty one hundred plus bouts under his belt in both the amateur and professional game at light heavyweight. After years of research, we finally managed to track him down, and here's what he had to say.

'I'd retired from boxing about a year and was in the pub one night when my dad rung me and says, "Eh, son, Bob Padgett's been on the blower and he wants to know if ya fancy a fight with Lenny 'Boy' McLean." Apparently they wanted my brother Sid, but my dad couldn't get hold of him. They had also asked Eddie Neilson who'd fought Bruno but he wouldn't fight either for some reason.'

Kev told us he knew all about Lenny – 'I mean, Lee, who fucking hadn't?' Apparently Len was due to fight Paul Sykes, and as it happened, Paul had had a tear up in his own town and had taken a cut above his eye, so his fight on 29 November 1979 at the Rainbow with Lenny was off, and this was where Kevin came in.

'Being from Southampton I get myself down to London and no sooner had I got off the train then I'm stepping into the ring. It's a lively old place. Donny "The Bull" Adams is the referee for the evening and Lenny steps through the ropes and murmurs something to me. I ain't bothered, I'm a fighter, it's what I'm paid to do, and at seven hundred notes as my purse in the late seventies, well, let's just say I'm more than happy. So, we're off and Len comes at me like a steamroller. He's smashing me to my body with some fucking heavy shots, lucky for my skills as a boxer I'm managing to duck'n'dive my way out of harm's reach, otherwise I'm sure I'd be bang in trouble. So, after a few rounds, Len had run down his batteries and he's flagging, so now I'm simply racking up point after point on the scorecard for the next five rounds. The bell goes for the end of the eighth and I've won on a point's decision. After the fight, he said to me it was like hitting a brick wall – he could hit hard but I could take a good punch. That's me sorted and I'm out of there with my bit of wedge, and that was about the size of it.

'Next time I seen Lenny was around 1981. Roy Shaw had just beat Lew Yates and I was told to go in and challenge Shaw. Lenny then jumps in the ring and challenges to fight the both of us there and then. All of a sudden there was murders there in the ring and everyone's getting pulled apart.

'I will just say that after my fight with McLean, my ribcage was as black as "Newgate's Knocker" for a few days. There was talk of a re-match, but for one reason or another, it never materialised.'

DOMENICO BERGONZI

'The first time I'd heard of Lenny McLean was when I remember my dad taking Lenny to work with him as a kid, lifting and delivering 300-pound blocks of ice. I then heard all the stories going round the boxing gyms. I remember the day in 1980 when I was training in a professional boxing gym called the Craven Arms in Lavender Hill, Southwest London. I was in my first year as a professional welterweight, an East London – Hackney – boy under the management of Sam Burns, who had the Finnegans, Chris and Kevin, Tony Sibson, Bobby Neil, and many more that I've forgotten. The man supervising and ruling the gym with a rod of iron was Freddie Hill, an old-school trainer who took no prisoners and let a few verbal Fs and Cs go on a regular basis!

'One sunny day in the gym in early summer and I'm skipping around the 4pm mark when I saw Lenny McLean and Johnny 'Bootnose' Wall, Lenny's cousin, come through the door of the small gym. Fuck, I thought, what's Lenny doing here? Lenny's big frame took up most of the door frame, Johnny was as tall as the door frame. The two cousins were greeted by a moustachioed Freddie, with his cap on the side of his head. Lenny and Johnny were assaulted by a verbal barrage of Freddie's colourful language, probably covered in globules of spit as well! With Lenny at later gym sessions was Frank Warren, a relative of his who sat there and watched the training and the sparring (Frank was promoting the NBC organisation at that time). Over time, Lenny gave me lifts home to and from the gym as I lived near him in East London. I was asked a few times to spar, getting Lenny and Johnny warmed up.

'One day I sparred with Lenny, with Frank Warren looking on. Lenny was stalking me down in the ring. Remember, I was under the welterweight level at around ten stone three, Lenny weighed fifteen stone plus. I had my running shoes on and Lenny couldn't get near me! He asked me to hit him so I did several times, whipping up and across fast combinations straight in the face. Lenny shouted loudly, "Did a fly land on me?" There was laughter outside the ring and he asked me to hit him again. So I hit him as hard as I could and as I moved away, I saw blood dripping from the headguard around the eye area. I stopped and said to Lenny, "You're cut, Len." He said, "What?" I repeated it, and in one move he undid the headguard with the glove on. On removal, a crimson sheet poured onto the side of his face. As he glared at me, I died in my boots. "Sorry, mate," I said. "It's not your fault," he told me. He then said, "I blame that old c***," looking at Freddie Hill. Frank Warren was having a seizure – Lenny was fighting in eight days' time and the fight was now looking like a no-go. I think they had to put the jump leads on Warren's wallet. His concern was that Lenny had sold hundreds of tickets and now the main man was injured.

'After a flurry of adrenaline and swabs and butterflies, Lenny set off to the doctors. He had twenty-six stitches in the cut but refused to pull out of the fight and knocked the next opponent out in two rounds, eight days later.

'Another story I remember was at Freddie Hills' gym one Saturday night after a session. Lenny and Johnny Wall took everyone in the gym downstairs for a drink for Lenny's birthday. The landlord wanted to close the pub as it was coming up to 2pm and was past closing time. Well, needless to say, Lenny kept the pub open all night and all the customers were happy except for the landlord, who was a lot wealthier but rather late for his Sunday lunch! We had pro boxers breaking curfews and orders on drinking on certain nights.

'Another day in the gym, Lenny and Johnny came in and they got changed into their gym stuff. About two-thirds into their training, these two women come in. I'm also training hard at the time and I saw these women sit down to watch Lenny and Johnny train – they must have been friends of them, with an interest in boxing. I watched on as other boxers started to up their groundwork rate to try and impress the two ladies, it was quite a funny sight to see with these men sweating buckets.'

ROY YORK

A name and a face many of you will have stumbled upon, a man who is no stranger to the Fight Game. The man we refer to is none other than Roy York, otherwise known as 'The Yorkie Bar Kid'. Now Roy first met Lenny when he was sent along to the Camden Palace in the late 1980s to work alongside him. Lenny introduced himself with all of the theatrical dramatics that we have come to know and love. He held out his massive mitt and said, 'I'm Lenny McLean, the Boxer,' and in turn, Roy replied, 'Good to meet you, Lenny. I'm Roy York, the Boxer, as well.' That broke the ice and cleared the way for a great many years of friendship to follow.

While minding the club alongside Len, Roy recalls how Lenny would always be the one at the front when trouble would arise, with no fear whatsoever.

THE GLOVES ARE ON

'He was just like that, Lenny, he always steamed in right in front of everyone, with that ferocious scowl and growl, to be honest, that stopped most situations from escalating without a blow being thrown.

'One particular evening, Lenny goes out on his own into the middle of the busy Camden street and confronts a rowdy pack of no less than twelve fellas. He goes in with his growling and snarling at the biggest and loudest one, a big Jamaican fella with dreadlocked hair. Lenny is shouting in that voice of his, which is enough to scare anyone. Well, at this point the fella realises just what he's up against and immediately backs down, with his entourage soon to follow.'

Roy went on to tell us that he also worked the odd night at the Hippodrome with Lenny, along with Len's cousin, Johnny 'Bootnose' Wall. Mick Theo and Johnny Madden were also working there. Lenny would always be your man at the front in any situation that arose at that venue too.

'Anyway, this one night the alarm's gone off upstairs and Lenny and I shoot up the stairs, expecting some trouble, but when we get up there, there's these two fellas in dresses fighting over a fucking handbag. Well, Lenny and I just picked up each of their bags and told them to kiss and make up. Some might see that as homophobic, but I can assure you that it wasn't. Let's face it, we weren't used to seeing that sort of thing, that was all. Funny too because Lenny had given me a call earlier that day and said, "Listen, Roy, we need the full firm out tonight. It's Gay Night," and with a laugh I'd said, "Right, son, if you work it, then I will." He was only joking, it was never meant with any malice. Suffice to say, we worked many an evening like that and got used to it in the end.'

It was around this time that Lenny asked Roy to get him into the film business – Roy already had a number of TV and film appearances under his belt. While working down the Camden Palace one evening, Lenny says to Roy, 'I wanna get in the film game like you, Roy,' so Roy says to Lenny, 'Don't worry about it, Len, I'll get you in.' So he introduced Lenny to the Ugly Agency, and they say to Len, 'Yes, Lenny, we're interested in working with you,' so Lenny tells them that he has a fight coming up over at Tottenham and do they fancy coming along? Anyway, they went along to the fight and afterwards almost inevitably they signed Len onto their books. So the Ugly Agency got Lenny his first job, but while on set unbeknown to them, Len had a row with one of the directors. Apparently Len really went into him, and obviously frightened the life out of him, and everyone else for that matter. Here, Roy takes up the story…

'So the company give Roy a call up and said to him, "Look, Roy, we can't have him if he's gonna be like that. The man's impossible, not to mention, of course, terrifying," so Roy says to Ugly's, "No, leave it with me. Get us a job together, and I'll go on it with him." Luckily enough, the job came up on *The Krays* [1990] with the Kemp brothers, and Lenny and Roy worked on that. As most of you will know, Lenny is sat ringside with Jack "Kid" Berg at the Krays' fairground fight.'

Needless to say, they all had to quieten Len down, Roy especially – you see Len and Roy had a lot of respect for one another. So that's Len on his way in the film game, and Roy was very glad that he could help. Roy told us, 'Lenny deserved a bit of a better life after the life he'd had to lead.' He went on to say: 'Lenny went from strength to strength and would've been in many more top roles if he'd have lived, bless him.'

Roy also went along with Lenny on a handful of debt collection jobs, Roy himself playing good cop to the role that Lenny did best as the most frightening character you would ever wish to owe money to. We asked him did they get their hands on it all, to which Roy, with a whimsical chuckle, simply exclaimed, 'No, believe it or not, they always fucking paid!'

As a great number of you may not be privy to, Roy was the referee for the first and, in some respects, most talked-about fight staged at Cinatra's in Croydon in 1977 between Lenny and Roy Shaw. We say 'most talked-about' for the simple fact that this event seems to be the only one that never circulated online in video format, so with this information in mind, let's put all of the hype and hearsay that engulfed this notorious fight to bed, with these accounts straight from the horse's mouth, our main man Roy, the ref himself.

'In my humble and non-biased opinion, so many things attributed to Len losing the first fight against Roy Shaw, not least the fact that I believe Lenny wasn't at all well, a fact of course that has been documented in the past by a number of people from the industry and beyond.'

Roy went all in from the off, in much the same way as he did in the two fights to follow, of which he has attributed losing the third and last fight to taking some kind of liquid relaxant, which greatly slowed him down. This, of course, we couldn't and wouldn't possibly comment on, owing to the fact that the Great Man isn't around to contest any such argument.

We then asked Roy if he could clear up a few questions we had with regard to the Brian 'Mad Gypsy' Bradshaw fight and he said contrary to popular belief, it was all reasonably calm at the Yorkshire Grey. There obviously was a strong gypsy presence, that was always going to be the case, but at first there weren't really any problems. As referees do in this game, Roy visited each fighter before they stepped into the ring. He went on to say that when he walked into Bradshaw's changing room, Bradshaw was punching and smashing his fists into the wall. As anyone who follows any sort of fighting sport will be aware, if your gloves have rips in them, it's quite easy to cause cuts to your opponent. This, of course, is villainy. Oh fantastic, we're off to a great start, he thinks, laughing as he tells us this.

Roy then visits Lenny's room and Len is sat as 'cool as a cucumber' with not a care in the world. We recall another pal of Len's saying that, an hour before the fight, Lenny said to him, 'You go take your missus and my Val to the Chinese restaurant, and wait for me there. I'll be there soon, son, once I put this fella to sleep.' Roy told us, 'Lenny simply didn't know what fear was.' He adds that the fighters then came into the ring – 'There's no need for me to go over the detail, I think that's been very well documented.' He did say, however, that when Len went cranky and went nuts, no one really knew what to do – 'I mean, we knew that Lenny wouldn't go into us proper when trying to stop him. Len was cranky at that point, he wasn't an animal.' Roy then says, 'Lenny left with no murders. We attended to Brian Bradshaw – I pulled his tongue out because I didn't want him to swallow it – and after some time, he came to. His corner helped him to the edge of the ring, where to his dismay, by the look on his face, someone stuck a microphone in his face. He didn't look very happy, to say the least!'

Roy also went on to tell us that Lenny offered himself up on behalf of his brother, Dave York (whose story you will read next), on account of Dave getting sliced up while working on the door one night by a couple of mugs that couldn't handle Dave in a straight-up fist fight and so resorted to pulling a Stanley knife out. The news obviously travelled a bit lively over from South London to the East End because in no time at all Lenny was on the blower to Roy, fuming – 'Right, let's go and sort these no-value c***s out!' Roy told Len how fantastic that was of him to offer his services, but Roy and Dave had it covered. Apparently Len took some persuading, but then he just said, 'Alright, son, but if you need me, pick up the blower.'

Lenny was always there if you needed him, Roy explained. Fortunately for the York brothers, they were well equipped in dealing with such situations themselves, unlike many others for whom Lenny sorted out problems over the years. He finished our chat by saying that he thought Lenny was taken for a bit of a ride at some points. After all, he did a hell of a lot to help many, many people, and in the early days sometimes without so much as a thank you. Roy said he was sure Lenny realised this himself in his last few years, but hopefully one day Lenny's film will give him the recognition he so richly deserves.

DAVE 'MAN MOUNTAIN' YORK

'Owing to the fact that I was in the same line of work as Lenny McLean, and also I had worked on a few doors from time to time for him, I was very aware of his well-vocalised reputation that echoed through the streets of London for a number of years. You see, being a doorman on a similar manor, I was very used to that way of life, and as Lenny has documented in his own book with regard to being shot and stabbed, etc., well, I too have been stabbed a few times, shot at, and occasionally set upon with bats and bars and chains and the like – it's just the way things are if you choose to enter our sort of world.

'My younger brother, Jim, was in the fight game. He'd had twelve senior fights as an amateur and for the record, he had knocked every one of them out with lightning speed. He could definitely have a row, could Jim, and that's a well-known fact. So, we're training in the gym in Southeast London called Shapes one day, and Jim's down there with us. Anyway, he decides to jump in and have a spar up with Lenny. They're in the ring gloved up, Lenny's got his arms flat down by his sides and he goes to my brother, "Right, go on, son, hit me," so my brother goes into Lenny, hitting him with everything he's got in his locker. Anyway, with that Lenny's just hit him with one shot, and knocked him spark out, and my brother's got up, crawled out from the ropes and gone to me, "For fuck's sake, rather you than me! You must be off your fucking nut, sparring with him." I go to him, "No, no, bring it on, son."

THE GLOVES ARE ON

'To be honest, my younger brother only got in the ring with Lenny to prove to me that Lenny didn't frighten him. Well, he was wrong about that little one, wasn't he? You see, back then, I used to get rid of my aggression down the football or in the clubs I was minding and I make no excuses, back then as I say, I did all of my fighting outside of the ring. I weren't a great boxer, I ain't stupid, I know that – I just liked having a tear up.

'My brother Roy knew Len very well, and had often talked about him. Anyway, this one night down the Camden Palace, where Lenny was minding at the time, Roy said to me, "Eh, Lenny wonders if you'd want to fight him." So I jumps up and shouts, "Yeah, no worries, son, I'll fight him." "Eh, Lenny," I shouted over, cos I'm a right cocky bastard, "I'll fight you," I says. "Where and when?" he shouts back, "Whenever and wherever you want, boy." So I goes, "OK, I'll fight you in here, if you want. Here, we'll have it now, on the dance floor." But Lenny's at work, so he just laughed it off. I think that he thought I was taking the piss, to be honest. He asked my brother, "Is he serious, Roy?" Our Roy just laughed – you see, I was game for anything back then.

'One thing I will say is back then, all of my brothers had fights for the glory of it. I was in it solely for the money – I was diving years before Tom Daley, taking bets against myself, even betting on which round I would go down in. I would've bet on anything back then. I didn't give a fuck, I just wanted the pound notes, simple as that.'

Still laughing, Dave says that's why he talks normal and his brother Roy talks like he's swallowed a bucket of sand – 'It's because our Roy's stopped too many punches with his fuckin' head in the ring!' He picks up the story...

'Anyway, we talked it up and the fight is on at Woodford Town Football Club, Snakes Lane, on 28 May 1986. I'm sure many of you reading this will have seen the footage on YouTube.

'So it was on a sunny Sunday afternoon in 1986. I was billed as "six foot seven" and "twenty-five stone" – a little bit off the mark. I'm about six foot five and a half, but eh listen, it sells tickets though, doesn't it? The fight poster slogan read, "The Guv'nor Has Had His Day", a little optimistic from my camp, but who gives a fuck? Well, I'd just come back from my wedding three weeks prior to this fight so I hadn't really trained much, to say the least. I ran to my hotel from the plane and back, if that counts, but to be honest, I think Lenny was a bit knackered too. Anyway, this was set to be his last fight with the 'things' on, as he called them (gloves). We get in the ring; Len's walked over to my corner, showboating, as we all knew Lenny would, my brother Roy stood between the two of us. My brother knows what I'm like, and we all know how Lenny is as well. So, anyway, we're off.

'One of the first shots Lenny threw broke two of my ribs and it was probably the first punch if you watch it back on the video. I sort of bend over a bit, with the pain of it, so anyway, we're moving around the ring again and I think I hurt Lenny too with a few shots, or so he informed me afterwards. So, Len's got me on the ropes and he's bashing me up, so I thought, right, fuck it, I'll stick the nut on him.'

Lee: So, I said to Dave, 'Crazy that is, Dave, because most people think Lenny started the nutting.' Dave told me, 'No, mate, that was all my doing, and I bit Lenny too.' He continues...

'So anyway, that's how it went. Len kept smashing at my ribs and I couldn't stand it any longer, and I went down. If you notice, I kicked Lenny in the bollocks when I'm on the deck although afterwards I realised that my brother Roy had already thrown the towel in, you can see it float past me as I'm on my back on the canvas. So anyway, we were still pals after that, that's just the fight game for you.

'Last time I saw Lenny was probably a couple of months before he died, in a pub just up the road from his house in Bexleyheath, and believe it or not, he still looked good. Anyway, he came over and asked how I was and that. You see, the thing is, Lenny had a hell of a lot of respect for anyone that dared to get in the ring with him because he knew that most people didn't have the bottle, and they thought he was way too scary. Like I said earlier, I was getting four and half grand – I would have got in the ring with King Fucking Kong for that sort of dough. As it turns out, I was working over Bexley on the day of Lenny's funeral so I was able to slip out and join the crowd outside the church and watch the procession go in and out. It was mad around there that day – you couldn't move it was that busy.

'One last thing I will say is Lenny done me a massive favour putting that show on, because let's face it, I'm still dining out on that story today, thirty years on. Cheers for that, Len! Funny how things never go away though; I own a bar on the Costa and my barman goes to me the other day as he's showing me a fight video on the big screen (I think it was on YouTube), "Look at these two big fuckers, they're off their fucking nut!" I says to him, "That's me, you soppy c***!" Everyone's laughing in my bar, so like I said earlier, I'm still dining out on it today, and I'm sure I probably will be for a fair few years to come and for that, I have Lenny McLean to thank.'

CLIFF FIELDS

Anthony: No Lenny McLean fan is a stranger to the name Cliff Fields, the ex pro boxer from Dunstable. After losing his professional licence due to stoppages from cuts, he tried his hand at the unlicensed fight circuit to make some money. I caught up with Cliff a few years ago and managed to interview him at his flat. He opened the door, smiled and welcomed me in, shaking my hand with some of the biggest shovels that I'd ever seen on a man. After settling in for a chat, Cliffy seemed a little confused about some of the details – I guess that with the alcohol dependency and the fact that we were trying to draw detail from fights that he had some twenty years ago, this was to be no easy task. So, after couple of hours chatting, I thanked Cliffy for his time and left with a few of our questions answered.

'This one night I was out and this man Johnny Stevens offered me a thousand pounds to fight this man from London named Lenny McLean. I was skint and it wasn't bad money for an unlicensed fight. I was told Lenny was a right fucking animal so I popped in to see him fight this bouncer at the Rainbow Theatre. Lenny done him in a minute, and looked powerful. At the end of the fight I stood up and laid down the challenge to fight him and straight away, he accepted. Frank Warren then approached me and said, "Lenny has accepted a re-match with Roy Shaw. How do you fancy reffing the bout, and then taking on the winner?" So I refereed their third fight at the Rainbow. The atmosphere was electric; Lenny caught Roy with some fast combinations. He was just too powerful. Roy Shaw didn't stand a chance, and very quickly, Lenny destroyed him.

'So, our fight was all set for the Rainbow Theatre too. A few days before the fight there was a rumour going around that Lenny was going to pull out as he had a virus but anyway, it went ahead. The bell went and he came out at me, throwing nonstop punches and really hard. The first round finished in Lenny's favour, but with his nonstop throwing of shots I could see that he could hardly breathe over in his corner. The bell went for round two and Lenny's come flying at me again. He then started nutting me, so I nutted him back, I *fucking nailed* him. He had simply worn himself out, so I took advantage and smashed him with the big right hand, straight on the button, and with that down he went, Lenny didn't make the bell.

'So, Lenny comes in the changing room afterwards

and says, "Well done, fair dos, you fucking beat me." We shook hands, but as he's leaving the room Lenny says, "I'll get you next time though."

'A few weeks later, I was training for a rematch with Lenny, and I was running round this park in London. Who do I bump into but Lenny having a fag. He then says to me, "Who are you training for, Cliffy?" I said, "You, Lenny, I'm fighting you." His face was a picture, he didn't even know the fight was on. "You want to stop smoking, Len," I told him. He said, laughing, "It don't make a difference, Cliffy, I can't breathe after two rounds anyway." We had a good old chat and then we continued to train.

'The second fight was more or less the same as the first. This time I finished him in the fifth round – I hit him with a combination and he went down and was counted out. He then got up and said to someone, "Who's next then?" – I think he thought he had won. I was glad when he got back up, as I liked Lenny. He came to see me again after the fight backstage and was great to me.' Cliffy went on to reveal in an article a few years later in the *Daily Mail*, 'Len was really tough, but I suppose I was that bit tougher [in the ring].'

'Lenny then asked me to come up and see him one night when he was working on the doors. We used to go around all the clubs and pubs in London, he was a proper gentleman and well respected everywhere we went.

'One day I took my son with me and went round to his flat, where I met his missus. His wife Val was a lovely lady and his kids took a liking to me too.

THE GLOVES ARE ON

'I became good friends with Lenny, he even gave me two of his suits some years ago, and they fitted me perfect. The last time I seen Lenny was when I stayed at his house for the weekend in the eighties. I never really heard from him after that. I speak as I find. He was good to me; I only ever witnessed a true gentleman. That's how I knew him, and that is simply how I will remember him.'

JOHNNY WALDRON

Lee: Going back to the early eighties and a little contentious debate that will be talked about forever is the one with regard to Len's bouts with pro boxer Johnny Waldron. Now Ant and myself, being trainspotting Lenny fans, would obviously never dream of running Len down, but the truth is the truth, and this by no means takes a single thing away from him as a fearsome fighting man and the ultimate 'Guv'nor'.

Johnny Waldron was a seasoned pro boxer with a great deal more talent under the strict control of the Marquess of Queensberry rulings than that of our man Lenny, a fact of which Len himself would never contest if he was sat with me as I type this massively debated piece of boxing history. For those of you who don't know, Johnny Waldron had a great pro rec under his belt consisting of nine wins, seven by KO (knockout), one loss and a draw. Not to mention the countless amateur and unlicensed fights that he had fought and won too. Big Johnny boxed in the ABAs for England and also went ten rounds with British and WBC Champion Dennis Andries, so let's just say he had some artillery with the gloves on.

Johnny then had his licence taken away from him and so joined the unlicensed circuit to make a few bob. In the unlicensed world he remained undefeated in twelve fights. Anyway, Johnny had been called in for his first bout with Len as a last-minute replacement for a fighter known as Dave 'Psycho' Spelling. In the weeks leading up to the fight, and for reasons we aren't privy to right now, Dave had apparently broken his hand and backed out of the fight with Lenny. What follows are the words taken from my brief, yet enlightening chat with Johnny 'Big Bad' Waldron.

Now I wanted to get to the bottom of this once and for all. Many an argument has reared its ugly head with regard to this matter on social media and I was keen to finally set the record straight so I started the conversation from the hip and straight to the point. Listen, Johnny is a man of few words and I wanted the few that he shared with me to be an all-encompassing envoi.

Johnny said that he first came across Lenny at a pub that he was minding on the Kingsland Road, Hoxton, called the White Swan. When he walked in this rough house he immediately spotted Len – it was difficult not to because Lenny was the sort of fella that once you'd seen him for the first time, you would certainly not forget him. Len was walking around the pub, big and brazen, with a copper's truncheon in his hand. Johnny immediately thought to himself, this ain't the kind of place that I want to be associated with and made a hasty retreat. He had heard many stories about Lenny McLean, stories that gave prominence to his reputation, and in turn could make any man a little weary of him.

Round about this time Johnny unfortunately had to

retire from pro boxing on account of a problem with his eyes – he could no longer get a licence. Anyway, the unlicensed scene was sort of flourishing at that time and so he thought, right, I'll get myself a few quid from this game. He knew that Lenny was number one in that world and often wondered if one day their paths would cross – 'So that's me back into a regime, and the training's going well.' Out of the blue, Johnny gets a phone call, asking if he fancied a spar up with Lenny McLean. He jumped at it, thinking, this will be my chance to find out just what this McLean fella is all about.

So the day comes and Johnny's made his way over the water to the desired gym. He remembers walking in to noise and the smell of sweat and blood – 'to be honest, Lee, that gave me a bit of a gee-up'. Anyway, no sooner had Johnny walked into the main area where the ring was than he spots Lenny. Johnny's thinking to himself, wow, the fucking size of the man! He looks even bigger in here. Just for the record, Johnny himself was about fourteen stone at that point. With that, someone shouts, 'Come on, Len, let's get the gloves on,' and Lenny jumps in the ring with some big wrestler fella. According to Johnny this fella had no technique to speak of. Suffice to say Lenny smashed him all over the ring. Credit to the wrestler fella though, he managed to stick with it for a couple of rounds, but Lenny just gave him a bit of a spanking. So with that the bell goes and it's Johnny's turn and he jumps in the now blood-drenched ring. He told me he remembered thinking to himself, there will be none of my claret mixed in with that fella's by the end of this session.

So they're off. Len comes out reasonably conservative, just throwing his weight around. Johnny bobs and weaves his way out of those massive shots that Lenny's throwing, now and then connecting with a left jab to Lenny, just to let him know that he's there. This carries on for the next two rounds while the pair of them get the measure of one another. Then Johnny starts throwing the odd jab'n'hook back at him. Len's face is getting a bit red and marked up, and he's looking increasingly angrier. Johnny told me, 'I was there to do a job, Lee, and that is the exact job of a sparring partner.'

Anyway, we're now into the third and final round and Len's come out of his corner like a bull. Johnny's thinking, fuck, I should've maybe gone at him a little harder, because now Lenny's punishing Johnny: his head's down, he's snarling and growling, and he's backed Johnny into the corner. Now he's going in on him like a madman. With that, Johnny says Len's lot around the ring are shouting for him to slow it down a bit, but Len did what he wanted and upped the heat ever more. So, Johnny's throwing jabs and ducking and weaving his way out of the onslaught. But Lenny is just going for it, so now it's a right proper tear up. With that, a couple of Len's pals jump into the ring to break them apart and Lenny is delicately eased away to his corner – 'But Lenny weren't happy, he had a right glare on his face,' said Johnny, adding that despite the vicious encounter, he was glad he'd done it, because it was a proper challenge. In Lenny he'd met a man that could push him to his absolute limit, and probably beat him. Lenny was a powerful man, and he'd been marked far more in a spar-up with Len than he ever did in the actual ring with him. A puzzler for Johnny, as it is for us, and I'm sure a great many of our readers too.

So anyway, Johnny's back to his training over at the Thomas A Becket gym. One evening, the phone rings: this time it's Alex Steene and during their conversation he suggests to Johnny that he fights Lenny McLean proper – 'There's three'n'half grand in it for you, John.' So Johnny thinks, right, I'll have a piece of that – 'I could do with a few bob' – and the first fight is on.

Forward to the night of the fight: we're at the Cat's Whiskers over [in] Streatham with Len and Johnny. Johnny has arrived at the venue and it's bouncing to Lenny's tune, full of top movie stars, etc. Johnny said, 'Lenny couldn't half pull in a crowd.' He waited patiently for the undercard [supporting fight] to wrap up and then it's his and Len's turn.

So they're off, just like the sparring session, easing into one another, letting out the odd shot here and there. Johnny said that he was expecting a bit more of a battle from Lenny though, but for some reason that wasn't the case. So they're moving for a few rounds. Nothing much is happening, although Lenny has hurt Johnny with the odd dig here and there, so Johnny's ducking and diving his way out of Lenny's reach. But nothing's really happening and the crowd are getting a little 'aggie' [agitated]. Anyway, they're now into the third round, and Jackie Bowers, the cornerman, says to Johnny, 'Right, hit him hard, people are getting bored,' so with that Johnny steps up his pace and puts a few shots in. Lenny is sent back a little and while he's a bit off-balance, Johnny unleashes a blinder and catches Lenny on the button, knocking him down to the canvas, with his head under the ropes. Johnny is a little alarmed by this because it wasn't meant to happen. But it has, and the ref has counted Lenny out. Len's cornerman, Bobby Warren, is doing his nut, the crowd are going mad and things are looking a little dodgy. With that, Lenny comes steaming over to try and start the fight up again

–'Oh, it was murders, Lee, I didn't know what the hell had just gone on,' Johnny told me. He said that Lenny had absorbed a lot of the shots that Johnny hit him with that most people would have gone down from. Also, that had he known Lenny had connected with him, it would have hurt and maybe he would have gone down himself.

Anyway, that was that: Johnny's first proper encounter with 'The Guv'nor' Lenny McLean. Apparently in the mayhem Lenny had told the announcer to call Johnny out for a re-match. Once Johnny has got himself dressed and sorted, things have calmed down, so he decides to head into the quiet bar. He's only been in there a couple of minutes when Lenny walks in and Johnny's thinking, oh this ain't good. Johnny says, 'Sorry about that, Len,' and like a true sportsman, Lenny says, 'Don't worry about it, Johnny, it happens,' then buys Johnny a pint. They sit and chat for a while, and that's about the size of it. Johnny told me that after the first fight, he did on occasion go up to the Hippodrome, the club Lenny was minding, to see him. He and Lenny would chat about this and that over a lemonade or two and always remained friends.

Now and again he also bumped into Lenny over Victoria Park and they always had a nice talk there too and even ran together. You see, contrary to popular belief, there was never any bad feeling between them, not on any level. Johnny said he had a lot of respect for the man, and that's the way it will always remain.

So, let's go back to the second meet and the most-talked-about fight that the two of them had. This was arranged to take place at the Ilford Palais, over in Essex. Again, it's another rowdy house, and it's packed to the rafters. All of the faces are there from the fight world and celebrity

THE GLOVES ARE ON

world. Let's just say, there was a few bob changing hands that night.

So, fight two... The referee for the evening was Patsy Gutteridge. He calls them into the middle, tells them to shake hands and be good boys. The bell goes and they're off! Immediately, Johnny's sticking some hard jabs into Lenny, again and again, but Lenny's hunting him down. Johnny is way more mobile than Len, faster on his feet. Len's coming at him with that growling snarl on his face, but Johnny dances out of harm's way. Lenny then moves into Johnny, but leaves himself wide open. With that Johnny hits Len with a left combination, which connects hard, and he watches in what feels like slow motion. Johnny told me as Lenny started to go down, he watched him tumble, all the while thinking, he ain't getting up from that, and so he retreats to his corner, watching on as Gutteridge counts Lenny out: One... two... three..., and Johnny says, 'Fuck me, Lenny starts to get back up.' He's grogging and spluttering a bit, but Patsy signals for them to continue. Meanwhile Johnny's thinking to himself, fuck me, he's a hard bastard! He told me: 'The punch was so hard, it's jarred my arm,' before adding, 'not many would've gotten up from that.' He continued: 'I had never hit anyone as true on the chin as I did with that punch. If I myself had taken a shot so damning, I would have been out for a week.' Lenny was made of stern stuff, although from that point on Johnny could see that he was out on his feet, but the sheer will and mettle of the man was so strong, he would have carried on forever.

So Johnny keeps pounding away at Len, with heavy shots from torso to head, but Lenny just keeps coming for him. Johnny catches the ref's eye as much to say, 'He's dead on his feet,' but Gutteridge indicates that Lenny wants to carry on, so they're off again. Johnny starts to think, fuck sake, is he ever gonna let up and go down? But no, Lenny is still in pursuit. So, Johnny just throws blow after blow after blow, raining shots in on Lenny and throwing everything he has in his locker. All of a sudden it's bedlam in the ring – everyone's jumped in, Roy Shaw, Cliffy Fields, Joe Carrington, the lot – and there's mayhem. Cliffy is shouting something over the MC's microphone. Johnny said it was bloody murders in there but it all calmed down and that was two wins in a row. Who would've thought it, Johnny thought to himself.

He went on to say, 'Just for the record, Lenny was a very tasty fighter, make no mistake. Not to demean Lenny or anything, but that's the difference between a cobble fighter and a seasoned pro boxer: once they step into the professional arena it's a different game altogether. That's just the way it is, you know.'

The last time that Johnny saw Lenny properly was over in Victoria Park. They had a brief chat and of course Lenny asked Johnny for a re-match, obviously knowing that it would never come off. I said to Johnny, 'I suppose it was a reversed Shawry thing, and like Shawry with Lenny, Lenny would have fought you until the day that he died, just to even the score up a little, eh?' To which Johnny respectfully replied, 'I suppose you're right, Lee, yes.'

Johnny paid his respects to Lenny at his funeral and how very honourable it was of him too.

So anyway, that was the end of that. The chat myself and Anthony had wanted to happen for many years. A no-holds barred, honest and true insight into what went on between those two fine pugilists, the street-fighting

Guv'nor of the cobbles, Lenny McLean, and the boxer and formidable contender Johnny 'Big Bad' Waldron. One last thing I would like to do is say a big thank you to Johnny Waldron's son, Jamie, for making it happen – you're a gentleman.

LESLIE GROOM

'I grew up in the East End of London and my dad was also called Leslie. My dad's best mate was Jack 'The Hat' McVitie. My dad knows anyone that's anyone and he's a proper character and was also good mates with Lenny McLean too. If you look at the vids doing the rounds with Lenny sparring Johnny Wall in Kenny Mac's yard – well, that's my dad in the background. Most of the people there that day at Kenny's worked for my dad in his scrapyard. I was about fifteen when they were filming at the yard. When I was there I was asked to put a ring up and I found these big gas bottles and the only thing I could think to do was to put ropes around them.

'Anyway, we'd go for a bit of lunch and then go into Kenny's to eat it, then Lenny and the others, usually Johnny Wall, would start training. At the time Lenny was in training for a fight with Dave 'Psycho' Spelling from Brixton. Spelling was fucking massive, one big bloke, but his camp had rung up a few weeks before the fight and said he couldn't fight for some reason. It was the worst thing that could have happened as Lenny had sold a lot of tickets and now the challenge was getting someone to step in at short notice. Next thing you know, Lenny himself was up against Johnny

Waldron. Also on the bill was Cliff Fields, fighting on the undercard against Gilberto Acuna (who was from Costa Rica and had lost to Frank Bruno, a few months earlier). So, Kenny had Cliff Fields down in his yard to train and spar and my dad put Cliff up in his pub, the Railway Tavern, so he was staying with us for a few weeks. We also used to have the weigh-ins for the fights and after-show parties.

'So this one day Lenny was sparring with Cliffy and there was no love lost between these two in the ring. They had done a few rounds and were having a real war. Lenny's then caught him with a combination and this cracking right hook, cutting his eye to pieces. The sparring was stopped and Cliffy was going mental like a madman, so Lenny gets out and you can see Lenny thinking, OK, we're on the cobbles now. They started pushing each other but both men won't throw the big one. Cliff's eye looked like it had been sliced with a knife and it was only two weeks before the fight.

'Things seemed to calm and then Cliff's off again. Lenny looked at me and said, "Boy, get me an iron bar." Now where the fuck could I get an iron bar from? Then I noticed next to the ring was this little blue gas bottle fire extinguisher you see in caravans. Lenny's shouting and growling, so looking back, it was the best thing I could have picked up as he would have hit him with an iron bar if he had one. Anyway, I've given Lenny the blue bottle and Cliffy sort of stopped in his tracks as he was moving towards Lenny. They both looked at each other and Lenny said, "How the fuck am I supposed to hit him with this, you fucking dozy c***?" Both then started pissing themselves laughing.

THE GLOVES ARE ON

It stopped them fighting though and they went off to check Cliff's eye out. Later on they were good mates again and were down my dad's pub the same night.

'Like I said, Lenny was good mates with my dad but I remember Dad banned him from his pub this once. Lenny had a fight with this bloke who also worked for my dad and Lenny had smashed him right up – you can't fight Lenny when he's in that mood. Now this bloke wasn't the biggest, but he kept coming back, proper hard case. In the end the bloke left, then around about two in the morning after hours there was a bang on the door and it's only this bloke with a sawn-off shotgun. Lenny had gone not long after him as he hardly drank then. Anyway, my dad said to Lenny the next day, "Len, you got to keep out of the pub, you're causing too much trouble in here and scaring my punters." The trade had gone down with Lenny being there and you didn't know what he was going to do next in them days.

'Obviously, you've seen the video of Lenny running through Victoria Park with his fist clenched, shouting, "I'll kill that Roy Shaw!" Well, what happened was Johnny Wall had a new convertible golf car and he wouldn't let anyone drive it. Now Johnny always had a video camera with him and they were also making a documentary for the upcoming fights. So my dad's other mate they called Dukie was in the back of the car, filming Lenny running and stuff. The distance around Victoria Park is about three miles roughly, so Lenny had been doing it for a few days, then on the last day he was going to get filmed. So anyway, Lenny's got all around the park and he's sweating his bollocks off and they've wrapped up the filming and Lenny's wiping himself down. Lenny then changes into his red polo-neck top and Johnny's got out of the car and taken the camera off Dukie. Next thing you know, Johnny's gone, "You dopey c***, you ain't turned the fucking machine on!" Everyone was laughing as Lenny's chased Dukie around the car five times and Lenny says, "You dopey c***, I'm fucked now!" so the only thing they could do is do the bit of a sprint with Lenny with his polo-neck on, but what Lenny should have been saying is, "I'll kill that fucking Dukie!" instead of Roy Shaw. Lenny was one funny, funny fucker.

'When I was about eighteen Lenny was working the door at the Camden Palace. Now every week, I'd go there with my mates and Lenny would always say, "You alright, boy? How many of you tonight? Now get in there quick and don't cause any aggro." So we've gone up every week like clockwise and always had a good night. We've gone up this one night and Lenny's not there – it must be his night off, I thought to myself. So we paid our money and made our way into our regular corner.

'We'd been in there a while having a chat, dancing with girls, and one of my pals says, "Les, you got a bit of agg." Now there was always about ten of us with our backs to the walls – we weren't causing trouble, we were just young and loud. So I says, "Who with?" We weren't frightened of anyone at that age if it did come on top. All of a sudden there was this Scotch geezer who worked the doors on nights when Lenny was off, he had rings on and tattoos all over him,

THE GLOVES ARE ON

and he was fucking massive. This guy was twice the size of me. Anyway, he's coming through the crowd and the crowds parting, and I'm thinking, fuck, he's coming for me or my mates behind me! As he's a few feet from me, he's now putting these leather gloves on and looking me in the eye. It's gone all quiet there as my mates could see what was happening. Next thing you know, all you can hear is, "You touch him and I'll break your fucking jaw!" Lenny appeared up on the balcony. Although it was his day off, he'd come in to collect his money and thank fuck he did. He then came down and grabbed hold of the Scotsman and said, "See him, he's my fucking son. You ever come anywhere near him, I'll bite your nose off and shove it up your arse!" Lenny and he didn't get on and he was always testing Lenny. The bloke then said, "Lenny, he was causing aggro." Lenny looked at me and said, "Leslie, was you causing agg?" "No, I wasn't, Len," I told him and Lenny believed me and said to the bouncer, "See the night in, get your money and then fuck off!"

CHAPTER 5

THE GUV'NOR IN YOUR CORNER

Many of you will not be privy to the facts of just how many people Lenny McLean helped out over the years. From a very young age and with almost no financial gain to himself whatsoever, he had taken on a great number of people's problems – friends and associates of Len's that simply never possessed the tools or wherewithal to iron out said problems for themselves. Over the course of writing this book we met up with a bunch of them. Here we have some of their stories.

RAY KENNEDY

'Lenny and Val took me and my mother in when I was about seven years of age after my dad had gone to jail for a bit. I'm from Belfast but my mother was from Bethnal Green and married an Irishman. When my dad had gone to jail, my mother was left homeless and Val let us stay until we went to Belfast. Lenny was one of the loveliest people I have ever met, a true gentleman. Not once did he shout at me or have a go at me and I was a right evil little bastard. Lenny once caught me throwing bricks at one of his neighbours' windows. I thought, I'm in for it here off Lenny, but he took me with him instead and made me clean out his neighbour's pigeon shed and it was fucking stinking. I think it was Lenny's way of teaching me a lesson.

'This one day the neighbour's son, who was a lot older than me – I'd say he must have been about sixteen – anyway, he was threatening to beat the living hell out of me after I'd cleaned that fucking shed so I went and told big Len what the man's son had said to me. Lenny at the time was stuffing his face with a packet of biscuits and spat them all over the place. He then said to me, "If this lad hits you and you don't fight back, I'll make you clean every fucking bird shed in London.' I took this advice on board as all Len wanted me to do was stand up for myself and I thought to myself, if this fucker touches me I'm going to fight because there was no way I was going to clean another bird shed ever again.

'I remember Lenny singing a lot in the time while I was there, and he was always smoking like a train. This one day I lifted up one of his roll-ups and he just looked at me and said, "Don't you think you're short enough, son? If you smoke, you will stay that size." I ended up not smoking until I was thirty-six. He was a right character with the things he used to come out with, he would have us all in stitches, laughing.

'I also remember this big tall bloke who was even taller than Len coming to his house and he would call Lenny, 'boy'. Thinking he was talking to me as he had said the word 'boy', I went to him and this big cheeky fucker then would tell me to sod off. Looking at it now, they were probably there to talk business and I may have been a cheeky little kid in the way.

'After two weeks of being in Len and Val's house my dad's brother came and took us back to Belfast. A few years ago I had a run-in with a few tinkers over some shit. The tinkers never paid me the full amount of money owed to me, so on the way out of the site I lifted up this little tiny puppy and put it in the back of my van. The pup went from being a tall skinny swine to a fifteen-stone powerhouse Rottweiler and I still have him to this day – he's called Lenny.

'I spoke with a bloke recently and he told me that when he was younger, he worked on the doors in London and every bouncer knew Lenny was unstoppable when he snapped on the street. When I think of Lenny being like that it just doesn't register as he was like a big kid when I was there. I think the best way he should be remembered is his way of doing things: he took no bullshit and a few people didn't like that. Lenny was a fucking angel, the hardest angel on the planet. I saw the real side of Len even though I was only there for two weeks. You could see everything he had done was for his family, and I was glad to have had the privilege to have met them all.'

MICHAEL JURY

'I never knew Lenny on a personal level but just from going regular to the Camden Palace for a few years and saying hello to him. We used to go there raving all of the time, and Lenny (or the big scary bouncer bloke) as we knew him, would look around and see just how fucked-up myself and my fellow ravers were. If he saw us in a bad way he'd grab a box of ice poles from over the bar and hand them out to people who were worse for wear. Remember, take into account they were charging two pound a pop for them, but Lenny didn't pay and was just helping people out to come around a bit – not many doormen done that.'

MICHAEL FLINDALL

'I met Lenny the once. It must have been about twenty-five years ago and I was working a one-man door in a place called Samantha's in Regent Street, London. I was having trouble with these three gangsters and it's gone off and while taking one or too blows, I was thinking, I'm in trouble here, then all of a sudden a car pulled up and a giant of a man got out. I was thinking, look at the size of him, I'm done for. The men I was then fighting clocked him coming towards them and started shouting stuff at the big man and then they run off. I would then find out that this man was Lenny McLean and he said to me, "You alright, boy?", to which I replied, laughing, "I had it under control." Lenny starts laughing and got back in his car and drove off. Funnily enough, the next six months

I had no problems at all in this venue – that was the sort of presence he had. That was my only encounter with The Guv'nor and he probably saved my life that day, and it always stuck in my memories.

DEBBIE MARSH

'My nan Grace and her family, the Copperthwaites, were born and bred in the East End. They were a very well-known family back in the day. Nan used to tell us stories of how her brothers would teach the Kray Twins how to box and that. Now being born and brought up in the East End in a certain decade, everyone knew everyone. Suffice to say, my nan, of course, knew Lenny McLean. She would often say to us, "Do you know what? Now there are a lot of things said about Lenny McLean, you know, saying he's this and that, but it's all a load of old fucking pony!" She would tell us that every year without fail at Christmas time, Lenny would come around to see her and he would always give her a few quid, always a tenner or more, never any less. Which Nan would say, "You know, Debbie girl, that was a fucking lot of money in them days."

'Nan told me also that she would on many occasions bump into Lenny down the market and he would go, "Right, give me those bags, Aunty Grace. I don't want you carrying that lot all the way home." Now let me just say this, Lenny was no relation to us at all, but that was just the way it was in the East End of London. Like I said earlier, everyone knew everyone; we were like one big family back then. Now Lenny wouldn't just walk my nan to the street where she lived and drop her off there, he would take her right up to her door and make sure she got in safe. Then Nan said, "You know what? He would put those massive fucking arms around my shoulders and give me a kiss and a cuddle and say, 'Well, Ta, ta, Aunty Grace, be lucky, gal.'" Now I must warn you to please excuse my French, because it's just the way they all spoke in the East End. So my nan would say, "Fucking hell, Lenny, ya nearly breaking my arm!" Nan said, "Cos you do know, Debbie, that Len was a right big fucking giant of a man, don't you? He done all that bare-knuckle fighting and that, and no one could beat him."

'I don't think Nan had ever seen Lenny fight – it was probably just what her brothers had told her because they were a right tasty bunch of fellas too, by all accounts. You see my nanna was a proper old-school feisty girl. I can hear her now saying to Lenny, "Fucking hell, Len, you big c***!" It's just the way she was. She said Lenny was a proper old-school gentleman, one of your own, a lovely man. She couldn't sing his praises enough. Well, I say, God bless you, Lenny McLean, for looking after my nan and making her feel safe.'

RICHARD MICALLEF

'I was lucky to have had the pleasure of meeting Lenny a couple of times through my old mate, John Huntley. I met John through a very good friend of mine, Glen Hibbert, who was an extra in *Lock, Stock and Two Smoking Barrels* – he used to do some modelling with John back in the day too. I always met Lenny in the

Emporium club in the West End when he would come with John.

'I was telling Lenny how I had always enjoyed the boxing scene, as my dad, George Micallef, used to box as well – Dad was also the cousin of Charlie Magri, the boxer. When speaking to Lenny, I asked him for a picture to put up in the café I had called Capones as I had old boxing pictures up on the wall there. I told Lenny that it would be good to have him up on the wall there, and you could see by his face that he was quite chuffed. I never thought for one second that he would do it for me, though.

'The next time John brought Lenny down we went into the VIP area in the Emporium and we had a couple of drinks and a good old chat, then Lenny pulled a signed picture out of a bag and gave it to me, as promised. I was over the moon with it. That was the last time I saw Lenny but I'll always treasure that I met him. He was a true gentleman and it's always been a nice little story to tell people that I've met The Guv'nor.'

DON DELANEY

'I first met Lenny McLean many moons ago when I first went to England. I was eighteen at the time and was working on a door in Tottenham. One Saturday night I was on the way to work on the doors and I met him on Holloway Road as I was heading to the Archway Tavern, which was a mad Irish pub.

'I asked him for advice as I was doing a lot of rough pubs and was only a fresh Paddy coming to England. Lenny then told me to get down the boxing club called

Thomas A Becket during the week and he would help me out. I already had a good number of years boxing behind me so I thought 'brilliant', until he got me to hold the bag for him down there. He was just jabbing, but his power was unreal and he hadn't even broken a sweat! It was then my turn and he said, "Oh, you fight southpaw," which seemed to shock him.

'He then helped me for a few months on and off and then got me a job on a door in Tufnell Park, North London. My God, was it a rough place! It was called The Boston and full to the rim with mad Irishmen. I met him the following week and he cracked up laughing and said, "Hope you enjoyed it, son." My nose had been broken and I was waiting to shit out my two back teeth.

'If anyone wanted a straightener, he would show me the way – "Get in quick and fast," he said. I always remember that about him. He got me plenty of protection work and I will never forget him for that as I went back to college and done my degree and started training in the close protection business. I will always be grateful to Lenny. I'm retired now and I've moved back to Ireland. Lenny was, and shall always be a legend in my eyes.'

KEITH HUNT

'I was first introduced to Lenny by my parents, who were very good friends with him. They were also friends with Lenny's father Leonard until his untimely death at the age of just twenty-nine. My family lived above Lenny's relations, the well-known Spinks family.

Yet another formidable character lurked among that family too – it was plain to see exactly where Lenny's fighting prowess was borne from. I had of course heard many stories with regard to Lenny over the year, as he had a very big reputation from a very young age. I went to school and was good friends with Lenny's younger brother, 'Kruger'.

'Lenny always had a lot of time for people. If you were down on your luck he would try and help you out. So, I had just come home from my first Nationals tournament in Karate and I'm with my mum, sat in our local pie'n'mash shop. Anyway, with that, would you believe it, in walks Lenny. So, he's having a chat with my mum and me and he goes to me, "Eh, you do all of that Kung Fu stuff, don't you, son?" I says, "No, Len, my one's Karate, Lenny, the one that I do." Anyway, we have a little laugh and joke about it, as you do, and we both walks over to the counter to get some more drinks and that for Mum. Len goes, "Here, boy, you wanna earn yourself a crust?" I says, "Oh yeah, Len, not half!" "Right," he goes, "get yourself over the Eagle Pub tonight, seven to seven thirty, and dress up smart. Alright, boy?" I goes, "Oh yeah, thanks, Len, I'll have some of that." But with that he goes, "Listen, boy, don't tell Mum." So, to be honest, with that last instruction from Len, I'm thinking to myself something's going down here, and what with me and my Karate background, it just all fitted together.

'So that's me, my word is my bond. Len just isn't the sort of fella that you say no to, not in an intimidating sense – he just had this way about him that made you sort of agreeable, you know. But as Len has said, Mum's the word. So I gets myself all suited and booted, as instructed. Remember, at this time I'm still only a boy of nineteen years. Anyway, I make my way to The Eagle, the boozer Lenny has sent me to. When I gets there, I can clearly see that something had or was about to go down. I'm thinking to myself, please, God, tell me that it's the former as Lenny doesn't look at all happy. I'll tell you this though, when you think of Lenny's signature music for his fight build-up, the popular tune 'Daddy Cool', I'm here to tell you, he certainly fucking was – 'Cool as a cucumber', as he would always say. But me on the other hand, my arse was twitching a bit. I mean, this isn't any run-of-the-mill job I'm on, this bit of work is for the formidable Lenny 'Boy' McLean. So anyway, I done a few nights for Len, and everything went great. I'd earned a good bit of dough, so I went and found Len to give him a drink for helping me out.

'Let me tell you this, Lenny was like the Scarlet Pimpernel to find. Mind you, not if you needed him though – in that case he just sort of appeared. Anyway, I goes, "Here, Len, thanks for that bit of work," and went to bung him a few bob for a drink, and he goes, in that fucking booming voice of his, "Piss off, now you go treat ya mum. Never mind me, you owe me fuck all!" I said, "I've already bunged Mum some, Len," and he goes, "Right, well that's that then, Keify boy, as long as you've treat your mum." So that was that – I knew Len would give me a shout if he needed me again.

'A while later, I was at a place called the Empire in Leicester Square and for some strange reason the Old

Bill would frequent there on a regular basis. Well, obviously we had no choice but to allow them in, it just kept things sweet. So this one evening I'm stood inside and these two plainclothes Old Bill are parked up opposite me, and with that, in walks Lenny, with his pal, Vince. So anyway, Lenny comes over, we had a little chat, he asked about my parents, etc., and then him and Vince had it away on their toes. To this day I'm sure that he had come up there on the lookout for somebody. So, like I say, Len's left, and with that the two Old Bill fellas come over to me. They were still looking at Len as he walked off, I don't think they could believe the size of the man. Anyway, one of them goes to me, "Is that Lenny McLean?" and I goes, "Yeah, that's Lenny 'Boy', why?" and they goes, "Fuck me, that's the first time I've ever seen him, he's a fucking big bastard!" I said, "Yeah, good man is our Len," and the copper says, "What did he come in for, is he after somebody?" I'm thinking to myself, this little mug is trying to stir up shit, so I says, "No, nothing like that. He's a friend of the family, he just popped up to ask how my mum and dad are." Then I goes, "Anyway, boys, if you're looking for a pull, you'd need another couple of van-load of blokes to give Big Lenny a tug." They sorted of nodded as if to say "no shit" and left the club. I swear to God, those two coppers could not take their eyes off Len. It was as if a top movie star had just walked in, I'm telling you, that was the sort of presence he had. Anybody would tell you the same, I guarantee it.

'It must have been a year later that I bumped into Len again, around 1994, maybe earlier. Anyway, he was in a car showroom on a bit of business, I think. We had a little chat as usual, and he goes, "Where you off to, boy?" I said, "Nowhere special, Len, why?" You see, a little while earlier Len had sorted me out with a nice motor from one of his pals. Anyway, he goes to me, "Listen, Keify boy, fancy nipping me down to a meet? I'm meeting someone from the telly and I wanna be a bit posh, ya know." I sort of chuckled and went, "What you doing, Len, you gonna be a comedian?", and he goes, "No, boy, I'm gonna give the acting a bit of a go."

'I thought, well, if anyone can jump into the acting, it was Len. I mean, he was like a movie star round London as it was. So I takes him from Kingsland Road to 79 Waldorf Street, where he obviously had his meet, and the next time I see him, he's on telly in *The Knock*. He was a grafter if he wanted something, that man. I knew he'd get himself in there, and he was fucking fantastic in it. Sad really because it wasn't too long after this that I found out that he was very poorly in about 1997, and obviously he passed away not long after. It was such a shame as he had just managed to leave the violent world behind and started to get himself a good name in the TV world – that has always upset me that, it really has.

'Like I said earlier, Lenny was always there to help anyone in need. It was just the same when my dad died. I don't think it was coincidence that all of a sudden Len would be around, and would pop in our local café to see my mum and ask how she was, and he always bunged her a few bob. She never actually told me this, but mark my words, he did. Lenny was a true

gent and a great friend, and my family loved the man.
I will certainly never forget him.'

ANTHONY CHANNON

'I first met Lenny in 1996 when I was out shopping this one day in Bexleyheath. I said, 'hello Lenny, how are you?' I put my hand out he said, 'hello mate' back to me and shook my hand. I told him I had not long started working the doors myself and asked him if he had any tips. He said, 'always stay strong and let no punter make a mug out of you'. I then shook his hand again and he said, 'be safe'. I then seen him again and he asked how I was getting on with the doors. He come across as a true gent but was not someone to be crossed.

CHAPTER 6

BEHIND THE DOOR

In 1991, Lenny was nicked on a murder charge for a crime that he would later be acquitted of. The court found him not guilty of the murder of Gary Humphries, but made an example of him with a charge of GBH. As a result, he spent eighteen months in the confinement of 'Her Majesty's Pleasure'. Now locking any man away from his loving wife and family is always going to be a difficult task, so imagine if you will, a man of Lenny McLean's size and ferocity locked away for a conviction that he wholeheartedly knew he was innocent of. This was always going to prove to be a very difficult ride for the prison hierarchy, and of course anyone foolish enough to cross Lenny. The stories that follow will give you an insight into the fraught and fractured state of our man Lenny's mind during his time spent 'Behind the Door'.

MARK DAVIES

'So I've just turned twenty-one, and I've got myself nicked on a charge and I'm being held in a holding cell in Lambeth. There's no need for me to fill you in on the bit of skulduggery that's landed me in the clink but let's just say that I'm bang in trouble and awaiting a hefty sentence. So I'm sat in this holding cell, absolutely fucking shitting myself, with about thirty other villains and what have you. Now if you've ever done a bit of bird, you'll know how it is when you're sat feeling sorry for yourself, listening as you hear the boots of some Nazi screw clumping down the corridor towards your cell, and you're hoping and praying it's you that they're coming for. If only to ship you out to whichever Grey Bar Hotel [prison] you will have to call home for the foreseeable.

'Right, so the screw's on his way and the whole room's eyes are fixed on that big steel door. So, the keys jangle in the lock and the door opens wide and in steps this fucking Goliath of a man. I've never seen anything like it, this fella had to stoop his head to get in the room, he was a fucking frightening-looking big c***, make no mistake about that. Anyway, in this big gruff and booming voice, with an all-apparent East London twang, this giant says to the whole room, "Right, listen up, you fucking mugs! I don't wanna hear any that, 'Sweet bruv, how's it hanging?' or any of that other street talk shit, or I'll bite your fucking noses off!" Then, cool as a cucumber, he turns to me and says, "Alright, my son, you fancy a roll-up?", as he sits himself down right by my side. Now it was great while he was in there, but he got called out for shipping way before me, so now I'm sat on my own with this bunch of fuckers, who by now think that I'm some sort of teacher's pet, for fuck's sake – they couldn't call my name quick enough, I'll tell you that! Now at this point I have to be brutally honest and admit to you all that at the time I had no fucking clue who the hell Lenny McLean was. A fact of which I was subsequently going to find out.

'So, anyway, Lenny gets shipped out to Brixton, and I'm sent to Belmarsh. So, it's all going well for me. I'm sorted out with a proper tasty little job as a hospital orderly and things are looking good. Now one particular day there's a load of commotion among the screws and that, so I liven myself up and go to find out what's going on. So I'm talking with one of the screws and he says to me, "Listen, we've got a right one coming in, apparently this fella is a fucking raving lunatic, an animal that they've sent along to us from Brixton." Apparently while in Brixton the doctor there had given Lenny a phone and it's obvious to me that the doctor has had to say that Lenny bullied it out of him in order to cover his own back. So, anyway, they bring Lenny in, and obviously I immediately recognised him, but he didn't recognise me. It's understandable really, considering who he is and the sort of people he runs around with. So, they put Len on the lower floor, in a dormitory. Now there are three dormitories on this floor, each accommodating five inmates. In the middle there is a Perspex room, where the screws are stationed in order to see into all of the three dorms. Anyway, I goes into Len's dorm and says to him, "Hello Lenny, you don't remember me, do you?" and to my dismay, he says, "No, sorry, son, I don't." So I goes, "Do you remember up Lambeth?" and thank fuck for that, he's jumped up and gone, "Oh hello, son, how you going, boy?" So obviously I'm as happy as a sand boy – I was just pleased he remembered me in the end. Listen, Lenny is the sort of fella you want as a friend.

'So, everything is going great, and due to my trade as a butcher in Smithfield Market, I've landed myself a lovely little job on fifteen notes a week in the kitchen. This is a double bonus because I have some good pals working in that kitchen too. So, of an evening, at the last knockings, the kitchen staff are sorting out the grub for the night screws and obviously I'm into my pals for big hunks of cheese and steak and such-like. This is a top-quality perk in any nick, because obviously I'm taking what I can back to my dorm and sharing it out with the five fellas I'm banged up with, and of course Lenny happens to be one of them. Now I will say this, Lenny always managed to get the lion's share of the fucking cheese – anything to keep the big man happy!

'You see, while Lenny was in Belmarsh, he was in a bit of a bad way. Not wanting to speak out of turn, but whatever was going on with Len, he certainly wasn't dealing with it too well. Obviously, the charge that he was in for, that he 100 per cent knew he wasn't guilty of, was the main reason, and at that time 'for one reason or another' the evidence hadn't come to light. Deep down, Lenny he knew he was innocent so you can sort of understand why he would blow hot and cold now and again.

BEHIND THE DOOR

'Lenny at one point was having to be sedated and believe me, sedated he was. I got on quite well with the nurse and she had told me that the doses of Valium and Temazepam they were giving to him were enough to knock a fucking elephant out. For me, Lenny always seemed his most down a few hours after he'd had his morning visit from his wife, Valerie. Lenny never stopped talking about her and his kids, of course – Kelly and Jamie – he worshipped those three with all of his heart. So I guess that after Val had gone, he'd be thinking about his family for a good while, and knowing that he was totally innocent, well, I guess that it was slowly killing the fella. At one point I walked into the dorm and Len was face down on the floor, sedated to fuck – he looked like a giant bear, he didn't have a clue that I was even in the room.

'Now I can honestly say that I always felt at ease around Len, even given the facts of how quickly he could fly off the handle. But other people, well, for fuck's sake! If someone upset him, that was another matter. So anyway, there was this one screw in there – he was a big c*** himself, must've been about six foot six – and for some reason he fucking hated Lenny. I said to him one day, "I wouldn't let Lenny fucking hear you, mate" – I think he said "fuck him" or something like that. Well, he didn't say "fuck him" after this! One day, this boy in our dorm had gone out to get breakfast and he brought Lenny's brekkie back with him too. Well, this big screw grabs the boy and says, "Eh, did he make you come out here and get that for him?" and the boy went, "No, I just do it. You know, he's a good fella, Lenny, so I just do it."

Anyway, Lenny is still asleep in the dorm so the boy takes him over his bit of breakfast and tells Lenny that the screw had just pulled him up, and what the screw had said. Well, fuck me, Lenny shot out that door in his pants at about three hundred mile an hour, done the fastest shadow boxing you've ever seen, an inch away from this muggy screw's face, picks the screw up by the throat and his bollocks, and Lenny's screaming at him, right in his face. Well, now all of the alarms have gone off, there's fucking POs [prison officers] and screws running around all over the place. I guarantee you now, that the big PO screw fella never took a liberty with Len again.

'Another quite odd story was this: like I said earlier, I never really knew exactly who Lenny was, or much about his bare-knuckle fights and his fearsome reputation. All I really knew was the impression he made on me and the rest, the day he walked into that holding cell at Lambeth – well, have a listen to this! We're all in the dorm one night, watching a bit of telly; even the screws were peering through the window. With that, some news article came on the TV and it's only fucking Lenny, I swear to God. It was that footage with the gypsy fella who nutted Lenny. Fuck me, none of us could believe it. I tell you what, everyone gave Lenny a proper wide berth after that evening. I mean, everyone was scared of him anyway, but that bit of news footage just added to it. Even the POs were kissing Lenny's arse.

'On a funny note, there was an old gangster in our dorm, called Albert Clark. 'Nobby' as he was known, well, Lenny thought the world of him, but he used to wind him up and play tricks on him. Now Nobby had one leg shorter than the other and so he wore one of those orthopaedic shoes. So Lenny would be on a visit with his wife, Val, and Nobby used to come and say to me, "Where's Lenny?", hoping he was out of the way for a bit, and I'd tell him Len's on a visit, so Nobby would go, "Right, I'm off for a bath. Don't tell Lenny now, will ya?" With that, Lenny's come back and gone, "Where's Nobby?" I never even had to answer, Lenny would go, "Never mind, I know, he's in the fucking bath, ain't he?" So, Lenny has sneaked down the shower block. He knows which bath Albert will be in, and he's turned the hot tap on full pelt, and run out laughing his head off. Two minutes later, out comes Albert, chasing after Len, red as a fucking beetroot, going, "You bastard, Lenny, you fucking bastard!"

Lenny would do all sorts to Albert. He'd hide his orthopaedic shoe sometimes, go back in his dorm and put it on his pillow, and Albert would find him and walk in to Lenny going, "Whoever this shoe fits, I'm going to marry" – you know, like *Cinderella*? Oh yes, he was a funny fucking fella was Lenny, loved having a laugh he did.

'Lenny got it into his head that he might need to wear glasses. Len goes to me, "Here, son, we need to have our eyes tested." And I said, "I don't need mine doing, Len. My eyesight is fine." To be honest, so was Lenny's – he had the eyes of a fucking eagle. But there was no telling him, he just went on and on about it until I gave in.

'Anyway, so the day comes for us to have the eye tests, but in the meantime, I'd cancelled my test beforehand so it was just Len. Lenny comes back from his eye test and he's like, "Here, son, apparently I have to wear glasses." To be fair, he was happy as Larry – I think he thought that they would go with his movie-star image... The movie star that he was going to be when he got out, because Lenny had told me over and over again that he had an Equity card waiting for him on his release from prison. He never let up about it.

'Lenny said to me, "These glasses I have coming, son, they ain't just your normal National Health bollocks! Nah, these are tinted glass, gold-rimmed fuckers. I'm telling you, boy, they look the absolute bollocks!" Anyway, he had to wait a couple of days for his glasses to arrive, but by Christ, those screws knew about it. He just wouldn't let up, every day with, "Are they here yet? Check for me, will you, son? They should have arrived by now." He never let up until finally the day came and they arrived. Oh my God, he was like a kid at fucking Christmas! He's in the mirror every second, doing impression after impression of some movie star or another. He was nonstop, he fucking loved those bins.

'I can picture Lenny now, bins on, head tilted back, doing a Marlon Brando impression. Christ, he must have spent hours looking into that plastic makeshift prison mirror. I remember at the time thinking, oh my God, I think he's losing the plot, until years after, when he had made it in the film game and I finally realised that he weren't losing it at all. Those episodes in the cell mirror were simply a rehearsal, a sign accenting Lenny's sheer dedication to succeed.

BEHIND THE DOOR

'There was this other time when I stupidly offered Lenny a smoke. My tin of Old Holborn is sat on my bed, lid off. Anyway, Len takes a few fingertip pinches and what's in the tin is almost in his fag paper. So anyway, I'm thinking to myself, he'll empty it back into my tin in a minute, but did he fuck! He rolled it up. Fucking hell, it must've been an inch thick and he's lit it up and it's gone up like a giant cascading firework. With that, Len goes, "You know that I'd help you out in return, but sorry, son, I've only got about 120 ounces left," and he laughed at the top of his lungs. What you need to remember is in prison you're on rations of about two to three ounces per week, but not with Len.

'Lenny's bed was right next to mine, our beds were literally a foot apart, and let me tell you, Lenny McLean snored like a fucking bear. So, anyway, in the morning I was always up first because I had my job to go to, so I would get out of bed, make it ready for bedtime that evening and with that, Len would jump out of his and jump straight into mine... with his fucking trainers on, I might add.

'So I'd go, "Oh come on, Len, that was all tidy," and he'd say, "Come on, son, look at my bed, it's a right fucking shit hole!" All the while I'm thinking to myself, yes, so is my fucker now, you big c***. To add to that, as I said earlier, Len smoked inch-thick roll-ups and he would put ash and that all over my crisp white hospital sheets, but eh, he looked after me big time, what was I supposed to say?

'Things could be a little contentious at times. I mean, I ain't slagging Lenny off, but he used to have bad days and at times I would be at the brunt of it. One day, I was proper down because the fellas from the other dorms were giving me a bit of a hard time with the piss taking, as if I was doing everything for Lenny, and I was his lapdog or something. So anyway, I walked into our dorm and Lenny goes, "You alright, boy? You look a bit down in the mouth, son" So I told him the score. Well, fuck me! With that he went from Mr Nice Guy to a raving fucking lunatic. He grabbed my hand and marched me into the main area, where all of the other fellas were. To be honest, I felt a bit silly. With that, he goes to the fucking lot of them, "Listen up, you no-value c***s! See this kid? Well, he's under my wing. If you have any problems with him, then you've got them with me, and I'll smash every fucking last one of you lot in a second." Anyway, he goes, "Right, come on, son," and marches me back to our dorm. He just went, "Alright now, son?" as if nothing had even happened. Honestly, he could turn it on and off like the flick of a switch.

'Funny story, you know how we all have our little stories? Well I ain't told any of these stories to anyone aside from my wife. All that my pals know is that I was inside with Lenny McLean. Anyway, we're sat there at my pal's one day – me, him and his dad – and they've tried to call me out on it. You know, catch me out, like. So they've gone, "Here, Taff," because I'm actually Welsh, you see. They've gone, "Jump in the motor, Taff, we've got someone you'll be pleased to see." Now they think that I don't know Lenny McLean, so they're trying to make me look like a mug. So I goes, "Yeah, come on then, let's have it. Let's go and see whoever this is you're talking about." Anyway, we've jumped in the motor and turned up at this café down my road, called Poppins. So, I've walked through the door and obviously the first person I've spotted is Lenny, and Lenny just happens to be sat with another fella I've known since I was like fifteen years old, called Dave 'The Bomb'. With that, Lenny jumps up and he's going, "Alright, my son? How you doing, boy?" Made my day, it did, and it was a right result because it made my pals look like a couple of mugs instead.

'It was so lovely to see Len too. I could tell that he wasn't well though, still big and strong and powerful, but I know Lenny, so I could just see it. I sat with him for a few hours and we had a right old reminisce, and that was the last time I ever saw him. Shame really but let's face it, due to my pals trying to pull a fast one, they'd inadvertently done me a massive favour because at least I got one last chance to spend time with my friend, Lenny McLean, and on the outside too, which was a huge bonus. I will never forget that man for as long as I live.'

DERRICK STRAIN

'The first time I come across Lenny McLean was when I ended up on remand in Brixton. I'd never really been into the fight game, so I never really knew who he was. I remember the day they brought Lenny in and they put him in a cell with a guy who was basically in for fraud. Lenny turned to the bloke and said, "I'm Tarzan, you're Jane." The bloke's face was a picture as he didn't have a clue what Lenny meant – I bet he was thinking, is this big fucker going to fuck me? Lenny kept winding him up but he was basically saying I'm taking over this cell and he didn't want any shit off him.

'When I saw him there, you could see there was something about him. He reminded me of some cartoon character, meat and chunks, he was just huge. You could see his muscles busting out of this blue vest. Lenny ended up getting a job on the hot plate, dishing out food. No one wanted to do this job because of the shit you would get from it, with people wanting more, and also the food was shit, but he was respected in there by the boys and the screws because of who he was.

'Lenny turned out to be very wise inside. Going by all the stories people were saying about him in there, I was expecting this loud-mouthed animal. But he wasn't like that, he was sort of quiet, an old-school gentleman who would speak to you every day and that was my experience of him.

'This one morning my mate and I were smoking a bit of pot and a guard had told us to open the door, so we told him to fuck off and he disappeared. A bit later, we had gone to slop out when Lenny's mate in the canteen had overheard a conversation saying that the guards were going to bust us. While we were eating our food, Lenny told his mate to come and let us know what was going to happen. We had our food and I got up and looked at Lenny and nodded as if to say thank you, he nodded back and we went back to our room. You could see he was proper old school. I don't know if it was an "us against them" kind of thing as he didn't even know us, I totally respected him for that. Anyway, we offloaded the stuff and as Lenny had told us, we were busted minutes later after getting back.

'I spoke with Lenny on a daily basis from then on, and he'd call me "jock" or "boy" and we'd talk about everyday things like boxing and run-of-the-mill stuff. I then got moved to Belmarsh Prison a few months later, and who do I bump into but Lenny again. In Belmarsh you could have family visits three times a day for twenty minutes at a time, but for some reason, Lenny used to get forty-five minutes. Usually you'd just walk into visits but when Lenny walked in, he'd always have a screw with him. He didn't show any sign of causing trouble and the screws respected him for that, but he just had that look like a pressure cooker ready to explode. No one would make a fuss about the time he had as we all just wanted to do our time.

'I was somewhat of a loose cannon inside too and I'd always end up arguing with the screws. A few times they smashed me up in there. This one day I was owed money from the canteen and I told Lenny if I didn't get it from them, I'd end up going to the block. Lenny sat me down and said, "Look, boy, it's not worth it. Listen, you just aren't going to beat them." Things ended up getting sorted and I got my money back.

'I later saw Lenny on TV programmes and then in the film *Lock, Stock and Two Smoking Barrels*. It's sad to think that he was just making the cream when he passed away, as I think that was the start of a big career for him.

'After coming out of Belmarsh I was never in any trouble for another thirteen years until I got caught selling some football tops in 2006. It was hard to believe how much jail had changed. I was then on probation and ended up getting into theatre and becoming a stand-up comedian and changing my life around. I ended up supporting comedians like Michael McIntyre and Frankie Boyle in places like Jongleurs and the Comedy Castle. Maybe Len's guidance had altered my destiny.'

PETER DUKE

'I first met Lenny McLean when I was doing a bit of bird on E wing in HMP Wandsworth Prison. I knew he was a rare breed as soon as I clapped eyes on him. I introduced myself and he told me that he had just come from HMP Brixton. I then moved on to B wing and got a job on the hot plate.

'The next day, Lenny pops up in the cell next to me, and he was chuffed to fuck because he had a single cell. It was good for him to get a job on the hot plate too so it could keep his mind off his court case.

'I came out of my cell one day and I saw this man who I recognised from TV. It was Gary Taylor, who also won the World's Strongest Man. Lenny and Gary had a lot in common with weight training and Gary was a gym orderly. Now as much as Lenny didn't like screws, there were a few that he didn't mind, owing to them being old school and they also knew he was innocent. This was obviously working well for him because when I walked into his cell one day, it looked like he had more contraband than they had in the fucking stores! Lenny also had the cons who were working in the kitchen on the wing with us, and that meant we never had to eat the shit we served up to the rest – Lenny, for instance, used to have whole roast chicken and chips most nights.

'Lenny had a good sense of humour and hated drugs and anything to do with them so this one day I can see two cons cleaning his cell and when they finished, he winked at me. They then had their hands out and Len says, "Go on, now fuck off!" They were taken back and he said to me, laughing, "These daft c***s do anything for drugs these days, they can fuck right off!"

'There was another screw that was into his boxing, so obviously he knew what Lenny was all about. One day the screw came down the stairs with a guy in this brown leather jacket and shades on. Lenny introduced me to him. Turns out it's his good friend, Alex Steen, who was on a cell visit. This one day we were outside and it was a nice sunny day. We'd been banged up for a few days due to a staff shortage or some bollocks like that, so the break was nice. So we had been out on exercise and Lenny didn't want to come back in as he had the sun on his back. He was asked again but refused to come in even when six screws approached him. In the end he was the only man bowling round the yard – suppose they didn't want their noses broken that day.

'I remember when this Colombian came in, who had just got an eight-year sentence. He'd been nicked at some airport for bringing coke into the country and couldn't speak any English. Now back then doing bird you had to slop out, no bogs or TV like now. Anyway, Lenny thought he'd shit in this fella's bucket in his cell. He sussed it was Len who'd done it and he had the hump; he then starts giving Lenny some mouth. We were all laughing, but he wouldn't let it go and was still on about it the next day. Len went in his cell, saw him and sparked him right out. A screw heard the commotion, opened the cell door, looked at us, laughed, shook his head and fucked off.

'This one day I nearly experienced Lenny's wrath. A few of us were fucking around near the hot plate and I chucked a roast spud at him. He turns and says, "I'm gonna rip your fucking lungs out!" I never banged myself up so quick – good job he calmed down over bang up [after lock-up].

'I had some great days with Lenny, and in my time spent with him he told me all of the stories about America – being shot, stabbed. Let's just say he certainly had a colourful life. But I must say, the best day of all was when he got released.

'This one day on the hot plate someone gave Lenny some mouth. I thought he was going to chuck a big tin of grub over him there and then. Lenny then looked at me and gave me the wink. There and then I knew the guy was bang in trouble. Then during bang up, Lenny cut his toenails and stuck it in the prick's grub at tea time. We could then hear him getting loud, shouting, and he came down, gobbing at Lenny again. Lenny said to me, "His cards are now marked, I'm not having that." He got someone to cover him, went up and smashed the man to pieces – it was a hospital job, that one.

'At the time Len always had his head in a script from Pinewood Studios. He was hoping good things were going to happen, and it also kept his mind off his court case and that bullshit charge of murder.

'There was always cons that would stick their chest out and try to impress Lenny. He loved winding them up. Lenny used to let them tell him their stories then he would just destroy them with his words. He said to this one guy, laughing, "Have you finished yet? I'm bored." The look on their faces was classic and they didn't stick their chests out after that.

'He had a great sense of humour and always had me in stitches. I don't think I'll ever meet another Lenny. Not a lot of people make a lasting impression on my life but Lenny McLean certainly did and it was a privilege to have known him.'

RICKY H

'I had a brief meeting with Lenny in 1990 when I was doing a short stretch and was put in Fraggle Rock in Brixton as overflow. Anyway, I was out on exercise one day and I would sit with my back against the wall as there were a few psychopaths and not well people in there. While sitting there, I could see this hulking figure sitting down, upset, with an old man talking to him. I noticed it was Lenny as he was very well known to me. The old man would try and get Lenny up and motivated, getting him walking around the exercise yard, saying, 'Come on, Lenny, you're The Guv'nor.' It seemed to work as Lenny got up and started jogging.

'Now I don't regard myself as a tough guy but I'm afraid of no one, and I've worked with some monsters, but it was very surreal seeing this legendary fighter at such a low ebb. It was just another indication as to the kind of loony bin we were in.

'After a few days some young lads came up to me and said, "Oh, we're doing a card for Lenny, do you want to sign it?" I declined as I didn't really know him or him me, and I didn't want to come over like an arse-licker. A week later, I'm sitting in my usual spot on exercise, feeling sorry for myself when I heard this big gruff voice say, "Cheer up, mate." I looked up and it's Lenny who was smiling and as I made eye contact, he repeated, "Cheer up, mate, think we got beans for tea," which of course made me laugh and gave me a real boost on the day.

'I remember him moaning one day about the way people talked in there with all their jargon, using words like "sweet" and "safe", etc. He said to me laughing, "What the fuck is all that talk about, why don't they just talk normal?" Another time this big tall man was giving the big one and made eye contact with Lenny, who promptly offered him out, which the guy wisely declined and moved on.

'I believe he was drugged by the prison as he was very slow-moving at the time but the man still took time to cheer me up a bit, which shows how much of a nice man he could be, and I'll never forget that.'

CHAPTER 7

LEN'S TASTY LITTLE FIRM

When we talk about Lenny's prowess as a cobble fighter, this of course spans over a wide spectrum, none greater than his life going to work on the doors. He and his formidable firm of bouncers minded some rough houses in and around London town. For a bouncer to gain the kind of respect that Lenny's name demanded, up and down the dark and dangerous world of Britain's door security, simply makes you wonder just what kind of artillery he held in those fast and vicious fists of his. Lenny was one tasty fucker on the pavement, the kind of fighter who would take on any amount of opponents, and quickly iron them out with ease. Take heed as you read the stories below that we have gathered from some of Lenny's firm, a handful of which had the arduous task of being The Guv'nor's right-hand men.

TOMMY MERRY

'Now the firm of bouncers Lenny had with him at the Camden Palace in the mid-eighties was one fucking tasty outfit. I worked alongside them around this time, and I must say I've never seen such a well-oiled machine as this one, comprising of Lenny, Basil, Brian, Ray and Johnny – they were a set of bouncers to be reckoned with.

The first time I was properly introduced to Lenny was in a club called Limelight's. I walk in and I sees Lenny and this other fella stood there, and they're asking people where they were getting their drugs from. Now these two were all suited and booted, and to me they sort of looked like Old Bill. So anyway, I'm a little taken aback by this. I call over my supervisor, who just so happens to be another well-known figure from Essex; anyway, his name was Carlton Leech (Carlton was running a promotion in Limelight's at the time, putting on dance parties and such-like). So with that Carlton shouts Lenny and his pal over, and says to Lenny, "This is Tommy, he thinks you two chaps are Old Bill." I'm thinking to myself, fucking turn it in, fella, have you seen the size of these two lumps? Anyway, Lenny took it all in good fun, took a hold of my hand in his giant mitt to shake it and said, "Here, boy. You're alright, son, just keeping you on ya toes." I obviously let out a huge sigh of relief because Lenny could have taken it all wrong and maybe thought that I was taking the piss. I mean, we know Lenny and his attitude towards the Old Bill. But anyway, from that day on, I seemed to get on great with him.

LENNY'S TASTY LITTLE FIRM

'Working alongside Lenny was something of an honour for the likes of me. He never suffered fools one bit, and he had the quickest temper I have ever seen: he could be stood laughing and joking one second, then someone would get a bit leery and flip. I suppose it could be a little intimidating, even for us working alongside him. This one time we're stood there and everyone's having a laugh and a joke, and this fella says, "Eh, I seen your boy Jamie up West. He looked a bit off it, if I'm honest, Len." With that Lenny belted him straight across the jaw and the fella is out cold on the cobbles. It was as easy as that, bang, and they're chewing the concrete.

'This other night, this other fella goes, "Eh, Lenny, you've put a bit of weight on," and Lenny's unloaded him right there and then, and no one said another thing about it. I mean, don't get me wrong, Lenny was no bully but if you were stupid enough to try and humiliate him, then I'd say you were offering yourself up for a slap.

'I remember one time we're all stood out front at the Pally, me, Len, and I think Ray. Anyway, if you look above our heads there's a thirty-foot neon sign saying "Camden Palace". Now you have to be some sort of a clown to not notice it. Anyway, these three big fuckin' geezers come over to Len and goes, "Excuse me, mate, can you tell us where the Camden Palace is?" so Len's gone, "Yes, mate, do a left here, take a quick right and an even quicker left, and you can't miss it." So with that these fellas have it away on their toes. Five minutes later, they come steaming round the corner, and we're sat there on the wall pissing

115

ourselves. Anyway, they start going off at Lenny, and I'm thinking, oh ease up, boys, or there's gonna be murders. Anyway, they carry on with the ranting and with that all of a sudden Lenny stands up, like a bear with the hump, and goes bosh, bosh, bosh... One with a left, one with a right hook and the other with a belt straight into the old Niagaras, and the three of them are laid spark out on the pavement. I mean, come on, Lenny was only having a bit of a wind-up. He'd played the same trick on many occasions, but let's just say that the others he'd done it to had obviously thought better of starting a row with Lenny about it. I mean, come on, it was only a piss-take, it's what fellas do.

'Back then at the Camden and I guess at all the places Lenny looked after, people used to always throw his name up. You know how it is – Len's my cousin, Lenny said we can have a free pass, and all the same old lines – but Lenny had left a strict code of conduct for us boys when he weren't at the club. He'd say, "Anyone throwing my name up and trying to act a bit Harry dash [flash], knock the c***s out," or failing that, we had to call Len up and he'd come out specially and knock them out. Once the name dropper had been given this information they slipped away a bit lively funny enough, unless of course they were fucking stupid. No one ever really took the piss on that door, and that was all down to Len.

'When Lenny moved on from the Palace to take over at the Hippodrome, I never really saw him again, and many years later, I found out that he had passed away. Of course I was shocked and saddened by this news. Lenny to me always seemed indestructible, but

LENNY'S TASTY LITTLE FIRM

I suppose I'm just thinking of the Lenny fighting on the cobbles, and drawing from those memories of the times I spent with him. Nobody, but nobody could beat him... I have in recent years read books that seem to dig Lenny out a bit, saying he was just this self-acclaimed Guv'nor. But let me tell you this, Lenny didn't need no self-acclaim, anyone that ever worked with him would tell you the same as me, and that is that the man was, and always will be, the absolute Guv'nor, and I felt it an absolute honour to have worked with the man.'

GARY BETH

'I first met Lenny McLean together with my father when I was a kid. Then another time Lenny was talking to my dad one day. While pointing at me, my dad said, "Take him with you, Len, he's looking for work," and that's where my path started on the doors. It was around 1984, I'd just turned eighteen and I started in a place called Benjy's in the Mile End Road. I worked there for about six months with Lenny and then he put me on a couple of his doors and he used to come round and check on everyone.

'This one time in Benjy's we had a phone call from this club called Treadmills, saying there was about forty Millwall football fans coming our way and taking over pubs, playing up hell. We were on the front door and Lenny sent me upstairs and said, "Whatever happens, do not come downstairs." I think me being new and young, and him knowing my dad, he didn't want me hurt. I thought to myself, well, if it kicks off, no fucking way am I going to stay upstairs, but he said it again, "Make sure you don't come down." Next thing you can hear is them coming up the street and Lenny's gone straight outside on his own. I'm now down on the front door watching and waiting for something to happen when Lenny says, "Right, who's your leader?" Then this geezer pipes up and says, "Well, what the fuck has it got to do with you?" Lenny sparked him straight out and shouted, "Right, who's second in command?" and no one would come forward. He then said, "Do yourselves a favour and pick this piece of shit up and walk away," and next thing they did was they all walked off, dragging their leader with them. The man had no fear, he claimed it for himself, and no one would go near him once the one was sparked out.

'The following week, the main man from Millwall came and asked to speak to Lenny. I knew who this bloke was, and I said to him, "Are you sure you want to speak to him?" Lenny came to the door and said, "What do you want?" The bloke said, "Look, I want no grief, I just want to apologise for last week. The little firm's been roasted over it," and Lenny said, "Ah right, that was that little shit last week who I flicked" – that was Lenny's actual words. He had a way with words and didn't give a fuck for them.

'Lenny also had a way with numbers as well, it was like he had OCD. Take, for example, the amount of bouncers he had working on the door: it had to be an odd number, it couldn't be an even number. It was just strange sometimes.

'I then started doing a bit of debt collecting with him. He would go to the door and genuinely ask nicely and most of the time people knew who he was and would offer him furniture and stuff. A few times we have gone to a house and Lenny's seen what circumstances the people were in and he would end up putting the money up himself. That's the sort of man he was, he had a big heart. Don't get me wrong, he was a fucking lunatic – he was more frightening than anything I'd ever known. I'd known him a few years and still sometimes I was petrified of the man as you didn't know what he was going to do next.

'I went on about fifteen debts with him. Sometimes Mick McDonnell was with us too. It was good money and easy money when you were with Lenny, as nine times out of ten people paid up to get him off their doorstep. Then other times he would have to throw a right-hander and it would only ever be the one. He had a dig and half, he used to slap people on the back to say hello and he would wind them up – his hands were like shovels. In the end I gave it up as I didn't like doing them.

'Last time I see Lenny was on the *Lock, Stock…* film set when I was doing security there and we had a good chat about the past. I was so happy for him as he always wanted to get into the acting thing.

'I have nothing but good memories of the time spent with him. He was a character to work with, he really was. He was funny; his sense of humour was second to none. He was strong as an ox. He was a fair hardman until someone fucked him off. I loved the man to death.'

PAUL WINSON

'I first got introduced to Lenny through my pal, Neil Garfield, who was friends with Turkish Richard, and Richard worked for Lenny at the prestigious Hippodrome. In a conversation one night, Richard said to me, "Here, Paul, come up the Club one night, and I'll introduce you to Lenny McLean."

'I was slightly nervous at the thought of meeting Lenny because I'd heard so many things about the man. So, I met Richard and he introduced me to Len, and within the first ten minutes of being in The Guv'nor's company, I could tell right there and then that Lenny was no bully: he didn't need to be one. However, it was like shaking hands with a gorilla – his fucking hands were like bunches of bananas! So, I said to Richard and Len, "Right, I'm off to Burger King," and Len said, "Here, my son, get me a banana milkshake, and then come in my office and we'll have a chat." Anyway, I says to Richard, "Fuck sake, Turkish, I ain't going in there! I mean, fuck that, I've only just met him," and Richard goes, "No, leave it out, Paul. Go get your bit of food, and come back and have a chat with Len. Listen, you've got to, otherwise, you'll make me look bad."

'So off I goes, with that Richard shouts to me, "Eh, Paul mate, for fuck sake, don't forget Lenny's milkshake!" I'm sure Turkish was laughing when he shouted that, the c*** – he knew how nervous I was. So anyway, I've got a bit of grub, and Lenny's banana fucking milkshake, and I'm back at the Hippodrome. I'm now in the office with Richard, Neil and the big man, Lenny. From that moment on, Lenny was funny as fuck, and as welcoming as you would ever imagine. He reeled off some amazing stories. I was relaxed and laughing like a child within minutes of being in his company – the man was an absolute fucking legend.

'One little story I remember happened while Len was on remand in Wandsworth Prison. Lenny said the doctor asked to talk to him, saying that he had a problem with his son because his son was being sexually assaulted by another inmate. Lenny said, "Give me the blower," and he done a bit of growling down the phone, and the problem was dealt with. The doctor asked Lenny, "What can I do, in order to repay you?" And Lenny simply said, "Keep me in this hospital until I'm getting out," and job done. So, Len's in a lovely clean hospital wing, with all the necessary perks, for the rest of his stay. Now you tell me, who has that kind of pull?

'In that office Lenny never bigged himself up, not for a minute. He just chatted to us as if he was giving us bits of his wisdom, like "always stay strong and fit, and don't be flash". Lenny hated a flash bastard. He used to say, "Listen, as soon as they come a bit Harry Dash, get them out of my fucking way." He didn't want those kinds of people around him. It wasn't worth sitting around with Lenny going, "I bashed this fella up, I done whatever to this other fella, because it ain't going to impress the man," so I never did, and I got on great with him. In my time working for Len, I never actually saw him that often, because Lenny would just turn up to the club for an hour or so, do what he had to do, and then he'd be off. He didn't have to be on any of his premises for very long because he was Lenny McLean. His name was enough, he didn't have to use any muscle; everybody just knew, McLean runs this gaff, and the business ran very smoothly. Let's face it, that's why everybody wanted to use Lenny's name. It was like the ultimate deterrent.

'One evening, Lenny was up the club in the VIP area with his wife, Val, and Kelly, his daughter, and a few others. Anyway, I was just stood there minding my own business when Len shouts me over. Now Lenny is obviously telling his friends a story and wants to use me as some sort of prop. With that he goes "flip, flip, flip," and lets loose this flurry of punches in and around my face and that. Fucking hell, he was only fucking around, but by Christ, the speed of that man. For fuck's sake, you wouldn't want him doing that to you for real – I wouldn't last two fucking seconds.

'I actually got the job at the Hippodrome the first time I walked up to the door on that first night. It had kicked off outside. Anyway, Len's bouncers were sorting it, so I stood back a bit. All of a sudden I happened to notice this one fella bend down and get a knife out of his sock so I grabbed his arm from the back, got him in a bit of a choke hold and took the knife off of him. It must've got back to Len because Richard called me up and said, "Len wants you to come to work for him." To my amazement the next night I'm working alongside the big man himself.

'After a few nights working the Hippodrome for Lenny, I'm in the club and me and Lenny are having a little mooch around, doing the usual end-of-night "come on, let's have you! Haven't you got homes to go to?" routine. Anyway, these two big fellas are having none of it and coming it a bit leery, so Len goes to me, "Here, Paul, give them a tug. Hit him before I have to hit him." So anyway, I'm thinking to myself, they'd rather have a clump from me than a fucker from Len. I'm doing them a favour really, aren't I? I'd heard about Lenny's fists and how he'd knocked out two fucking massive Welsh rugby players with one shot each a few weeks earlier for asking Len, "Who the fuck are you, old man?"

'So, I think to himself, go on, son, don't mug yourself off. With that, I give one of them the punch of his life and knock the geezer spark out. Listen, it must have impressed Len a little, because the next night at work, I was asked to move from the door. So that was my stint working under Lenny.'

Paul did also say that he left a little abruptly. I'm not sure what he meant by that was that he felt like he was pushed out by the management, whether they were having a shake-up and wanted all of these new school, "never had a tear-up in their fucking life" style of bouncer taking up the jobs, Paul said he really didn't know, but anyway, he had to go, and Paul told me that Lenny bunged an extra six hundred notes in his last pay packet as a little sort of severance, again Paul says, 'how many head fucking doormen would do that sort of thing?'

Before I wound up the interview, I asked Paul how the photograph that we had obtained actually came about. Paul said that Turkish Richard asked Lenny one night in Cairo Jacks to have a photo taken with the three of us. He told me that Len said, 'Right, you can have one with me smiling, and another with me growling.' Paul said 'he was a born fucking film star, was Lenny.'

Paul told me that Lenny's nickname for him was from a *Carry On* film, *Carry on Screaming*. Lenny used to call him 'Paul Oddbod Junior'. I think I'll end there as Lenny would've liked that.

PAUL KNIGHT

'I worked, fought and laughed alongside Lenny McLean. I have many memories about the big man. Whenever he saw that you were down, pissed off or just had a run-in with some punters, Len would turn to you and say, "Give us a cuddle" and squeeze you in those solid arms of his. He was that lovable uncle that you always enjoyed being around, a giant amongst men and a mentor. I liked Lenny. He was an empowering man, with a funny and caring side.

'Lenny McLean was a monster: the man was six foot three and weighed over twenty stone. He was strong and intimidating, and you didn't want to be on the wrong side of him – in or out of the ring! Lenny also used to sort out Cliff Fields' brother, Roger, whenever he was in town with free entry and drinks . He just didn't bear bad feeling towards those that you think he would be bitter towards. It was during these unlicensed years that the crown title of "Guv'nor" was used. People today argue how could Lenny be known as The Guv'nor when he lost certain fights? Well, sorry to burst anyone's bubble, but the title wasn't like a belt that gets handed to the winner, it wasn't an automatic right to be named that – it came from the respect of your peers.

'I remember this one incident that took place with Lenny at the Hippodrome. We were on the door when two Japanese businessmen, a little worse for wear, approached the door and wanted to gain entry. It was Leicester Square in the West End of London. Rich businessmen weren't uncommon at the Hippodrome, but on this night, one of the gentlemen was sporting a very nice wristwatch – very expensive, very shiny – and it caught Lenny's eye. He even commented on it, but the inebriated businessman just laughed in regard to his comments. Len let them in.

'About thirty minutes later, Lenny went inside the club. Another ten minutes after that, the fire alarm went off, signalling that one of the fire exits was open. A couple of the guys ran around to see what was going on: it was Lenny, throwing the two Japanese businessmen out for being drunk and disorderly. Anyway, he came back and stood on the front door. I couldn't help but notice that he was wearing a very expensive, very shiny wristwatch that also caught my eye; it was also too small for his wrist. Whether he found it after throwing them out, I do not know, but I certainly wasn't going to enquire.

'Another time, I was on the door of the Limelight in Shaftesbury Avenue. This was a little while after Len had done his eighteen months sentence for GBH in 1991. So, now he was working at Cairo Jacks up the road, and was popping down after work. At the reception desk was a bloke called Tommy. Now

Tommy was from Canning Town and was a friend of Lenny's. I mean, these guys went back twenty years. Anyway, we were taking the piss out of each other, like doormen do about our physiques and that, and we were calling each other fat, etc. Then all of a sudden Lenny sticks his head through the door, his gravelly voice piercing the laughter. He joins us. We're all still laughing when Tommy looks at Len and says, "Lenny, I haven't seen you for ages, you've put a bit of weight on," and proceeds to pat Len's stomach. Now Lenny hadn't been with us to know exactly what context the comment had been made, but he went from smiling to growling and started to hit Tommy, his friend of twenty years, repeatedly. It took six of us to pull Len off of him, and let's just say Tommy wasn't in a great shape afterwards.

'You see, Lenny's reputation had its benefits. For example, we had just secured the security contract for the Roadhouse in Covent Garden, and it was filled with bikers and other quick-tempered folk. Lenny came down and sat at the end of the bar. The manager went up to my boss, Steve, not knowing that it was Steve that had invited Lenny down, and told him to be on his toes as the word going around was that there was going to be trouble, and looking at Lenny, it was going to start soon. Anyway, Steve puts his mind to rest by saying, "That's Lenny McLean, no one's going to start anything if they come in. If they're a real threat and connected, they'll know who Lenny is, see that he's with us and leave." The manager replies, "And if they don't know who he is?" Steve laughs, puts his hand on his shoulder, looks him square in the eye and says, "If they don't know who he is, they're no one of importance and Len will single-handedly make sure they'll never forget him. Either way, it's the start of a new era," and that was the start of two decades of contracted work at the Roadhouse.

'Over the years, I gathered a few little stories like that about Len: he was to you what you were to him, plain and simple. I went through a phase and had to see a therapist about my anger issues. Len would always ask if everything was all right whenever he saw me. We weren't great friends, different circles, etc., but Lenny always had time for people. He was generous and funny; he would cheer you up when he saw you were down by coming over and saying "Give us a cuddle" and he would squeeze you so you knew you had a friend who cared. Despite all that is said, whether fact or fiction, anyone who actually knew him will say the man's heart was as big as the rest of him, if not bigger. May he be raising hell in heaven's tranquility, with all those from our gang who also went before their time.'

MANNY CLARK

Manny was a well-respected name from the unlicensed fight scene – we had seen him for years on posters and that. We then started a new page on Facebook about the unlicensed fight scene and dropped him a message. Manny was in training for an unlicensed fight on a charity show, which also featured boxing legend Sugar Ray Leonard as a guest. He took some time out of his busy schedule to have a chat.

'I first met Lenny McLean when I was around twenty

years of age. I'd been brought up around bouncers and boxers all of my life and I'd just started bouncing myself. I saw Lenny outside the Hippodrome this one night and I went up and spoke to him and mentioned my dad as he knew my dad from the boxing and bouncing world. My dad, George Clark, was a good amateur boxer and his brother, my Uncle Fred, who was fourteen years older than Dad, were both well-known bouncers in North and West London. They had some big battles on the doors while working at the White Hart in Acton. A few other heavyweight boxers, like Joe Seabrook, Mori Bush, Cliff Fields and Peter Lanaghan, worked the doors there with them too. My dad and Joe Seabrook were also bodyguards for The Bay City Rollers and The Rolling Stones, and my uncle, Fred Clark, was rated fourth in the British Heavyweight ratings and he even fought Bruce Woodcock in the 1940s. Years later, he got into a fight in a scrapyard and these men smashed his head in with wheel braces and starting handles and he ended up with brain damage. So, me and Lenny hit it off like a house on fire as we basically had the same interests in life, so we talked about my dad and his brothers and other stuff.

'Years and years later, I was running one of the biggest security firms in London and I was supplying bouncers to all the clubs, like the Gas Club, the Buzz Bar, Slap Harry's, Cairo Jacks and the Camden Palace. Well, a lot of the clubs I ran were owned by a company called European Leisure and what happened was I got nicked for shooting a fella in Canning Town when I was twenty-six and was found not guilty. When I got out, Lenny McLean got nicked for that incident at the Hippodrome.

'When Lenny came out of prison, European Leisure had a problem and came to see me and said, "Look we can't employ Lenny no more. Is there any chance you could take him on your books with your company and put him in one of your venues, like Cairo Jacks?" After some consideration Lenny was now working for me in Cairo's and ended up working there for about two years. Now Lenny being Lenny, he didn't like many other bouncers so we kept sending some of our doormen around to Cairo's to work with him and they would come back, saying, "Lenny had fucking shouted at us and told us to fuck off." Lenny was used to the other venues before he went down and always knew who his team was. So, I've walked round to see Lenny and said, "Look, Lenny, what's the problem, mate?" He replied, "I don't want to work with none of these mugs, I only want to work with you, Manny," so I said, "Listen, Lenny, because I run the security firm, I don't work at one place all the time, I go around and work now and again, but usually I supply the bouncers and I'm usually at the Gas Club if I do work." I then said to Lenny, "Look, what I'll do is send my brother Elliott here with you." Now my younger brother Elliott is six foot five. I have four brothers and they're all big and all worked the doors. Lenny was alright with Elliott working there. I also put another bouncer named Huey Robinson there, who was a boxer, and Lenny was happy enough.

'So, this one day, I've gone round to see Lenny and told him I'd signed up to box professional for Greg

Steene. Lenny said, "That's lovely, son. Why don't you come and see me tomorrow at Slim Jim's, over in Greenwich? I've got a good middleweight for you to spar with. He's had six pro fights, he's a young black kid, and he'll be good sparring for you. Now come and meet me tomorrow." At the time I was a light heavyweight. Anyway, I went around and told Greg Steene, and he went mad and said, "Manny, you're becoming a professional boxer and we don't want you training with the likes of Lenny." (I think it was to do with Lenny being involved in the unlicensed scene in the past.) I said to Greg, "Listen, I've got to, cos if I don't turn up at that gym tomorrow, Lenny's going to think I'm frightened of him and it will cause me problems when I'm working with him.

'Greg Steene then said, "Alright, go then, but don't make a habit of it, we need you training with us." Anyway, I went along to this gym with my girlfriend and my girlfriend's dad – he was also an ex-heavyweight pro boxer named Desie Cox and Lenny knew him well. I've got in the ring with this kid and done three three-minute rounds with him and then Lenny says to the geezer, "Right, out you get!" Lenny then sticks this great big geezer in named Mickey Theo, who I had known from the doors – he was well respected and knew a lot of people. Lenny was training Mick to become a prizefighter although I'm not sure if he went on to have any fights.

'So, I was now in the ring, looking at this monster that was about eighteen stone, and there's me, thirteen stone, soaking wet. Mickey was muscular, being a bodybuilder, but he just wasn't quick enough to hit me and he was going wild at me, swinging punches, and I was just jabbing him. I then thought rather than just looking flash, I'd slow down so he could land a couple of shots when Lenny shouts, "Right, out you get, Manny," and then Lenny climbs in the ring with Mickey. Mickey starts throwing little shots into Lenny like he was frightened. Lenny then said to Mickey, "look here, Mickey, when you were sparring with Manny, you were trying to knock his head off, now I want you to try and knock my fucking head off! I won't hurt you, but you can't hurt me." Mickey wouldn't do it and Lenny said, "You're insulting me now. I told you, you won't be able to hurt me. Get out of the ring and watch how Manny goes to work." Lenny shouts, "Get in here, Manny!"

'I was shitting myself as he was a big frightening man – he reminded me a lot of my dad, with similar mannerisms. The way he talked was much like my dad. As I stepped into the ring with him, I'm thinking, fucking hell, I'm going to have a right hiding here. Lenny says, "Right, son, how old are you?" to which I replied, "Twenty-six, Len," and he said, "Well, I'm forty-one and I've been boxing all of my life, I know the game like the back of my hand." Lenny then asked, "What weight are you, Manny?" So, I told him I was nearly thirteen stone, to which Lenny said that he was twenty-one stone.

'Lenny then said, "Let me tell you now, I'm twenty-one stone, I'm built like a brick shithouse, I'm strong as a fucking ox! You can't hurt me, so when you spar with me I don't want you to piss around and ponce around like normal sparring, I want you to try and knock my fucking head off. What I'm going to do, I'm not going to try and hurt you, I'm just going to block a few, but every now and then I'll let you know I'm there." I thought to myself, what should I say here? So, I've come out and thrown two left jabs and both have hit him on the head. Lenny's not throwing a shot so I threw some more shots. I then caught him with a cracking left hook and a straight right cross, and he kind of wobbled and stumbled backwards. I said, "You alright, Lenny?" He shouts at the top of his voice, "Am I alright? That's fucking lovely, son! That's what I want, no one's sparred with me like that for years, and that's fucking lovely!" He then came at me, hitting me with body shots that were lifting my feet off the floor. The bell went after three minutes and he shouted, "Don't stop, don't stop," so me and him stood there trading punches. The bell went after another three minutes and he shouted again not to stop. A few minutes later, I got two black eyes, my nose is pissing with blood and I'm loving it and fighting for my life. The bell went again after nine minutes and Lenny grabbed me in this big bear hug and said, "Well done, son, that's enough. You done fucking really well!" He turned to my girlfriend and said, "You tell your dad, Desi Cox, this boy is the fucking bollocks as he's just done nine minutes sparring with me!"

'A little while later when I was training with Lenny I ended up getting into a punch-up and got locked up. By the time I come out, I had lost interest in pursuing a pro career.

'Another time I was working on the door with

LENNY'S TASTY LITTLE FIRM

Lenny at the Gas Club and a mate of mine says, "Manny, are you hungry as I'm going over to McDonald's to get some burgers?" I said, "Yeah, get me something," and I was about to order when Lenny lifts his head and says, "What's that, Manny? Don't eat that fucking shit!" Lenny turns to my mate and says, "Go on, fuck off if you're going to get a burger but Manny don't want that shit, he's boxing." He then said, "If you're hungry, son, come with me," and off we went around the corner to Shaftesbury Avenue and he took me into this place to have a cheese and salad roll. What a fucking character he was, he was laughing and winding me up because he knew I was hungry.

'While working on the doors with Lenny only twice did I see him hit someone and I don't mean with punches but just a slap, which was pretty much all it took to wise them up. This one time in the Gas Club this geezer was getting lippy so he was given a slap and was sent on his way. No one was hurt, but they knew not to mess with Lenny or cause trouble again.

'I was working on the doors with Lenny one night and this man came in, asking for Lenny MacLane. Lenny was standing near me and said, "I'm Lenny McLean, not MacLane. Get it right, it's McLean like the toothpaste." I was laughing to myself as Lenny hated people calling him MacLane. I didn't talk to him about his fights all the time as he'd get it all of the time from other people, and it probably gets to you after a bit, so when we worked on the doors together, we just had a good laugh about ordinary things.

'Lenny was a very funny character, an old-school

character, and I have good memories from the time I
spent in his company.'

KEVIN SUMER

Working the doors in the eighties, in and around London,
you're definitely going to know the name Lenny McLean,
and of course Kevin Sumer was no exception. As he says,
Lenny's name sort of ruled over clubland. Everyone knew
he was the absolute bollocks and the main force to be
reckoned with, in and around the world of bouncers.
Here's what he had to say...

'So, I'm working at a place called Moonlights, just
round the back of the Hippodrome, where Lenny and
my great friend John 'The Neck' were minding at the
time. I'd started to pop round when we were a bit quiet
to chat to John and that, so Lenny had seen my face
on a few occasions, or at least that's what I thought.
I was a pretty big fella back then and often trained
with John 'The Neck' and Scotty amongst others, and
I suppose I looked a bit like a bodybuilder.

'So, anyway, this one night I was asked to go round
and help out at the Hippodrome with John and, of
course, Lenny. So, I goes down there and as I walked
in and introduced myself to the other bouncers that
worked for Len, one of them said to me, "Don't stare
at Len, just let him spot you and come over, and oh,
by the way, Lenny fucking hates bodybuilders!" So,
I'm like, oh for fuck's sake. I'm twitching a bit, but
I'm not one to back down, even if I know I ain't got
a chance – I'm going to give it my best shot, anyone

that knows me will tell you this. So, I'm leant up against the bar and I sees Lenny walking my way, chatting to people as he's moving through them, and he's getting bigger and bigger as he nears towards me. Anyway, he gets right up to me, leans on the bar, and squares his face right up into mine and in that fucking gravelly nuts'n'bolts voice of his he goes, "I fucking hate bodybuilders," so I goes to Len, "Well, it's a good job I ain't a fucking bodybuilder then." I'm thinking to myself, is this the point where he gives me a slap? But with that, he just bursts out laughing, slaps me on the back and says, "You'll do, son, you'll do." I'm thinking to myself, thank fuck for that.

'So, I'm up there at the top of the tree working under Len, so this one night I'm having a mooch around the Hippodrome and it's gone off big time near the dance floor. I'm on my own, but I steam in, and knock one of the c***s to the floor. He's at my feet; I grab the other one in a loose choke hold, and the one at my feet grabs hold of my legs and he isn't letting go. So, now I'm struggling to stay on my feet. With that, the big door's smashed open like it's gonna come off the hinges and Len's there with two little rounders bats in his hands. So, I've gone to this fella on my ankle, "Fucking let go of my legs," and he's going, "No, no!" I said, "For fuck's sake, let go! Look, he's gonna steam over here and go fucking beserk!" I goes, "Listen, you fucking mug, that big c***'s steaming our way and he's gonna smash you to pieces and probably me in the process, so fucking liven yourself up and let go of my fucking legs!" I think this fella can't believe what I'm saying. I'm thinking, I don't give a fuck about these two mugs, I just wanna get out the way of Lenny, because when he goes off, you ain't stopping him. Because let me tell you, Lenny wouldn't worry about any collateral damage afterwards, he'd probably just say, "Well, you should've been quicker and got out of the way, shouldn't you, son?" It's funny, thinking about this now, but it wasn't at the time. So, anyway, Len's gone berserk, and all hell's let loose and you can imagine the rest for yourselves. Let's just say, it weren't a pretty sight, to say the least.

'This other time I'm walking round the club and there's this Chinese waitress bird on skates. Well, she's going past me, winking and all that. I'm thinking, fucking hell she's gorgeous! So, as she teases past me again I'm thinking to myself, I'm having a piece of that. Anyway, I goes outside the club and the other two lads, that being my pal, Terry Moss, and Leo, are out there with Lenny, and I'm like, fucking hell, I think I'm in there, she's a right tasty piece! I'm gonna try and get her home after work. Anyway, they're all laughing their heads off, and Len's going to them, "Fucking tell him, fucking tell him!" I'm like, "What the fuck you going on about, you lot?" and Lenny shouts to them, "Just fucking tell him, you lot, or I will!" Well, these lot are still laughing, and Lenny goes, "Listen up, the tart on the rollers is a fucking geezer, son!" Oh my fucking God, I'm thinking to myself, how the fuck am I ever going to live this one down? And for the record, I never fucking did!

'Around this time I was working in a club and got in a bit of bother with this right bully boy. So, this one night he comes in and he's kicked off and to cut it short, I've stuck a left hook into him and he goes down like a ton of fucking bricks, and he's crouched over, going, "Alright, I've had enough!" I go, "Fuck off, you c***! I'll tell you when you've had enough," as I've booted him out through the doors. Well, that's done it – there's gonna be murders over this, and there was. He's gone round my house one night while I'm at work and the wife and kids are home alone and stuck a bayonet through my front door. The line now has well and truly been crossed.

'So, anyway, I goes to see Lenny. Len first said, "Let's have the pair of you in the ring and you can smash him up in there." "It's gone past that, Len. I mean, what would you do if he'd been round and terrorised your wife and kids?" I said. Len says, "Well, you know, I'd have killed the c*** stone dead," so anyway, I thinks to myself, that's done the trick. Suffice to say, this fella and his boys got done bad one evening. By all accounts it looked like a massacre. I mean, don't ask me what happened – I was up the other end of the country at the time. Makes me laugh to myself today, thinking what would've happened if Lenny would've encountered this fella at first instead of me. Lenny would've fucking unloaded him with the first wrong look. He would've smashed him to bits, probably with one punch, if I'm honest. Lenny certainly didn't like bully boys.'

Lee: Right, as I'm sure you've all realised by now, any stories that were discussed between myself and any interviewee with regard to Len's funeral, I do like to slip in the middle of a write-up and end the piece on a nice note. Well, this is a slightly tongue-in-cheek thing that happened on a very sad day. Kev Sumer and Billy Isaac were in the car behind John 'The Neck' and Alan Crossley, and as they pulled up and got out of the cars, Kev said to Billy, 'Look at those fuckers in the bushes with cameras, they can't even leave poor Len alone on his funeral day.' Billy goes, 'Yeah, fucking piss-takers!' Well, as it turns out, they weren't there for anything to do with Lenny, they were actually from the National Crime Squad, under surveillance, and were following Billy and Kev. Just goes to show how despicable these Old Bill can be. Well, everything went as it should. Len's wife, Val, and their children, Kelly and Jamie, had done the big man proud, with a service fit for a king. Here's Kev again...

KEVIN SUMER

'So back to business and the handful of shifts I'd done for Len at the Hippodrome, we would often sit over in the café right opposite. You see, Len had this walkie-talkie thing in case anything big went off. So, we're all sat over there and Len's just told us a joke. Us lads are all in bits, laughing – all except Rick, one of my pals from Options. I'm thinking to myself, what's wrong with him? Anyway, Lenny goes into talking about something a bit sensitive and serious, and with that, Rick's laughing like fuck at the top of his voice, With that, Len's gone to Rick, "Oi, what the fuck's so funny, you c***?" So, Rick goes, "What, Len? I was laughing at that joke you told," and Len's gone, "Oh, for fuck's sake, boy, that was about ten fucking minutes ago! Catch up, son." So now we're all laughing. I thought to myself, what a time to start laughing when Len's just talking all serious. Good job it wasn't something too sensitive, or Rick would've probably ended up getting a bit of a backhander off of Len.

'Another funny little story – Lenny sent John 'The Neck' and I out on the pavement to pick up a debt one day, so John and I are in the motor. John's a funny fella just like Len, he likes to have a laugh and a joke, you know. Anyway, we're out near Windsor, so we pulls up to this right big posh mansion place; this bloke owed thousands. So, we pull up to the massive gate and it's locked, but the fella must've seen us, so this fella, who's quite a big bloke, drives up to the gates in his little Mercedes Sports and goes, "Can I help ya?" and John goes straight away, pointing to me, "Yeah, he wants to talk to you." So, I says to the fella, "Eh, look, pal, you owe hundred grand, mate, and my Guv'nor says you gotta pay it today," and the fella went, "Well, what if I don't pay it?", and John goes, "Well, listen, son, if you don't pay it, he's gonna hit ya." The geezer goes from behind the gates, "Oh yeah, and who the fuck are you then?", so I went, "The geezer that's gonna smash you, if you don't fucking pay up today, my friend." Anyway, he pays up, probably for the reason that he knows who my Guv'nor is. So, we get back to the office and Lenny and John are ripping the piss, acting it out between them like a pair of clowns. I must admit it was funny, though.

'One thing I do know, and I got this from day one with Lenny, he got right up to me and said, "Listen, son." Pointing from my head down to my bollocks, he said, "When you get into it, and you're having a tear up, you hate 'em, hate 'em, son, and you smash 'em to bits, all around this area," as he's tapping my chest and stomach and that, "hate from here to here, and smash 'em to fucking bits." I thought, yeah, OK, Len, I'll take that on board, as long as I never upset Lenny and he has to do the same to me.

'Lenny was truly one fucking hard and tasty fucker, and one fella you wanted on your side, and not on the other side that you were in any sort of row with. One thing I will say is this, thank fuck Lenny McLean was a pal of mine and never my enemy. Rest in peace, Len, I miss you, my friend.'

AL CROSSLEY

Lee: 'During many meetings with my now-close friend, John 'The Neck', we have chatted many times about the fella of whom we have all researched a little over the years. A man with such fighting prowess that his name rang through the streets of his hometown in Ireland, and reverberated through his working life in the capital. The formidable Irish unlicensed street-fighting heavyweight and strongman that I speak of is "The Viking Warrior" himself, Al Crossley. Al had appeared in a documentary about himself in 1991 called *10 x 10 Hardmen*, in which he had mentioned that if he ever needed a hand to sort things out, he could call on London's finest, Lenny McLean.

'It's funny because it was my dad that first mentioned Al to me, way back in the late eighties. Dad used to say, "Eh, son, I wouldn't fancy upsetting this fella, eh?" I remember thinking to myself at the time, maybe if I had another ten fellas behind me.'

It's now thirty years on, and I'm sat with John and he calls up Al. Immediately a confident Irish booming voice replies, 'Hello Johnny Boy, how you going, son?' John goes on to tell him that he's with his friend, Lee, and would it be OK to have a few words? So, I'm now on the phone and with my ample knowledge of Al, in addition to the opinion that I gained within the first two minutes of chatting to him, it was easy to imagine the kind of fella I was dealing with, and I wasn't at all wrong. Al spoke with the utmost respect with regards to Lenny: Lenny was indeed a very tough and powerful man, he said. He added that he and John had worked alongside Lenny for many years on the doors and spent a lot of time together on various jobs.

Lenny and Al fought a few similar battles in the ring, one of them being against the six-foot six inches doorman Dave 'Man Mountain' York, who of course Lenny beat very quickly. As is documented elsewhere in this book , the bearded Al cornered Len for this, as you may have seen on YouTube. Also, he was pictured in Len's book, *The Guv'nor*. Then a few weeks later, Al fought York with Len in his corner and beat him in under a minute. Al went on to say that himself, Lenny and John worked on many jobs together, always bringing home the bacon – 'Well, imagine these three chasing you for a few bob,' 'Yes, I'm quivering at the thought of it too.'

It was a brief yet insightful chat, and in closing, I asked him how his health was, as John had mentioned to me that Al had suffered a heart attack a few months earlier.

THE GUV'NOR REVEALED

In true warrior fashion and in that whimsical Irish twang, he simply said, 'Aye, Lee, I said to the nurse as I gained consciousness, well, that was a pleasant experience.' For goodness sake, if that don't show you the worth of this man, I simply don't know what would!

CHAPTER 8

THE NECK

Lee: A name you heard about in the last chapter, as mentioned by Kevin Sumer a few times, is John, otherwise known as 'The Neck'. John an ex bodybuilder, who first met Lenny through mutual friends and ended up working with him on the doors and other jobs, and they became the best of friends. Not that Lenny needed any bodyguards at his last ever book signing, but John was the one who was rung, along with their other good mate, Al Crossley. This just goes to show how close and how respected John was to Lenny.

John Houchin is fifty-three years of age. He is known in and around London as John 'The Neck', owing to his many years as a bodybuilder on the British circuit. Not being the kind of fella to talk himself up, he did eventually inform me that he came fourth in the Brits qualifying. Suffice to say, John was and still is a very powerful man in his own right.

THE GUV'NOR REVEALED

Now let me just give you an idea of the sort of power he wielded. Our man John was a little bit shorter than Lenny, coming in at around six foot one inch tall, weighing twenty-two stone, with a sixty-inch chest, twenty-two-inch upper arm and a staggering twenty-three-inch neck, hence the apt nickname. By all accounts he was, and still is, one tasty bastard, and with the sort of artillery he had in those fists of his, you can easily imagine that anyone crossing him was bang in trouble, to say the very least. Also, the fact that Len handpicked 'The Neck' to be his right-hand man, his second-in-command, is some accolade.

I had chatted with John by phone for around nine months before finally meeting him, and I have to say the gentle yet gruff Cockney tones that he adopts while chatting down the phoneline are a far cry from the giant and somewhat intimidating figure I was greeted with. Luckily for me, John and I have become very close friends so our meet was of an almost 'family member coming home' sort of affair, but listen, I would certainly not fancy John 'The Neck' knocking at my front door with the right raving hump if I'd crossed him and Len, back in the day.

OK, so most of you will recognise John from his appearance in *Lock, Stock and Two Smoking Barrels*, playing the part of a doorman alongside professional Irish heavyweight, Steve Collins. Cast your attention back to the scene in which they throw the fella out of the gym, where the big card game is being played – well, the big geezer with the shaven head is our man John. Oh, and just to give you a bit of film fact history, the fella they threw out of the gym was himself a big fighter on the scene called Jim Flynn. As Lenny would say, he took John under his wing, a statement that carried a hell of a lot more weight than any of you could ever imagine, and believe me when I say it, from the stories John went on to tell me, on and off the record, that our man John was well and truly under The Guv'nor's wing. Anyway, here's what John 'The Neck' had to say.

JOHN 'THE NECK' HOUCHIN

'I first met Lenny at a very popular club Len was minding around about the mid-eighties in London called the Camden Palace. We met through mutual friends of ours, Col Camwell and one of my closest pals then and still today, Al Crossley. Col and I used to work the doors together. Fans of Lenny would have seen Col stood with his back to the camera in the changing room before the "Man Mountain" York fight – Col is the fella saying to Len, "I'm Lean, I'm mean, I'm Lenny McLean."

'This meeting at the Camden Palace then led to John working with Lenny at the Hippodrome, along with a bunch of other bits of work that required muscle to settle disputes, etc. Myself, Lenny and Alan went on many minding jobs together and we also collected debts for the Underworld and the odd celebrity from stage and screen. Also, Len would always have about a good few bob of his own money on the street at all times, so anyway, every Friday, we would be out picking up cash from people that owed debts to whoever we were working for.

I am known in our industry as John 'The Neck', owing to my neck measuring almost twenty-three inches. I am quite happy to have this nickname for the simple reason that many people over the years have struggled to pronounce my surname. Lenny, of course, was no exception. Picture it if you can, stood on the door of the Hippodrome, Lenny says, "Go on, son, your last name, say it to me." I said, "Well, Len, it's the same as how you say 'house' with 'chin' at the end, like 'how-chin'". "Oh, fuck all of that cobblers, let's stick with 'The Neck'," says Len. I'm laughing now, picturing him saying it. Lenny thought that was hilarious, he liked to laugh at his own jokes – mind you, it's funny, most people laughed along with him.

'Now let me start by saying this, most people never did and unfortunately never will know the Lenny McLean that the likes of me and my very dear friend, Al Crossley, had the pleasure to know. Lenny was comedic and kind, generous and loyal, witty, and of course a fearless fucking fella, all wrapped up in that colossal frame. He was everything you'd imagine – he had hands like King Kong and a voice that sounded like a bucket of spanners. Let me tell you this, when Lenny McLean got the raving hump, he doubled in size and was a frightening site to behold.

'Once I got to know Lenny, he let me know that he'd heard a lot about me through stories he'd heard from Al and Col – all good, I hoped. You see, I go back a long way with them. Col used to arrange unlicensed fights for the pair of us. He was the sort of fella to always try and test you, not in a bad way to see you get hurt, no, nothing like that, he just liked to test your muster. Well, he did the same with me, throwing up top fighters, one after the other, to fight me. Each and every one of them I smashed in no time at all. Anyway, once I got to know Len, I realised that Col had told him that I was a force to be reckoned with. Saying this to Len could almost be seen as some sort of a challenge – well, so I thought – but for me, this wasn't the case. Lenny simply whispered to me, "Don't worry, son, I've got Col's number," and from that day on, a fantastic friendship began to bloom.

'Now a lot of Lenny's fans probably don't know this but he was a very big joker and always playing tricks on people. Sometimes as we were stood on the door at the club and he would say, "Here, John, watch this, son." With that, he would bend down and pull the massive rug from under the newbie doorman's feet. The newbie would be on his back, holding his nose that he'd smashed with his own hands when he fell to the ground. He'd quickly jump to his feet, going, "For fuck's sake, what happened, what happened?" Lenny and I would just be stood there, pissing ourselves laughing.

'Other times there could be two hundred people lined up to come in the Hippodrome. All of the management would be stood there too, and out of the blue Len would go, "Here, John, let's practise our lines'". I'd say, "But Len, there's like two hundred people waiting to come in," and Lenny would say, "Oh, don't worry about them for a minute." With that he'd spin around on his heels, walk off and then quickly walk back towards me. I'm stood straight up as if I'm minding some club, and Len would go, "Alright, me son?" and this particular time I replied, "That ain't in the script, Len." He'd chuckle and go,

"I know it ain't, John. I'm just saying, 'Alright, me son?'" Honestly, this whole time the management are looking over, thinking, oh my goodness, how long's this going on for?

'This was the Lenny that no one really ever saw: he was a proper comic, and believe me, he really was. All of a sudden from inside the reception there's a voice shouting for Len, "It's kicked off!" Now Len being Len always had his own very individual way of putting things and in instances such as these he would go, "Right, John, jump in the motor!" People would look and think, jump in what fucking motor? I'm in bits, thinking about the looks on people's faces. No, what Lenny actually meant was, "It's gone off in the club or wherever, let's go to work." Now in the driver's seat, and always fronting the trouble was of course Lenny himself, and I'm in the passenger seat – his wingman, let's say. Now listen, not just anyone would get in that car, you would've had to have earned your stripes so to speak, you had to be "mustard", as Lenny would put it, because let's face it, you had to be able to back up The Guv'nor, which I'm sure you'd all guess, even for me was no easy task at times, and I've been about.

'So, this one time Lenny's flying through the club with me in his wake. The trouble's out near the back doors. As he's piling through them he picks one fella up by the throat while grabbing another one by his jacket collar, then he smashes the pair of them through the doors. I'm right behind Lenny, with this other mug in a bit of a choke hold. Apparently what they had done was touch some fella's wife's arse and he'd gone off at the lot of them. A bit brave, but it was his wife after all.

'So, anyway, we push them outside and let go of them. With that they turn back to have a dig, and just like something from a cartoon, Len does one with a left hook and the other with a straight right into his chest. I stick the nut on my one, and it's all over with, the three of them stretched out cold on the cobbles. Now we're back into comedy mode, Len goes, "Good work, son! Listen, do the bin men come tomorrow?" So I says, "Yeah, Len, it's Thursday," and he says, "Beautiful, son! Sling these fucking no-value c***s in with the rubbish, I'll have a chat with the other fella and his missus in the office." So there's me humping these three big lumps into the big yellow skip, down the back alley, and Lenny goes to me, "Eh, John, mind their heads, son." I'm thinking to myself, mind their fucking heads after you've just smashed them to pieces? Now come on, you couldn't write this sort of stuff, could you?

'With regard to power and strength, Len and I used to train together down the gym. I remember this one time Lenny had been down a particular gym in Bethnal Green called Muscle Works Gym, and when he gets over to Slim Jim's in Greenwich, where I was waiting to meet him for training, he says to me, "Eh, John, I've just been down that poncey fucking gym to look for someone and the c*** in there didn't even know who I was, so I'm screaming and shouting, "Don't know who I am? I'm the hardest man in Britain, you fucking soft, silly c***!"'

'Another time as we're boxing training down there

I'm looking around the place, checking it out, and Len goes to me, "What you looking at them fucking bodybuilders for, son? They're all full of fucking air!" I used to piss myself laughing. Anyway, we're on the bag, doing a bit of bag work, and Lenny's going for it. All of a sudden there's a slight pause between Len's shots, so I popped my head round the bag and goes, "Have you finished, Len?" and Lenny goes, "Get your fucking head out of the way, son!" I'm there, swinging up and down; as Len's hitting the bag, I'm almost hitting the ceiling.

'We also used to do boxing training down the gym. Lenny would always get there before me, and by the time I got there I'd say to him, "Eh, Len, how many rounds have you done?" and every single time he'd go, "Eighteen, John, eighteen." So, we're sat in the gym this one day, while Len's having a five-minute roll-up break, of which I will say at this point he was the only one allowed to smoke down the gym. Anyway, I said to him, "Eh, Len, you know eighteen?" He goes, "Yeah." I said, "Well, is eighteen your favourite number?" He goes, "Why, son?" and I goes, "Cos every time I come in and ask you how many rounds you've done, well, you always say eighteen." Lenny replies, "Do I, son?" and then laughs like a fucking nutter. Well, from that day on, it became a bit of an in-joke with Len and myself.

'Down the gym we used to go in the ring together, but it wasn't really sparring, it was more Lenny holding back, just to test my speed, etc., and to see how I coped with him. I mean, you couldn't really do proper sparring because Lenny would go right into it and unload you. One of our good friends, Mick, tried to do that, and he got a bit cocky one day and tried to unload a bit with Len. With that, Lenny gave him a body shot and put him on his arse, just to teach him a lesson – all in good fun though, of course, it was just the way it was then – but let's just say this, Lenny was way too powerful. So, I stuck to the bag work from then on with Len, and left the sparring to the others.

'You see, like I said earlier, not many people were fortunate enough to be privy to the softer side of Lenny. He was sort of a father figure to me, and of course in turn this made Valerie McLean almost like a mother to me too – funny, really as my own Mum's name was Valerie as well. Lenny always had this way of asking for a drink. He'd shout through to Val in the kitchen, "Babe, John wants a coffee," obviously meaning he wants a cuppa too, and Val would shout back to him, "Oh, and I suppose you don't want one then, eh, Len?" She had Len's number down, probably from the very first day they met.

'As you would expect, because of Lenny's reputation and notoriety a great number of well-known faces would park up in the club. Most weekends there would be TV stars, boxers, presenters, radio DJs, etc. and of course many faces from Gangland Britain. On occasion you would see Nigel Benn in the club – he was big pals with the boys from Essex. Now Lenny never really mixed with these lads very well – I think that the line of villainy these boys were involved in was the sort of thing he found deplorable and hated with every fibre of his being. Lee goes on to say that he has read on many occasions that the odd person linked to the Essex lot has slagged Lenny off in books and tours, etc, and Lee has also heard on YouTube and various other places like that, how these lot call him a bully – well, I'll just say this in retaliation to remarks like that, none of them ever said it while Lenny was alive, not one of them, and just for the record Lenny really had no time for those types of people anyway.

'Right, let's just set the record straight: with regard to Len's criminal activities, he dipped in and out of the Underworld, but only really as a third party. He would settle disputes over money, collect debts for the kinds of people that simply didn't have the muscle that Len had to retrieve large sums of cash – most of the time running into many thousands of pounds. But of course Lenny was paid handsomely for his services in these instances, which had a knock-on effect down to Al and myself, and we would be well looked after too. Let's just say, it was a very good payday for the three of us when we went to work.

'One particular day, we were in one of my Range Rovers on our way back from a bit of work, and we pulls up down Avenue Road, Bexleyheath, where Len and Val were living at the time. There's me, my pal, Al Crossley, and another fella who goes by the name of "Prince" – well, that's what we always called him. Anyway, Avenue Road is like a main thoroughfare, with cars and buses whizzing along all day long. So I get out of the motor, but then notice that Prince has left his window open, so I run round to sort it and wallop, this bus smashes my arm and it's smashed up proper. I'm screaming in agony, leant up against my motor. Al has already made a beeline for me because my arm is in a real bad way, so he's seeing to me, calming me down and that. Now just as the mayhem is heightening because people are rushing around me, the ambulance pulls up and the paramedics jump out and Len comes running over, but in the furore of it all he thinks that everyone is stifling me, so he picks one of the paramedic fellas up in the air to move him out of my way. Anyway, they get me down to Barts and I'm seen to by the doctors. Turns out I need all kinds of wires and pins in my arm to save it, a token from that day that I'm still having pain with today. The doctor did, however, say that I was very lucky to be alive, because if the bus was just half a foot closer when it hit me, it would probably have killed me.

'What I failed to tell you was that it was Friday the thirteenth and also the day that Lenny got the results about his illness. Which brings me on to The Guv'nor and the only fight he could simply never win: Lenny never really talked too much about his illness although once while we were sat having a cuppa in his house, he noticed me pondering for a moment at the mention of it, and he said, "Listen, John, I know you think everything will change for you once I'm gone, but it won't, son. Believe me, you have nothing to worry about." To which I replied, "I ain't worried about me, Len, I just don't want you to go, my friend," and those few words were the only ones he and I ever really said on the matter. Lenny was truly The Guv'nor, in every sense of the word.'

Lee: On that note I will just let you, as the reader, know that I thought I'd get this part of John's life with Lenny over with in the throes of the story, because I know John would want me to end his union with Len on a high note. I also do not want to dwell on Lenny's funeral day – it was, and will always remain one of the worst days of John's life. John went with his two great friends, Al Crossley and another doorman and minder, Kevin Sumer. He takes up the story again...

'Right, so myself and Al were in one of the second family cars, which of course Al and I found to be a great honour. Kev was in the car behind ours with another big friend and sadly no longer with us, Billy Isaac. Now as fans of Lenny McLean, I'm sure you will have seen the photographs in the national press of the procession with its thousands of well-wishers lining the East End streets. It was a procession and service fit for a king. Lenny's wife, Val, and the family did the man proud, and well-deserved it was too. Now that is just about all I have to say on the subject, because it's a very private affair and one I do not feel the need to detail.

'So, just to finish this section on a lighter note, I will tell you a funny story. Lenny was in bed towards the end of his illness and Val came up to bring him a cuppa. Lenny lay there as if he had passed away. I mean, talk about the strength of the man, to fool around this close to his own death. However, I don't think that Val took it quite so funny – I think Len probably ended up wearing that cup of tea. I think he just did it to see Val's reaction, I don't think he played that trick again.

'Right, so let's go back to our little firm... Now as collectors of debts you need to have a certain way about you and as we all know, Lenny McLean was born with it: he simply had to puff out his chest and growl a bit, and the money was paid in full. Now some of us may have to work a little harder at this, and for the chosen few Lenny would test your muster. So, we're on our way to collect a vast amount of cash from what Len informs me to be one proper gruesome, nasty, vicious fucker. He says to me in the car, "Right, go on, my son! You can front this one up." Now I'm used to taking all kinds on in a row, as you will well know by this stage in the story, but I'm thinking, oh shit, I hope I can sort this proper and not let Lenny and the boys down. Anyway, it's too late to think, we're at the desired property. Look lively, John, I'm thinking to myself. So, I'm at the door with Len and Al behind me and Lenny goes, "Give that door a boot then, son, let him know we're here." As I pull my foot back, the door swings open and the fella is stood there. "Oh, one sec," he says as he grabs a pile of cash and hands it to me with not a hint of any hassle. He then shuts the door. I turn to Len and he's got this big grin on his face and he's laughing – "Well, I had to make sure you cut muster, boy." I'm laughing to myself now and thinking, you won't get me with that one again, Len, I'm ready for you. Well anyway, that was a nice bit of scratch for a half hour's work and a bit of Lenny skylarking. Anyway, on to the next one we go...

'I got this pal of mine – Phil's his name, we don't need surnames, but he knows who he is. He and I go way back: we've worked on almost everything together, at one time in the eighties we were inseparable. Anyway,

Phil's got a bit of bother, some fella, let's call him Baz – well, as it happens he owes a few bob to my pal. Let's just say that he's into my pal for a couple of grand. So anyway, Phil's been on to the fella, saying, "Look, stop fucking about and just pay me the money you owe me." Next thing, he's on the blower to me, putting me in the picture. As it turns out, this Bazza fella has put Lenny's name up as front, so I've said to Phil, "Leave it with me, I'll see what I can find out."

'Within two minutes my phone's gone and guess who it is? Yes, it's Lenny. He says to me, "Alright, son? What's happening with this Phil fella?" So I says, "Oh yes, that's Phil, he's my mate, Len," and Lenny goes, "What's he done, what's all this about then, son?" So I said, "I'll tell you what it's about, Len. This Bazza owes my pal, Phil, a couple of grand. He wants his money, he ain't gonna do anything to him, but if he don't pay him, well, let's put it like this, if you didn't get involved, Len, then this fella wouldn't be about, that's all I'm saying." Lenny goes, "John, leave it with me, I'll sort it." Five minutes later, I get a call back, quick and simple as that, from Lenny, saying, "John, take Phil down with you. It's done, he's gonna pay it." Lenny's name carried that much weight, it just took a phone call and bosh, it was sorted.

'Lenny was always messing around: we would be sat round a big table on a meet with about twenty people round it and Len would lean over to me and whisper out of the corner of his mouth, "Here, listen, John, don't laugh, whatever you do, and act tough," because he just knew that I was going to end up laughing. It was always like a comedy sketch with Lenny.

THE NECK

'Another thing that Len always used to say, if you watch all the footage of him on YouTube, he would go, "Well, I unloaded the lot of 'em, killed 'em all stone dead, and they took them up Barts and revived 'em." My pal goes to me, "Eh, John, ask Lenny which hospital that was, cos they always seemed to revive 'em back from death. We could do with knowing which hospital that was, the stuff we get up to." I says to him, "Well, you ask Lenny yourself. Go on, ask him," and he goes to me, "No, you ask Lenny, you're closer to him than I am. He'll know you're joking, he might go off his nut with me."

'We would always be parked up in the little café across the road to the Hippodrome, and if Lenny was needed, one of the doormen would run across and shout us. We were either there or in the office, we were hardly ever actually stood on the door itself – well, not when I worked with Lenny, we weren't. You see, around that sort of time Lenny's name was deterrent enough: once all the wrong'uns knew that a certain place was looked after by Lenny McLean, it would pretty much put a block on any likely lads trying it on. Lenny used to say to me, "Look, John, we don't need to be stood on that door, because all I wanna know is, if there's trouble, we'll go sort it out," so when trouble arose, that's exactly what would happen.

'One night we had just had this tear up with a bunch of no-good c***s and we've gone back to what was Lenny's office. It's just off the side of the main corridor, we used to sit in there most of the evening; all of the staff knew that's where we were in case it went off in the club. We used to park up in there, having a bit of food and that – Lenny loved his Chinese grub. So, anyway, we're just sat in there after this row and the manager comes steaming in through one of the doors. Remember, we're still revved up a bit, anyway the manager comes in one door and Lenny hurls him with some force straight out the other door. A little later on, Lenny said to the manager, "Here, sorry, son, I never realised it was you. Come and sit on my knee," and Len was bouncing him up and down on his knee like one of those puppets. Lenny said to me later on, "Here, John, I can't believe it was the manager. I smashed him right round the side of the fucking head!" Well, believe it or not, the manager fella knocked on Len's office door from that day on.

'As a seasoned doorman with a good few years under my belt and, as I said earlier, I had had the good fortune to have worked alongside London's finest bouncers, minders and fighters, my great friend Alan Crossley being one of the very best, I would say at this point in my story that Lenny and Alan were by far the best two I have ever had the pleasure to have worked alongside. So it's safe to say that by the time I was taken under Lenny's wing I was already quite a confident fella. Don't get me wrong, subconsciously, however, I probably did feel the need to show my muster in and around Lenny, and at times when it did kick off and we would engage in a tear up, in the calming after the melee shall we say, Lenny would say to me, "You done good there, son. I'm proud of you, boy." You see, I've always been one to listen and take on board what someone that I saw to be an authority on such things believed, and in this instance that just happened to be Lenny. You know he would say to me, "John, be smart, be quick, always talk nice to people and above all, don't bully anyone."

'Lenny would also say to me, while looking my clobber up and down, "Always wear something baggy, John, cos if you can't throw a right-hander like this [as he gesticulates a flurry of shots] then you won't be able to do anything," and of course Lenny being who he was, and being head doorman, I would listen and sort of do as he told me. I mean, I could tell how strong Lenny would expect me to go when it went off or in any given circumstance, just with a look from him. A look alone from him could indicate a thousand different things. This one time, he had popped out on some business and it went off big time on the dance floor, so I've smashed into 'em and bashed 'em up, and was just giving 'em a bit of afters for taking the piss. Anyway, Len comes back and has to watch what happened on the CCTV. With that, he goes to me, "John, son, how much rope did you give 'em?" I said, "Eh, what, you're asking me how much rope did I give them?" and Len's like, "Yeah, how much rope did you give 'em, son?" I said, "Did you have a look at the videotape?" and Len went, "Yeah, fuck me, couldn't you have given 'em a little bit more rope, boy?" So I said, "Well, OK, Len, how much rope would you have given 'em?" and he went, "Ha ha ha ha, not a lot!" But then he goes, "Fuck me, John, I think you went a bit over the top." So I said to him, "Oh, that's fucking good, coming from you!" Anyway, he phones me later and goes, "The Old Bill are on their way down, John. I'll stick you on a pension for a week or two, son."

'If you go back to the days of the mid-eighties to mid-nineties, Lenny was getting a nice wedge of cash from a good few of those places that used his name as a deterrent, a front against any likely lads. So, on a Friday night for instance he would be on the pavement, going round, picking up his wages. This one night I'm minding a place called Lacey's and the gaffer's son is winding me right up – sort of undermining me at the front door, simply over what people are allowed to be wearing to come in. Anyway, he's given me the right hump, so by the end of the night we're stood at the counter of the reception area, my pal's missus is on the other side of the counter, counting the takings, and I've heard him go, "Is he a bit slow?" pointing his head over at me. I thought, here, son, I'll show you how slow I am, so I've unloaded into him and smashed him over the counter, nearly into my pal's girlfriend. Anyway, he's spitting blood and teeth out all over the place. His dad's on the warpath with all kinds of threats, wanting me sorting out and the rest of that old cobblers. Later, when I gets back with Lenny, he's taken me in the office to find out what's been going on because obviously if they're upset and Lenny's on the payroll, it could come back on him. So, I'm telling Lenny what's gone on and he's laughing, picturing the whole scene, and then he goes, "Right, I'm going to have to have a mooch round there and tell him he needs to calm down a bit." I think the gaffer's son's teeth bill ended up costing the son a few grand. As it turns out, as was always the case back then, Lenny and his reputation got it all sorted out and we're back to business as usual.

Lee: In closing, I ask John how much he misses those days with Lenny and Al and the rest. He ponders for a while before saying this:

'Like Lenny said on so many occasions, it wasn't a life that I chose, it just sort of crept up on me. But having said that, I wouldn't have had it any other way. I mean, meeting Lenny was the business at that time, everybody wanted to be in and around the man – he was a very charismatic and formidable character, to say the least. But of course on the flip side to that, you had the other side of Len, which could on occasion make for a hard day's work. You see, with Lenny being on offer twenty-four seven, you had to have your wits about you and in that I simply mean you couldn't really have an off day, and obviously Lenny had that on his head tenfold. Let's just put it like this, anyone doing a normal nine-to-five job can take a day off sick – well, that was never the case for Lenny because there was always some firm out there that would want to challenge him, and of course myself and Al being so close to Len at that time sort of meant the same for us too. Look, it goes with the territory.

'Lenny was there for each and every one of us, and in turn I would like to think that Al and I were there for him too through the good and the bad, right up until the sad day that he died. Lenny McLean taught me many life lessons, of which since he was taken from us, I have tried to adopt into my everyday life.

I would like to reiterate something Lenny said on the *Richard Littlejohn Show* months before he passed away. Lenny said, "There are ten thousand street fighters out there who ain't earning a tanner [Cockney slang for a sixpence], I'm a one-off," and he never spoke a truer word. Suffice to say, there will never be another man like my great pal, Lenny.

'Lenny McLean was, and always will be "The Guv'nor" and to echo his very words, Lenny was simply a one-off.'

Above: Lenny and John 'The Neck' Houchin minding the Hippodrome.

Below left: On our travels to meet those who knew Lenny.

Below right: Lee with John Houchin.

Above: Lenny with Rachel Rebecca Halliwell and his daughter Kelly.

Below: Lenny minding the Hippodrome – pictured with fellow employee Paula Morrell and a friend, Vanessa.

Above: Lenny with Kelly and Val at the Guv'ners pub.

Below left: Lenny and Val together.

Below right: Val with Kelly and Jamie.

Above: Lenny and his friend Bernie in Brixton.

Below: Lenny, Kenny Mac and Johnny 'Bootnose' Wall.

Above: Lenny the family man.

Below left: Len with Kelly.

Below right: Lenny with Karen Latimer, who he saw as one of his own.

Above: Lenny and Johnny Madden gloved up at the Camden Palace.

Below left: Lenny at the Camden Palace.

Below right: Suited up for work.

Above: Lenny with Johnny Nash and his wife Linda.

Below left: Lenny in happy times.

Below right: A tribute to Lenny by Charles Salvador (Charlie Bronson).

Above: Kelly, Len and Val.

Below left: Lenny with the Walls' dogs Bugsie and Mugsie.

Below right: Lenny with Val.

CHAPTER 9

THE PALLY DAZE

After years of roughing it, minding the doors in the dark and dangerous suburbs of East London, Lenny finally made a big step up and moved on to club nightlife, a scene blitzed and pulsing with electronic pop and parachute pants: the world inside one of London's most popular of night-club venues, the Camden Palace, known locally simply as 'The Pally'. The Pally would certainly have been an eye-opener, once witnessed through the eyes of those testosterone-fuelled doormen. Here are some stories taken from interviews we have conducted with a few people who stood side by side with Lenny on his journey into this vibrant new age.

DAVE CHIPPING

Lee: Dave was manager of the Camden Palace for a very long period, and of course as every one of you will know by now, Lenny ran the security there for many years too. Over the years Lenny's name alone became such a strong deterrent that the mere mention of it would be enough to iron out many a dispute. That said, it also brought many a likely lad along to the club, claiming to be Len's family, his best pal, and that sort of thing. Dave, however, had a very effective way of dealing with said people: in his words, this is how it would have gone down.

'Right, listen up, I'm going to give Lenny a call right now, and offer your name up to him. Now if I call him up and he doesn't know you, then you're up for a right-hander off of Len. Now if he does know you, and I'm causing him aggravation on his night off, then I'll get a telling-off instead. So, fellas, whichever way this ends, one of us is in line for a clump. Now I'm willing to take that chance, what about you?'

Maybe nine times out of ten, punters would take a walk with their tail between their legs. Job done, and Dave was a happy man.

He tells me that Lenny was very useful to their working firm and for many business dealings simply because his name carried so much weight across London and many other cities across the UK. Dave had some business over Basildon at a very well-known club known as Rachel's so he made his way down to this place to sort this bit of business out, but on arrival, he was met by the club's security team – I think you can guess exactly which team he is referring to. Anyway, they are less than welcoming and tell him in no uncertain terms to go fuck himself, to which Dave replies, 'OK, OK, that's fine, gentlemen, but I will go and have a chat with my head of security and we will take it from there, but for now I'll bid you a good day.'

Anyway, Dave had a meet with Len and they arranged another meet with the team at Rachel's. Would you believe it, when Len and Dave arrived at the club just a few days later, they could not do enough to help him. He got all of the flannel – like, 'Oh well, if Big Len's in charge, we will help and assist you in any way possible. No problem, just let us know what needs to happen and consider it done.' Lenny and Dave left the place and went back to business as usual. All the while Dave's thinking to himself, isn't it funny how people can have a change of mind in a heartbeat?

As you can well imagine, they had some rough nights down the Camden Palace. It was a very lively place, with faces from all walks of life and of course many celebrities frequented the Palace, or 'Pally' as it was favourably known, on a regular basis. This one evening, they're about wrapped up for the night, but there's a bunch of about nine fellas – 'not kids, fellas that have decided they don't want to leave'. Anyway, Len's in his office so Dave walks over and says, 'Come on now, fellas, time to go,' and immediately he's bombarded with a torrent of abuse. So, Dave says, 'Well, OK, fellas, but remember, I did ask you to leave very nicely.' Anyway, he goes to fetch Len from his office and let me tell you this, even Dave don't like pulling Len away from his cup of tea. So, Dave and Lenny make their way back over to this bunch of nuisances and Lenny tells them in no uncertain terms that they have to leave. Well, with that two of the braver ones out of the bunch jumped forward as if to have a row with Len – how silly they must've been. Within a split-second Len pings one with a left and the other fella with a right, and they're both out cold. Len had done his job and they were up and out of the club a bit lively, the lot of them.

Another time this group of fellas had been coming it a bit around two young ladies. Anyway, the girls came over to where Dave and Len were sat, parked themselves up on the sofas and started telling them about it, and pointing to the group of fellas as they explained what had been happening. With that, Len jumps up out of his seat in a rage, the two girls grab hold of his jacket to try and stop him from doing his nut, but due to his enormous size and speed, the whole of his jacket is ripped right down the seam. Anyway, that was the end of that, but someone was going to be doing a bit of suit tailoring that evening...

Lenny went with Dave on many business meetings, from Newcastle to France, the odd bit of business in Spain, and as I said earlier, a whole plethora of towns and cities up and down the UK. He was a very useful fella to have around in any capacity. Len was very sharp and witty with a beautiful turn of phrase, but even while he joked with people on many business meets, you could always sense that air of menace: anyone who was anyone knew not to fuck with him. 'Lenny McLean was a considerably valuable asset to our organisation,' says Dave.

DARREN JAMES

'I knew Lenny McLean from a young age, when I became a DJ. This one night I was at the Camden Palace, I'd been smuggled in through the fire exit to do some warm-up for the DJ. Lenny was on the door with about five other blokes, who were all big lads. A couple of geezers came up to the door, who were a lot older than Lenny and big lumps, and they started dropping names of faces from the London area. Lenny then says, "Well, do you know who I am?" The blokes then start shaking their heads, saying, no, and Lenny says, "I'm Lenny McLean." "Well, who the fuck are you?" they say. Lenny then went at them and smashed them round the front of the club. No doormen could pull him off; they were dropping off his shoulders, trying to stop him, but he was just pummelling these geezers. He gave them such a beating and these guys were no mugs. Apparently about five men came back a few nights later to sort Lenny out. I wasn't there to witness it, but from what I heard from people at the club, he took them to the cleaners too.

'One incident happened in the Hippodrome when I was a DJ on stage and it literally kicked off, it was a really bad fight. A load of English were fighting these foreigners on the dance floor and we had pressed the security alert button, and the first one in as usual was Lenny McLean. He's throwing them around like rag dolls, knocking them out, banging them out... Without exaggerating, he must have knocked out about six to eight people. They were pulling out blades and he was knocking them out before they had chance to use them, and what were the other doormen doing? They were just picking people up off the floor. I've seen some really tough people in my day but he was the cream of the crop, he really was.

'One Sunday afternoon, around about 1989, I was the DJ-ing in a pub in the East End and there must have been about a hundred men in there watching Chelsea and Sheffield Wednesday. There were two doormen and I'm playing music, and all these men are slagging Chelsea off as they all supported West Ham. All of a sudden in walks Lenny McLean and he has this smart light grey suit on. You could hear a pin drop. It must be about five in the afternoon, everyone just looks at him and Lenny says, "I want this fucking geezer, where is he?" I can't remember his name but all of a sudden a few blokes push this bloke forward who Lenny was looking for. Lenny then picks him up with one hand and takes him outside. The bloke was whimpering and screaming, and next thing you know, the fella's in a bad way on the floor. Lenny got back in his car and cleared off. No police or paramedics were called and the bloke was taken downstairs to be cleaned up.

'I don't know what the bloke had done but no one stepped in to help him. One of the doormen never came back to work that door ever again – whether it was to do with this, I do not know.

'One of my old mates used to go out collecting with Lenny. He used to pay him a hundred pounds a day plus 10 per cent of what they collected, that was twenty years ago. Now this bloke was a hard guy himself, all he had to do if it kicked off was to stand there and try and stop Lenny from killing someone. Lenny didn't want to kill them and they usually paid up – he was a bit of a gentle giant until crossed. Two things that come to mind when I hear the name Lenny McLean are the light grey suit which he was always looked immaculate in, and these words whenever I heard him talking, "I will rip his fucking head off". I think this was his favourite saying as he said it all a time and every time he said it, you just knew that he was the type of guy to go and do it.'

JULIE FARLEY

'I used to love Lenny working as a bouncer at the Camden Palace in the late eighties. He was a real puppy-dog charmer, singing Frank Sinatra songs at the ladies one minute and then in a flash, his gravelly concrete voice would put the chills up anyone trying to take the piss in there. He used to kiss my hand and sing me a Sinatra song, and then he'd say to me, laughing, "What you doing with that pussy?", looking at my ex-boyfriend who he used to make shake whenever he would talk. He wasn't coming on to me, he was just like your favourite uncle. He wasn't too keen on my dungarees though, which were fashionable at the time – he once said to me, "So what's is a lovely girl like you doing in painting overalls?" as he laughed to himself.'

MATT MARTINEZ

'My Uncle Billy worked on the door in a club in the Caledonian Road. Lenny had to go and straighten it out for him this once as they were having murders there. This one night in the Camden Palace, I saw him personally manhandle some scrote who was saying he was going to stab someone in the queue. He gave it the large one to Lenny. Well, next thing you know, unfortunately for him we were stepping over the scrote on the way in.

'Another night, some fucking joker put his finger inside his jacket, pretending to have a gun, and was larking around at the front of the queue. A few seconds later, we stepped over that one as well – Lenny didn't take any chances with these idiots.'

DANIEL WATTSON

'I first met Lenny McLean from going down the Camden Palace. We knew him from Bobby Franklin, the Gypsy, and Lenny used to let us in for nothing all of the time. I'd go down with my mate, Tony McMahon, from *Lock, Stock and Two Smoking Barrels*, who also knew Lenny through his son, Jamie McLean.

'This one night, I was by the bar with my mate who we called "Cola", where the backstage is on the right, and someone had been stealing a few drinks from behind the counter and all the bouncers came down and thought it was me. I could see all of these bouncers running down with their black gloves on, with leads in them, and I thought my time was up. They called me over and were just about to do me when Lenny came over and said, "Oi, get over here, son! You're alright." He then let me slip off – Lenny had saved my bacon that night.'

MARK TIBBS

'I first met Lenny McLean at the Camden Palace when I was about twenty years of age. I had gone there with my missus for a drink. I remember him towering over me and saying, "Come here, boy, and have a drink" – he always used to call everyone "boy". He knew I'd just signed with his relative, Frank Warren, as a professional boxer and he looked after me and made me feel welcome. I then met him a few times in the West End when he was on the door of the Hippodrome – he was one hell of a big character. I then bumped into him a lot in the West End on auditions for TV work as we were in the same offices. I used to hear him before I saw him: Lenny drowned everyone out with his audition. I'd be in one room and you could hear him in the next with his booming voice. I never seen him fight in the ring but I watch him still to this day on YouTube, etc. Lenny was a proper gentleman to me.'

JO TAYLOR

'I grew up in the East End, very close to the McLean family. As we grew older and into our pub-going days, we would often go up the Camden Palace. Lenny knew that our lot were all too young, but back then it didn't really matter as we were well protected in the Pally. Len would give me a nod and a wink as I went in, and ruffle my hair up with those fucking humongous hands he had.

'I'm glad Lenny can't hear me saying this because I would probably get a right telling-off, but I was a bit of a pothead back in the eighties, and when I was in the Pally, I would find a quiet spot and have a bit of a smoke. It was a good job Len never saw me – oh my fucking God, he'd have done his nut. You see, to me I just used to think that Lenny was like a big teddy bear and because he knew my dad, he would always watch over me.

'One night, something went off with a group that had a problem with my mates – one of the girls from the other crowd slung a drink over one of my pals. With that, Lenny came steaming over and picked this fella up from the other crowd with one hand and promptly threw him flying across the room. Well, unbeknown to Lenny, in the melee one of our boys got a bit of collateral damage, because Lenny's arm caught him as he was dealing with the other lot. Anyway, as it turns out, our boy ended up in hospital – fuck me, I'm thinking to myself, that's the power of Lenny, if that's what happens from just accidentally getting caught in the after-shock.

'The boy from our lot apparently said later, "Fucking hell, I'd rather have got a clump from Lenny, at least that'd be something I could brag about for years to come." Lenny would've hated to have thought that he had hurt one of our lot, so we never actually told him. But Len, if you're listening, watch what you're doing with those fists of yours up there – don't go knocking someone's harp out of their hand! I will never forget Lenny; he was like my very own minder in the Camden Palace for many years. God bless him.'

JOHN WILKINSON

'I first met Lenny when he was on the door of the Camden Palace and over time we started having a bit of a laugh and built up a bit of a relationship borne out of respect for each other. I see Lenny do a few people down the Palace but it was usually over after one punch.

'This one night, I'm standing outside the VIP bar by the stairs, talking to a pal, when some German bodybuilder starts nutting me out. I always carried something in them days but before I could even get my cosh out, the geezer's done me right under the chin. I'm only nine stone and my pal still laughs about me going two foot up in the air. The first thing I remember is Lenny's massive smiling face and he said out the corner of his mouth, "You got done there, son, good and proper. Don't worry, we've got him downstairs."

'Len picked me up and carried me downstairs – it must have looked like a father carrying his kid off to bed. Downstairs, one of the other bouncers with greyish hair has got hold of this German, already looking a bit worse for wear. Len took his arm and bent it the wrong way and snap, one broken arm. Lenny didn't even bat an eyelid. I was then given the chance to give the German a few whacks myself before he was sent on his way. My jaw ached for months and every time I see Lenny, he always called me "China" after a point he made clear was because my jaw was like china and not that we were mates.'

ANDREW LOIZIDES

'I used to see Lenny McLean on the doors down at the Camden Palace all of the time. I remember this one story he told me. One night at the club, it was nearing closing time and a group of drunk blokes were making a bit of a racket while still stood at the bar. They had been asked to leave by the barman but they weren't budging anywhere. Lenny then goes over to them and politely says something like, "Alright, lads? Looks like you've had a good night but will you please now leave?" He continued to be polite and have a bit of banter with them. Lenny then asks them to drink up again and quietly leave as the club is now closed. He tells me that these mugs thought he was a soft touch because he had been so nice to them, and with them being a bit drunk they felt a bit brave and decided to abuse his kind nature until one of them swung a bottle at Lenny's head. Well, that was it: in Lenny's words, he "fucking ripped them apart until they were a bloody heap on the floor". He leant over them and said, "Never mistake kindness for weakness" – wise words from a wise man. I later heard him giving this same quote in a TV interview.

'Lenny was the man, he always had time for me and was nothing but nice. He always had a story to tell and would greet you with a smile. He would never hit anyone unless they deserved it. Lenny was a great talker and a warm person but if you took the piss, you would be bang in trouble, like you would not believe. Believe me, it was a real privilege to have befriended such a great man.'

STEPHEN POULTER BISSETT

'Now I knew Lenny from going on holiday down the caravan at Saint Osyth, a lot of the other boys had only seen him fighting on the video I had shown them. So, roll on a few years and we had started going out. Now we knew Lenny did the door at the Camden Palace. Lenny was to me the sort of guy that made doing the doors glamorous.

'When I first met Lenny, the man projected an air of simmering violence – his body movements, the way he held his hands, the way he turned his head on this thick bulldog's neck, he just had this thing about him. I could also see behind that gruff exterior was a switched-on fella, either that or an animal in him which could just smell who was gonna be agg and who weren't.

'He must've noticed us straight away, and his hands come up, the whole of his bottom jaw would come out, and he would say in a loud growl, "Now, behave yourselves, boys, no agg tonight!" then simply laugh. I think it must've been all of our faces dropping that he laughed about, we were like a load of peacocks tucking in their feathers. It's funny because as I remember it, it was that night that I saw him perform, and I'm not just talking about smacking a geezer's arse down the caravan, I'm talking about throwing solid right-handers, proving to many why they called him The Guv'nor.

'Some grief or other had started over a long-forgotten beef by the people involved. It had kicked off, I've told my lot to stand down and watch this, as Lenny goes to town.

'I remember him hitting this crowd of geezers like a bowling ball hitting fucking skittles. Anyway, with beer and gear inside them and having the greater numbers, one went for him, and with speed belying his size, crack! He caught this fella on the chin and the funniest thing happened: the fella's head stayed on the end of Lenny's fist, but the geezer's legs and body left the floor – it was like something out of *The Matrix* or an old cowboy movie.'

PAUL LENARD PARADISE

'My pal and I used to sell tickets outside of the Camden Palace on a Friday night. I remember Lenny used to run the door there at that time. It's funny because he used to drive a little blue Mini – I will never forget the size of the fella pulling up and getting out of that little motor.

'Anyway, this one night it's kicking right off at the main doors: two of the doormen have been stabbed, one of the doormen was sat on the steps holding his stomach, and there's claret [blood] everywhere. The other bouncer was laid out on the pavement, screaming in agony – it was fucking mayhem. Then from nowhere came this raging Lenny McLean, fucking growling and shouting at everyone in his way. He then ordered the other doormen to chase after the one who'd done it and bring him back. Anyway, Lenny and the boys get everyone out of the Pally, all except me and my pal – we were still in there, hiding behind some fucking plants.

'One of the knifemen's mates happened to be there and he's shouting at Lenny's staff to let his pal go. With that, Lenny walks over to this mouthy fella and goes to him, "Listen up, shut your fucking noise, you no-good c***!" and promptly gives the fella one hell of a backhander – not a punch, just the back of his hand. I'm telling you now and this is no word of a fucking lie, this fella went down like a sack of shit and he's spark-out cold on the floor, just with a backhander from Lenny, for fuck's sake. It was a scary half-hour for me and my pal that night.

'The Old Bill arrived and said to us, "Did either of you boys see anything?", and almost in unison we innocently went "Yes"! But obviously now my arse is going a bit, because we knew that this turn of events could easily upset Lenny, so we're proper shitting ourselves.

'A couple of weeks later, we were ordered by the police to go into the station. So the following week, we're back out front at the Pally, doing our usual ticket selling, and Lenny's there, so I thought it would be in our best interests to tell him about the Old Bill and that we were due to go to the station and make some sort of a statement. So, with this information, Lenny said, "Right, OK, boys, come up to my office on Monday and we'll get this all straightened out."

'Anyway, Monday came and Lenny takes us upstairs to the VIP Lounge and he asked us what we had actually seen. So we told him straight – I mean we weren't going to lie to Lenny McLean, ya know what I mean? Anyway, we said that we had seen almost everything. The truth is this, you see, and a point which Lenny so passionately pointed out, we never actually saw the stabbing take place. I mean, obviously we were there, that's a given, but could we out-and-out swear that anybody had been stabbed? No! I mean, it was obvious the two fellas had been stabbed, but we could in no way be positive witnesses to the fact. So, anyway, we're happy that Lenny is happy.

'We spent a little bit more time in Lenny's company up in court and that – he was there in support of his door staff. I don't recall Lenny at any point in the proceedings giving evidence at all – well, certainly not to mine or my pal's knowledge. So, anyway, that's about all I can remember with regard to the case at court.

'My pal and I continued to frequent the Camden Palace and Lenny would always treat us like royalty. For at least a year or two after the stabbing event, he would always let us go straight into the club without paying, and once we were inside, he would have us looked after like some sort of VIPs. I will say this one last thing: intimidating as Lenny McLean could be, he was always a true gent to my pal and I – I mean, come on, he could've easily growled at the pair of us and put a stop to us making a few quid outside the Pally, but he didn't. He was as good as gold like that was Lenny.

JASON LEE HYDE

'I'm a close friend of Lee, one of the authors of this book, and we're both born and bred about a mile apart, way up north, in a small fishing town called Grimsby. I moved to "The Smoke" in the late eighties and unlike Lee, I had never heard of Lenny McLean until this one night I brushed into him on the door of the Camden Palace – I honestly thought I'd walked into a wall. This massive giant with a voice that would frighten King Kong voiced over in my direction, "Facking Mods!" I glanced up, gulped and almost shat myself. He immediately laughed, slung back the door and went, "'ere, go on, boy, get yourself in." I never said another word, I just slipped off into the club double-quick.

'I must say that in a weird way from that moment on, I felt strangely protected. To be fair, he weren't wrong though, because at that time I was sporting the obligatory Paul Weller attire. I said to Lee recently, "Hey Lee, mate, that Lenny fella was lucky I didn't get my mad up, eh?" To be honest, I think I can still hear Lee laughing now.'

CHAPTER 10

THE KING OF CLUBS

After head doorman and close friend Johnny Madden left the Camden Palace to take on the task of running the door team at the Hippodrome on Charing Cross Road, a suitable position became available at the club and Lenny was quickly offered the chance to join him. The Hippodrome, being one of the largest club venues in the UK, would soon see Lenny gaining a very high profile as he applied his trade in his unique and effective way. Although, unbeknown to Lenny, what seemed from the outside to be a fantastic move in his career as a top minder would very quickly prove to be a catastrophe of major proportions. We caught up with a bunch of Len's colleagues and associates, who recall their time working alongside him.

THE GUV'NOR REVEALED

PAULA MORREL

Paula worked as a telephonist by day and also in the reception area of the Hippodrome in the evenings. She says that under Peter Stringfellow, the team of bouncers they had worked alongside were a very different proposition to the bunch fronted by Lenny McLean and Johnny Madden. Stringfellows' lot were more like 'American coolers' were, and Lenny's firm were very much your hands-on sort of fellas. Paula says, 'I don't necessarily mean that in a derogatory way, it's just not at all what they were used to.' She picks up the story here...

'In all honesty, when that lot took over it was horrible, and it wasn't the sort of set-up that any of us were used to. For want of a better word, they seemed to come across like a bunch of thugs. This wasn't going to be how it was forever, it's just unfortunately how it seemed at the time.

'This one time some fella had smacked this random girl's backside. Anyway, Lenny grabs hold of this fella, drags him into the reception area bit and goes to town on him. He didn't damage the fella, Lenny knew just how much muscle to use, but he gave him a few backhanders and the fella ran off. Lenny's back on the job as if nothing has happened. Maybe this was the norm at the Camden Palace but we weren't used to it at all, and let's be honest, we were all very wary of Lenny at first: he had a reputation that preceded him, and of course we were all very aware of that fact. Once I got to know him, he was a lovable rogue, a big cuddly, teddy bear. It was much the same after we'd got to know the rest of the boys too. Everything settled down a lot, and it wasn't quite as hands-on as we'd initially imagined it was going to be. But I tell you something, if anyone showed us any disrespect then by fuck, Lenny was there like a shot. Most of the time it would just take a growl from Lenny and off they would go.

'Me and Len would sit together in the daytime reception area and chat over cups of tea and stuff like that. I remember at the time that the book that he had said he was writing was almost like an obsession. Not in a derogatory way, just Len was Len, and as we all know, once Lenny had got a bee in his bonnet about something, then until the day that it had been dealt with, it was all he could think about.

'Listen, it wasn't annoying at all. Don't get me wrong, it was just that it was Lenny's main focus in life at the time. I do remember at one point he brought like a mock-up of his book to work with him and read a few parts of it to me. To be honest, I was so happy for the man – he just seemed to want to better himself and life for his wife and kids, Kelly and Jamie. I mean, they were his world. It was understandable, especially after the life he'd had thrust upon him from a very young age.

'The other side of Lenny was a very funny man – he loved to wind people up, like the other bouncers, just for a laugh. Also, he would tell me stories of how he used to read to his kids Kelly and Jamie, when they were young and he'd change all the words and put the odd little cheeky swear word in, and the kids would giggle. Lenny used to make me laugh a lot. I left the

Hippodrome in about 1991 and unfortunately that would be the last time I saw Lenny. I always wished I'd got to know him even a whole lot better. I was so happy to see him get his wish to act on the big screen, and of course, get his life story out there, in the form of his bestselling book.'

ROSS BIAGINI

'I worked with Lenny McLean at the Hippodrome where I was the general manager. Lenny, as we all know, was a larger-than-life formidable character. I tell this story in good humour and wish to offend no one as I simply relay to you how funny a guy Lenny was, at the same time being very ruthless and tasty with his fists.

'I recall in the summer/autumn of 1990, one night Warner Brothers had hired out the balcony of the Hippodrome – they were celebrating the conclusion of Prince Rogers Nelson's London gigs. Prince was a massive star at the time, arguably the biggest star on the planet. There were a lot of music industry and nightclub industry in attendance and it was quite a stressful evening for me as we wanted to make a good impression to all who was going to the gig. The night was going along all well and good but Prince had not turned up yet, and it was getting late, perhaps midnight or so. I was positioned on the front door, in reception with our security and hospitality team to make sure he was welcomed accordingly. Sure enough, Prince did arrive at the club with a small group of people, but his minder-cum-driver had to park the limo, so he was to follow a few moments after the rest of the entourage had gone through. Obviously, we all made a very big fuss in welcoming Prince, So, anyway, I said to Lenny, "That's Prince, Lenny," and Lenny laughed and just said, "Alright, my son?" Just at that point, Prince's driver returned, a big heavy-set guy with a thick Irish accent.

'Now this minder fella was very cross-eyed and I was trying to avoid eye contact as you usually do when there's a cross-eyed person. Lenny looked at me though and crossed his own eyes and started speaking with an Irish accent really taking the piss. With that, the Irish minder asked him, "Where's Prince?" To which Lenny replied, "Prince? Prince? He's barking his fucking head off outside! You fucking mug, how the fuck should I know where that little fucker is?"

'I couldn't even stand, I was buckled up laughing and couldn't stop for ages – in fact the whole of our staff were in fits of laughter. Lenny was indeed a very funny man.'

LEE MACDONALD

'This one night, I met Lenny when he was bouncing at the Hippodrome. His big hands grabbed hold of me and I thought he was going to chuck me out. I don't know if he noticed that I was Zammo in *Grange Hill*, but he started singing me a nursery rhyme in my ear instead, laughing. It was a very surreal moment, one hell of a character.'

BOB CLEARY

'Years ago, Lenny's son, Jamie, invited me and the boys to the Hippodrome – I think it was his mother Val's birthday. We were upstairs and it was my shout so I went to the bar and Lenny was standing there. I introduced myself and asked if I could buy him a drink. He smiled and said to the barman, "I'll have my usual". I piped up, "I'll have the same as him". Lenny came back a couple of minutes later with two mugs of tea, he was pissing himself laughing. So when people ask me if I knew him, I always say we once had tea together.

'Also, this one night we came bowling out of the Hippodrome at silly o'clock, looking for somewhere else to go, and Len appeared from nowhere and said, "Now, go straight home, at this time of night the West End is full of wrong'uns," and there we were, six grown fucking men, saying, "OK, Mr McLean," and we all went home. We laugh about it now as we're thinking back, but that's just how much he cared about people.

'I met him a few times through Jamie and all I will say is he was proper old school, a family man with a great sense of humour until you upset him.'

MARTIN FERGUSSON

'I grew up in London and my dad and family were from Camden Town. I then landed a job as a police officer before making my way up the ranks to CID. Part of my job was working the West End on foot and building a rapport with staff and doormen at places like Stringfellows and the Hippodrome nightclubs. It was at Stringfellows I first come across this man named Lenny McLean. Listen, I speak as I find and Lenny was a lovely man and a proper gentleman. I don't think his face fitted there though so Peter [Stringfellow] had put him in the Hippodrome instead. So basically, Lenny used to move around venues as the same firm had the doors and Johnny Madden was usually running the doors with Lenny. Lenny had a good team there, with good guys like Johnny and Robert Lopez.

'Anyway, after a while of visiting these venues regularly we all go to know each other and had a good working relationship. Because I was in the CID I was never on response and called there, but a lot of the times I would go in there drinking with my mates. I see me getting out there at five the following morning sometimes.

'There was a big difference between uniformed officers and the CID. Lenny had the time to talk to people and like I said, a lot of the CID drunk in there and he was always friendly and polite, but the uniformed didn't have the time to build up that rapport with him. So I basically knew the manager, doormen and all the staff there, and it was more or less my local if I was out with my mates.

'My girlfriend at the time, who later became my wife, used to drink in there before I met her, so Lenny knew her too. So the first time I've gone out with her there Lenny said to her, laughing, "What the bloody hell are you doing with him?" We had a good bit of banter. And then Lenny went and sorted us out with some champagne, he was a proper gentleman and charmer like that. Like I said, being the head doorman,

Lenny had built up a good friendship with the police, helping them out all the time.

'There was one incident when a young WPC who was wandering the streets patrolling was being attacked by a bunch of blokes on the edge of Leicester Square. Lenny's come off the front door and gone over into them and dragged the policewoman out of the way and saved her a right good kicking, but the following week an allegation of assault's gone in and the Old Bill turn up and accuse Lenny of punching these men. He said to them, "Now hold on, I saved one of your mates last week." Nothing came of it, but it had to be followed up. Now Lenny didn't have to do that, but that's the type of man he was – he didn't care how many were there, he was out to save her.

'You got to bear in mind he was working on one of the busiest street corners in the UK. You had all sorts coming there to the Hippodrome so maybe they were a little bit strong sometimes, but then you had to be. You may get some bouncer now and again who may have been a bit punchy, but Lenny didn't need to do be – he just stood above them all and told them to shut up. The man was a man mountain, you only had to look at the size of his hands and his shoulders and you knew you weren't going to fight with him. So, basically, Lenny was the emergency cavalry if it kicked off big time. He very rarely went on the front door in the end but if they needed him, he was there. What Lenny used to do was sit in this room by the front door and if there were problems he'd come out and just by being there and them seeing him growl, nine times out of ten it would work. You may get someone there for the weekend fancying their chances but there was only going to be one winner and then what's the first thing you do when you come off second? You phone the police and say you've been assaulted.

'It was only on the Monday when the allegations came in of assaults I'd hear stuff of what happened on the weekends. Most of my mates were also door staff in West London and I knew that nine times out of ten, it was trouble drinkers who had come off worst. I do vaguely remember Lenny coming in for a chat, but he was bailed and no further actions came of it. The Hippodrome wasn't the place people came to fight, there were plenty of other pubs around if you wanted that sort of thing.

'This one Monday morning though I went into work and I'm told there's been an incident on the Saturday night and an allegation of assault. They then asked me if I could phone Lenny and find out what the situation was. So I rung Lenny and asked him what had happened. He said, "I'll tell you about it." It turns out this young lad has gone in with about twenty quid in his pocket and tried to order three bottle of champagne. Then he wouldn't pay for them, so they have called the security over and Lenny said, "Well, how are you going to pay for this then, son?" The cocky fucker said, "Well, I'm just going to drink them, I'm not going to pay for them. What you going to do about it, old man?" With that Lenny tells me he gave him a slap. I said, "Lenny, did you punch him or slap him?" to which Lenny replied, "I promise you I gave him a slap with the palm of my hand. If I'd punched him I would have knocked him across the room." I said, "Len, his jaw's broke and he got a perforated eardrum." He gave me his word it was a slap.

'Anyway, I phoned the man back and said, "Look, if this goes to court, you've tried to get three bottles of champagne for nothing, you've taken the piss out of the doorman and when he's given you a bit of a slap for being an idiot, you were out of order. If this goes to the papers, you'll look a proper c***. Now have a think, do you want to forget about this and chalk it down to experience or you being on drugs, or end up in court?" Next thing he said, "Let's forget about this." I then rung Lenny to tell him it had been dropped but please don't go slapping anyone anymore as he may not be so lucky next time, although in his eyes he hadn't done anything wrong and was just doing his job.

'As everyone knows, it's well-documented that Lenny ended up getting arrested for the murder of a man who he had given a slap to in the Hippodrome in 1991, although the man didn't die until hours later. He ended up doing the time for the assault but to try and pin a murder charge on him, it was totally out of order. I seen Lenny after he came out of prison and he seemed OK, but he had to keep his head down from now on as he was too high-profile. So he was moved to quieter venues like Cairo Jacks, near the Hippodrome.

'I then left the police force and I had a pub just up the road from there in North London and there was this bloke in there, dealing drugs to these lads. So I've gone up to them and said, "Listen, lads, this stops now, you're not doing it anymore." This bloke then says, "Why not, what are you going to do about it?" I said, "Well, I won't do a lot about it, but a mate of mine owes me some favours and he only works about a mile from here." The bloke then says, "Well, who the fuck's your mate then?" I said, "His name's Lenny, Lenny McLean." The bloke just left mumbling under his breath with his tail between his legs. That soon sorted the problems out there. I then heard a while later Lenny had become ill and it was a shame we never met again.

'The one thing that always makes me smile to this day is that he always used to say to me, "They'll write a book about me one day and they will make a film, Mart, the scripts in development." I never thought it would happen at the time, then *Lock, Stock…* came out and it was nice to see him on the big screen. All he had done was play himself, he had finally made it.'

DEAN KAYNE

'When I done my first stint in the Hippodrome, Lenny would be on the front door most of the time with his cousin, Johnny Wall. The doormen were legends, always looking after you. Some doormen would look down on you but not this lot. They were always welcoming people and spent time with you and would have a drink and a chat.

'This one story, I'll always remember. Lenny hated pickpockets and used to catch them all the time. They had a little green room by the side of reception in the Hippodrome and it was some sort of storage room. Lenny would catch them and keep them in there until Charing Cross police came down. The police would be saying, "What's your name?" and they would say, "I not speak English," and Lenny would be saying, "Fucking speak English, you c***!" and giving them a little shake. The police would be laughing, it was so funny.

'I didn't see Lenny much in action as he was on the front door and I was inside but I did see him going straight through the club once or twice – he'd just grab someone, pick them up and take them out to the door. Lenny was a man mountain and a proper old-school bouncer, but also a gentle giant if you never got on the wrong side of him.'

PETER BERRY

'Many years ago, when Lenny was head doorman at the Hippodrome, I was a new young doorman who had heard of but never met The Guv'nor. I was sat alone in the office one day, where Lenny used to watch the security monitors, when I saw his huge figure heading towards the office where I sat, unannounced. I was bricking myself, thinking I was in for trouble for being in his office. However, he was the nicest guy ever, shaking my hand and saying, "Alright, son, I'm Lenny McLean, welcome aboard."'

GREG KEMBLE

'I met Lenny several times when he was head doorman at the Hippodrome. I saw both sides of him, the polite gentleman and Lenny with the arse ache.

'This one particular night he was wearing a Prince of Wales check suit, a white shirt and burgundy brogues. I asked him, "You OK, Len?" and he replied, "No I ain't, I've got the arse ache," then from under his jacket he was sporting some sort of boxing glove and said, "I'm going to knock some c*** out soon." I didn't know whether he was serious or just messing about with the other lads with him but I kept moving on.'

CHRIS HAWES

'I saw Lenny on a few doors when I was working on the minicabs in the eighties. This one Saturday night, I was working and gone past the Hippodrome, and I saw Lenny chastising a gang of football Herberts and he caught up with them outside a pub in Poland Street in Soho. I don't know what they'd done but there were bodies flying everywhere. I could tell they was football Herberts from up North, going by their accents. I was with a punter, just going past the pub, and Lenny was on his own and from what I could see, he made short work of them.'

ELIE MARCO KHOURY

'I moved to London at the age of sixteen in the early nineties. I couldn't speak English for the first few months here but then picked it up quick. Then not long after that I met this man named Johnny Wall. I worked for Johnny in the day in his shop in Oxford Street and also worked the Hippodrome, bringing people in from the street. I was then introduced to this big man called Lenny McLean, who worked there too.

'Lenny had helped me out this one time when I

could have gone to prison for a stretch. What it was, this one night I had a fight with someone in the Hippodrome, and when the police caught up with me a few months later, they charged me with GBH section 18. Now I knew Lenny could have some influence on the guy and his manager because the guy also worked at the Hippodrome. So I spoke to Johnny and then we went and spoke to Lenny about it. At the time Lenny knew me but not that well. He knew I was working with Johnny, so straight away, Lenny said, "Leave it to me, son, I'll see what I can do" without any hesitation or even knowing the full story.

'He spoke to the guy in question and I remember he told him, "If you have issues, you can solve it with him like a man. Do not involve the police, because if you do and Elie gets in trouble, it's going to be like you grassing me up and not just him." The problem was solved and the guy didn't pick me in the ID parade. Plus, on the first day of the trial in the Crown Court, one manager who did pick me in the parade had decided not to give evidence all of the sudden. No prizes for guessing who had a word with him the night before. So the judge said, "No witness, no case," and he threw it out of court.

'After that every time Lenny saw me he'd put his hand around me and say, "You alright, son?" Then he'd put his hands in front of his face in a boxing position, like he wants a boxing match, and he'd start punching the air in front of my face if you know what I mean, he was so fast and accurate. He then used to refer to me when he was talking about me as, "Elie the Leb", like Elie the Lebanese.'

THE KING OF CLUBS

CHRIS RHODES

'I remember the year was 1990 and I'd gone to Wembley Stadium to watch the FA Cup Final between Man United and Crystal Palace. After the game we had gone around London and ended up queuing at the Hippodrome at the end of the night. As we were standing there, all of a sudden a lady came running out of the club in tears, followed by a load of Cockney grunts and growling, and Lenny, now he was furious and had a bouncer lifted off the floor with one hand, which was around this lad's neck – his feet weren't on the floor. This bouncer had done something to the lady and Lenny weren't having any of it.

'After he disposed of the other bouncer, Lenny was parading up and down the queue and was in a right foul mood. I popped up, a young lad from up North, and shouted, "Lenny!" to which my dad pulled me back into the queue. Lenny then came up to me and asked how I knew him (no internet then). I told him I'd read the odd story in the papers, we got chatting and he said, "Come with me". My dad, who was an old bouncer, weren't having any of this and Lenny politely told him to stay in the queue and not to worry – "He's with me now, no one will touch him".

'We walked down an alley to his dressing room, where he sat me down with a can and talked about me, him and his dreams and upcoming projects. He then signed me the Hippodrome monthly newsletter and went back to the queue. Lenny then took my dad, my friend and me inside and sat us at a table with a bottle of bubbly or two. All through the night he was asking how we was. A few weeks later, my mum and dad were down in London and walked past the Hippodrome and Lenny shouted, "Hey Arthur, how's ya boy? Send him my best." Although we'd only met him that night, he made us feel like we knew him well – he was nothing but a true gentleman.'

CHAPTER 11

THE SHAPE OF GYMS TO COME

L enny was always a big fan of boxing as a sport, and as a result he studied and practiced this art form for most of his adult life. It was obvious that at some point he would start hitting the gyms and weights to a very high degree. In his time spent in and around various gyms, he met a great number of well-known celebrities, including TV stars, singers, sports personalities and the odd movie star to boot. The stories that we have gathered here with regard to Lenny's gym exploits are indeed legendary, and for that we felt that they needed to be documented.

JOHN CAMPBELL-MAC

Anthony: John Campbell-Mac is a BAFTA-nominated British producer and actor based in Hollywood. He undertook extensive acting training at the City Literature

Institute, The Impulse Company and The Actors Centre in London and has been working regularly for the last twenty years in many movies and TV shows. JC has starred in several British feature films and won numerous awards as an actor and producer, including the BAFTA-nominated *Winner Takes All* (2004), which he also wrote.

I approached him in 2011 and he got back to me straight away, saying he loved Lenny's work in *Lock, Stock...* and that 'Lenny was never anything but respectful, charming and very supportive of what Chico [Slimani], who went on to have fame in *The X Factor*, and myself were trying to do back then and that was break into the music industry'. He went on to tell me that he liked Lenny and he was flattered to be approached by ourselves to contribute.

'I first met Lenny McLean around 1994 when I used to train at a gym in Greenwich, Southeast London, called Slim Jim's, which used to be above Iceland's supermarket on Trafalgar Road. It was a rough-and-ready gym with a great vibe and a mix of everyone from boxers and bodybuilders to regular guys putting in a decent workout and even a few actors and models between the various geezer types. Every type of person, all ages, colours and creeds, what a great place it was.

'I used to train there regularly along with Lenny. I would watch him pummel a heavy bag, he was a big man and when he hit the heavy bag, he hit it hard. I watched him spar on the gym floor with a few well-known faces and generally knocked everyone about. I had heard of his reputation and knew who he was but I have to say as I got to know him he was nothing like I expected. He always treated us with respect and was interested in what we were up to. At the time me and Chico were trying to make a career in the music industry and called ourselves Machico, we would come into the gym with cassettes of our latest demos, which Kenny the trainer would play on the gym system, so everyone would have to listen and enjoy.

'Lenny would always be supportive and want to know what progress we had made that week and always ended the conversation with "Good lads, that's a smashing song that is, that's great! Keep at it, you'll get there." At that time, he was trying to get a film made about his life story – I guess trying to make it in the entertainment industry was something we had in common and whenever I saw him we would swap stories of meetings or opportunities we had had that week and laugh about them. At that time he had a scrapbook with various pictures and newspaper articles about him. If he was going to a meeting from the gym, he would have it with him – it was very impressive to look at.

'Lenny would love to hear stories of crazy things that might have happened to us each week on a gig or in a meeting, or whatever. He was also a great storyteller and when he was in full swing, half the gym would gather round to hear and he would re-enact certain fights and situations he had found himself in. It was good times, I'll never forget.

'One day this Australian friend of mine was visiting London and trained with me and Chico. After the workout, Lenny starts telling us some of his stories.

Lenny decides to set up a demonstration: he takes two of the gym regulars and our friend and positions them around him as he talked us through. I never realised just how fast he was. In a split second he demonstrated how he would headbutt the middle one then punch out the other two with two swift hooks. It happened in less than a second, we were all dumbfounded. The shocked look on my friend's face was priceless and still makes me smile now.

'I was no stranger to a rough-and-ready background. I boxed myself for seven years and Lenny was present at one of my last fights, that he didn't even tell me until we had probably been training at the same gym for about six months and got to know each other. The Lenny McLean I knew was fun-loving, encouraging, hard training and even supportive. I liked him and was proud to call him my friend. He always said to us, "Alright, boys? You're good lads. If you ever get into any bother, you know a bit heavy, you can always call on me" – I'm happy to say we never did.

'Lenny also loved his acting. At the time he was a series regular on *The Knock* [TV series, 1994–2000] and he had high hopes of getting his life story made into a movie and had already had a few good parts. When Anthony approached me to contribute to this book I wasn't sure I was really qualified to comment, it wasn't like we were close friends but some of those hours we spent in the gym were magical. I never imagined all these years on I would be living and working in Hollywood or Chico would have had a No.1 record or had just made the final of *Dancing on Ice*, or that Lenny would no longer be with us. I like to think that wherever he is, he's smiling, looking down at us, maybe saying, "Well done, lads. I told you, you would do well, good boys."

YOUSSEPH 'CHICO' SLIMANI

Lee: Right, so, often when it comes to TV personalities, especially ones from the world of reality TV and our much-loved large-scale talent shows, some of the faces that rise to fame soon fade into insignificance; this was not, and would never be the case for our man Chico. No, Chico is not the kind of man to allow the great British public to cast him asunder with the rest of the fallen debris from *The X Factor* fame. Also, Yousseph or 'Chico' as he is popularly known, is one true gent who has to be credited for his sheer will and desire to succeed, and having a powerhouse like Lenny McLean in your corner giving you the gee-up of all gee-ups, what more could you need? That said, I will let the man himself explain to you in his own words about his short, yet fruitful relationship with our man Lenny. Before he begins, though, I have one question to ask him: 'Chico, what time is it?' And in time honoured fashion, he replies, 'Lee, go fuck yourself!' No, of course he didn't. Chico is a trooper; he obviously said, 'It's Chico time!' Chico is a solid gold star. Sorry, I just had to do that. Anyway, away you go, Chico, my friend.

'So, believe it or not, I had never really heard of Lenny McLean, but having said that, I was born in Bridgend in South Wales, and was brought up in Morocco, so I can be forgiven for this. Anyway, my spiritual brother, or let's say my brother from another mother, John Campbell-Mac, and I were a duo at the time. I'd say this would've been in about '94, Lenny was about forty-five years old. At that time, we were right smack-bang in the middle of our training and wanted to look good at all times, so we used to train at a place called Slim Jim's over in Greenwich. As you walked in Slim's gym, all of the equipment was on one side and the punch bags were on the other. Now Lenny would always be training on the bag, smashing a granny out of it – man, that fella was a fucking size!

'So, one day I'm in there and he comes over to introduce himself to me. He was like that, was Lenny, he liked to know who everyone was. Anyway, I was in good shape at that time, quite a good physique, trim and cut, you know the score. Well, Lenny comes over and spins me around as he's looking me up and down, and he's going to me, "Alright, my son? Looking good, boy. Here, how do you get yourself looking like that then?" With that, he like grabs my hand and he's showing his pal my physique, he's going to me, "Come here, boy, come here," as he's showing me off to his pal. Lenny would always big us up at the gym, telling people, "Here, listen, these boys are gonna be stars, you know."

'You see, Lenny was so charismatic. He was just a very special character, you could do nothing else but listen to him, he was just a very larger-than-life fella. Like I say, before that time at the gym I had never even heard of him, but let me tell you this, after watching him hit that bag and the way he held himself, you just knew never to fuck with him, not that me and my bro would ever have tried – we were lovers not fighters. Lenny had that much respect up at Slim's, it was like a movie set when he was about the place.

'I remember one time we was up there, he was telling us about the film they were making about his life. He was saying to us, "They're making a movie about me, you know, boys, cos I'm The Guv'nor, you know." I said to him, "Wow, Lenny, that's amazing!" I said, "Eh, Lenny, could I play you in your movie?" and Lenny said, "Nah, ya fucking joking, son! Ya too fucking pretty to play me, boy. Anyway, you've got too much fucking hair in the first place." He was so funny, he used to have us in bits laughing. Mac and I thought the world of him.

'This one time we had this friend of mine and Mac's with us called Paul Shire (he was a big well-known male model at the time). Anyway, we introduced him to Lenny. We said to Len, "Here, Len, tell our pal some of your stories." Well, obviously Lenny immediately obliged, so we're all circled around him and as he's in mid-flow with his story. He just went into a flurry of shots towards us, a headbutt, and a left and a right hook, so fast you just wouldn't believe it. Well, I looked at our model friend and his face was transfixed, like he'd just seen the Second Coming.

'So, as Lenny has stopped and he's shaking himself down, he goes to us three stood there, dazed in bewilderment at his speed, "You see, boys, by now you three would all be a goner. But listen, boys, I never took a liberty with no one, but if they step out of line, then I'm coming for 'em, and if I'm coming for ya... Well, that's another story., I'll let you boys read about that bit in my book."

'Lenny said one time while he was collecting a debt for one of the well-known gangsters in London, he walked into a packed-out restaurant up the West End and shouts across the room, "Right, people, don't get up, don't be a fucking hero, because we're not here for you. Now carry on enjoying your meal, cos we ain't here for any of you, we're just here to give that c*** a pull," as he gesticulates, pointing to some poor fucker who's bang in trouble sat with his pals, over in the corner of this restaurant. Oh, for fuck's sake! I wouldn't have fancied being that fella, would you?

'I remember Lenny used to do some sparring over at Slim's. Mind you, it was always the same fella that sparred with Len. Let's face it, I don't think he had many takers, do you? But the man that he had sparring with him was Mick Theo. I know this now, because Lee has just informed me of that fact. Now I must admit that this bodybuilding fella, Mick – who was a big fucker too – well, let me just say that he never looked that happy to be in there with Lenny. I think Lenny used to let him hit him with everything in his locker and then he would just go, "Alright then, son, now it's my go." This isn't me doing Mick down, Lenny never took a liberty with him, it was a bit of fun because Theo and Lenny were great pals.

'Lenny was always a gentleman to me and Mac. He would always say, "Listen, boys, I'm always here if you ever need me. If you ever get yourselves in any bother, ya know." Anyway, we never had to call upon Lenny for any such backup, although I must say, it was nice to know the offer was there, especially from a man with Lenny's kind of reputation. I used to say, "Eh, Lenny, we're lovers, not fighters. We just ain't that kind of people, you know that," and he would say, "Yeah, fucking too right, boys – 'ere that's what I should've done, eh?" I have to say, I never saw Lenny with the hump in the gym. He didn't have to use his aggression, it just oozed from every sinew of Lenny McLean.

'When Lenny told you a story that centred on the violence he may have had to use in a certain situation, I'm telling you this, my friend, you could feel it, and you were simply transported to that moment in time, a time and place I'm glad I wasn't a part of. I will take the Lenny that we knew, that gentle giant bear of a man, over that of which the stories behold any day of my life. We loved him. The man was a gentleman and a funny one at that, God bless him.'

LESLIE BUCKINGHAM

'I knew Lenny for roughly twenty years. Firstly, from the Thomas A Becket gym, then many years later, in Slim Jim's. Personally, I liked him, not through fear but we just got on and gelled together. Despite his size and appearance Lenny had a very dry sense of humour and was a very funny man most of the time. I remember the guys that he worked with for years and they were one good door team. There was Steve Jarman, Baz, Colin Madden, Alan Crossley, Ray Jezzard and John Madden, the head doorman at the Camden Palace and the Hippodrome. Lenny, Baz,

Crossley and John Madden all held the door at the Music Machine before it became the Camden Palace. The Machine was a gladiator's pit, but it was run by a strong door team. Also working there was Ken "The Dog" Farrel. Ken's hands were bigger than McLean's and Lenny used to look at him and say, "Fuck me, Ken, you've had some wars with them hands!"

'I also knew and trained with all of the doormen from the Camden and Hippodrome, and often visited both places as a guest. I remember once going up the Camden with my cousin from Ireland. Lenny took us up to the cocktail bar, got us a drink and told the staff to look after us, and said, "You're better up here and not down in the pig's trough with the lowlifes." We broke our bollocks laughing.

'Another time we were at the gym and having a break from training. Lenny always said to Darren, who worked behind the ramp, "Give us a coffee and a pink one, son." He loved his pink strawberry milkshakes. Anyway, there were some off-duty cozzers training there, who were sitting in the rest area. One of them said to Lenny, "Are you a minder or doorman?" Lenny said, "Not me, son, I'm a recognised children's author." Another fucking side-splitter from Lenny.

'I was up Slim's with him one day and we had just finished some pad work – he had amazingly fast hands for a man of his size. Brian who owned the place calls Lenny to say there's a phone call for him. Lenny takes the call and all I can hear is him saying, "He fucking *what*? Keep him there, I'm on my way." Imagine this, his hands are still wrapped as he runs downstairs and gets into his car, which at the time was a navy blue

THE SHAPE OF GYMS TO COME

Convertible Mini – yes, a Mini. You can imagine when he was in the car there was no room for passengers. So, he was gone about an hour, then he came back in and sat down and called to the counter, "Give us a coffee and a pink one." I said to Len, "What the fuck was all that about?" He said, "Some slag in a gym in Sidcup is calling himself The Guv'nor, so I sat him down and gave him a stern talking to, and told him, 'I ain't retired, you ain't beat me, so don't you fucking dare give yourself my title!'" I then asked him how it had ended and in true Lenny style he said, "Well, he was shaking a bit, but I think he was scared of the dark," and again in Lenny McLean patter, he added, "I gave him half a quid for the electric." We sat and had a giggle about it.

'Len was then telling me that interest had been shown to fight the late Bartley Gorman but at the time Lenny had started filming *The Knock* and was out of the fight scene by then.

'This one time, Lenny brought Mad Frankie Fraser up to the gym. They had been on the set of *The Krays* and Frank was interested to see where Len trained. I had met Frank many times in the past and knew him from others, he was a nice man. Frank was always well-turned out – shirt, tie, blazer, highly polished brogues – proper old school. We had a chat and while we were talking, Lenny was telling people about Frank being a proper chap in the same league as Charlie and Eddie Richardson and the Krays [Ronnie and Reggie] and how he was to be respected by all and if he heard of anyone doing otherwise he would be paying them a visit.

THE GUV'NOR REVEALED

'When we trained at Slim's there was a guy training who also done karate. Lenny said to me, "That's too fucking poncey, that karate thing. A good right hand and it's goodnight, God bless" – that's exactly the type of thing he used to say when we all trained at Slim's.

'We were sitting talking one day and I had done a couple of marathons and he said, "Do you know something, son? I done a marathon once, then a Kit Kat, then a Mars Bar," as he laughed with me. He could make a joke out of anything.

'Another day at Slim's, I had just wrapped up training in the morning. There was this big guy training there, who was a right arrogant c***. At the time we had a young Irish girl working behind the counter. Anyway, as I'm walking out to the rest area, I could see she's standing there, crying. It turns out she had apparently made the wrong milkshake for this bloke, who had then mouthed off to her, calling her stupid. Lenny, who was not far behind me, came walking out, not noticing her crying because she had her back to him and said as he always did, "Give us a coffee and a pink one, babe." She then turns around, upset, and Lenny could see she was crying. The girl then starts to tell him what had happened. Now fuming, Lenny walks back into the gym, goes up to this bloke and tells him to go out and apologise to the young girl and treat people with respect. The man went straight up to the girl and apologised. As he was going back into the gym, looking like he'd had the wind knocked out of him, Lenny then starts abusing him with words you couldn't print here. There was just no way he was having this man bully some innocent young girl trying to make some money.

'This one day outside Slims, Lenny had parked his car in a place it wasn't supposed to be. He left the gym after training and goes outside and there's this traffic warden looking at it and about to write something out. Next thing you know, Lenny's shouted at him, "Take your fucking eyes off my car! If you wanna look at the car, then come to Hackney where I live, now fuck off!" The traffic warden didn't even argue and walked off with his head down.

'Before I wrap this up, I'd just like to say I liked Lenny and all of the guys from that era. I hate it when people expect you to show allegiance to certain people, but they were all my friends and I trained with them all except Roy Shaw, who I knew from the Becket – he was always a very polite man. Like I've said, I trained with Lenny, Madden, Baz, Steve, Mark and Ray, and I found them great guys to train with, and I'm still friends with them all other than Lenny and Roy, who have obviously sadly passed away.'

DARREN BUTLER

Darren was another of Leslie Buckingham and Lenny's mates who worked behind the counter and trained at Slim Jim's. Here's what he had to say about Lenny.

'I was sixteen when I first met Lenny and that carried on till the unfortunate time when he got banged up. He taught me everything I needed to know when I started doing the doors at eighteen, and he was The Guv'nor. I had many good years spent in his presence, they were great times. Lenny would have a classic face when he would talk about ripping some mug's face off.

'One day some soppy c*** decided to pinch Lenny's Convertible Mini from outside the gym and Lenny went fucking mental. Well, Len knew I was born and bred in Greenwich where the gym was, so he said, "Ginge, put it about that my motor's been nicked." So that day I put the word out to the local idiots who were into nicking cars and told them whose car it was, and fuck me, within twenty-four hours the car was parked in the exact spot it was taken from with not a mark on it.

'I wish they had invented iPhones back in the days when I worked at Slim's, I would love to have shared with the fans Len training and working the bag. I can tell you it was a sight to behold, and listening to his stories of what had happened on the door of the Camden Palace each week... Well, put it this way, he would have us all in stitches. I miss the big man. There will never be another Lenny and I'm proud to say that I knew this man well and was friends with him. He was ten times bigger in person, his hands were like shovels and when he hit the bag, it was like an earthquake through the gym.'

JAMES MENZIES

'During the eighties I used to train at a gym in the East End of London called Broad Street Boxing Club.

THE SHAPE OF GYMS TO COME

I was only fourteen, and I got to know a couple of my uncle's mates who were boxers and they took me to Slim Jim's, a place where I had heard that Lenny trained a lot.

'Now when I was in my teens I was a proper little cheeky fucker, and just after I had been introduced to Lenny, he came over to me and said, "Here, son, pop down the shops for your Uncle Lenny, yeah?" and like I say, me being a cheeky little twat, I said to Lenny, "Alright then, but what do I get out of it?" Lenny just laughed at the top of his lungs and from that point on, he seemed to take to me. I think he probably saw himself in me, back when he was a cheeky teenager too.

'As I say, I was cheeky which was harmless, but I also was a naughty little boy, and I swear as I'm relaying this to you now, if it hadn't been for the guidance Lenny gave me at that time, I don't think I would be chatting with you today. Lenny always used to say to me "Listen, boy, all of that naughtiness and villainy you have inside you, just put on your blinkers and channel it into your training," and I'm telling you now, that's exactly what I did. Lenny used to say, "Look, Jamie, you have good speed and a good heart with the stamina to back it up, so just keep on doing what you're doing, son."

'Back at Slim Jim's I even used to go in the ring and do a little sparring with Lenny. Remember, I was only a young boy at that time, so Lenny would obviously just be tapping at me, but I'm telling you now, even in those little taps on my arms and that, I could feel the sheer power of the man. But Lenny was forever the gentleman and would let me hit him with a few. I mean, I must have been OK, because he always told me to keep boxing and training and getting my head straight. He was a great man.

'I would on occasion go round to Lenny and Val's house with two other well-known fighters back then called Tony Stamford and Jimmy Dublin. Now this was an eye-opener for me. You see, Lenny at the gym and around the East End was this big fearsome fighting man that literally everyone was afraid of, yet in that house in Avenue Road, he was every inch the respectable husband and father, and Valerie, his wife, was so sweet to me. For a very short period I looked up to them as if they were like second parents.

'Anyway, I had to deal with an illness of my own a few years ago, which in turn led to the British Boxing Board of Control revoking my licence. As an avid boxer this came as a very big blow to me, because boxing was and always will be my life. But like Lenny so rightly said, "I've had the roughest, toughest life, I think it's about time I had some cream." Well, anything that was good for Lenny McLean is well good enough for James Menzies. So with that in mind, I've hung up my gloves for the last time, because now is the time to look after the things that are most precious to me, my wife and my kids, as I'm sure that's exactly what my good friend Lenny McLean would be doing if he hadn't been cruelly taken so young. Here's to you, Lenny, you taught me how to be a true man.'

THE SHAPE OF GYMS TO COME

TED BERESSORD

'I used to train at a gym called Shapes in Eltham, which was run by a man named Reg Parker, who has now sadly passed away. Reg was a good friend of mine and I started doing weights and a bit of boxing there. Anyway, I remember the first time that me and Lenny crossed paths. Obviously I'd heard a lot about Lenny and this one day I was walking from the main gym to this little bar area Reggie had, selling coffees and stuff.

'I then heard this voice say to me, "Alright, son? Have you got any change for the machine?" As I turned round, I thought to myself, fuck me, that's Lenny McLean. He was bigger in real life than he was on the TV. I kept my composure and said, "Sorry, Len, I haven't, mate." He then says, "That's alright, I'll get some change elsewhere. Do you want one, son?" I replied, "That's nice of you, Lenny," considering he didn't even know me.

'He took to me from then on and used to say I looked like Kevin Finnegan, one of his sparring partners from years ago from his other gym. I was still in awe of him at the time and we became good mates. The funny thing was, I was a few years older than Lenny but the lads at the gym used to say to me, "Don't tell him how old you are." I was confused and asked them why they said, "He's younger than you," but I looked younger. With the life he had, with all the fights he'd had, he looked older.

'We then started training together and what we used to do is go around the back of the gym as there were two heavy bags and a speedball, so what we would do is start off hitting the heavy bag, each for a half-hour nonstop. Instead of having a minute break, we would just swap bags. We were fit then and would be soaking wet; we'd also go and do some skipping to finish off. What Lenny used to love after training was going to the bar – that was probably his favourite saying, "So, you want a coffee, boy?"

'I then got into a bit of trouble and one thing led to another and I ended up in prison. Anyway, I done my time and heard Lenny was now down in Slim's, training. Shapes was closed that day so I went down to Slim's and who comes out of the steam room but Lenny. I said, "Alright, Len?" He replied, "Hello boy, you alright? Have you just come home? I heard you went away." We had a good chat and he asked me how did it go and other stuff. Also, when I came home, Reggie Parker had thrown a little private party for me with a good few mates and family, and Lenny turned up, which I thought was nice of him. I got a photo of him standing by the bar, which I took that night.

'Anyway, back at Slim's, Lenny then asked me, "What are you doing next week?" I said, "Funny you should say that, Len, as it's my birthday next week" – it was also my ex partner's birthday that week too. He then said, "Right, think no more about it and bring your wife and bring another couple of your friends up to the Hippodrome and ask for John on the door." Len was the main honcho up there and if there was a big lot of trouble he was called in. John Madden on the door was also a double handful; he was a big old boy and always wore leather gloves on the door.

THE SHAPE OF GYMS TO COME

'So I went up and I've taken seven couples with me. I went to the front of the queue and John looked at all these people and said, "Does Len know about this amount coming in?" He then called Lenny, who came to the door and said, "Is this your crowd, Ted?" He then said, "Come on in, Ted, I've got a table all sorted for you." He sat us down, we had food and drink, champagne, and we didn't pay a penny. He said, "Have a good a time," and one thing I remember and I'll never forget it, he said, "If you got a problem, come and see me and you ain't got a problem." God knows what the bill come to that night. We thanked everyone at the end. Lenny also introduced me to the manager – he said, "These are friends of mine, especially this one, his name's Ted."

'I didn't see him for a week until I seen him in the gym and then he said, "You have a good night, the other night, Ted?" He didn't mention the bill or how much it came to. I said, "Thank you, Len, my wife was well happy." She thought a lot of Lenny and used to call him a big teddy bear. I'd think to myself, fuck me, love, you ain't seen the other side to him.

'I remember Lenny once giving me this funny look. We'd been training and we was having a coffee in the bar area. As we were chatting, he started doing a roll-up. I said, "You aren't going to smoke that, Len, and then coming training?" Fuck me, if looks could kill! I then said, laughing, "You do what you want, Len. I'll be in there training, see you when you're ready."

'I remember my mate telling me this one story of when Lenny was working in the Camden Palace. Now my mate who was an ex-boxer accidentally slipped and fell down the steps into Lenny. Lenny's turned around after getting bumped into and said, "See what happened there, there's about one hundred fucking people that seen that, they go away and tell their mates and then there's two hundred people, and before you know it there's a fucking thousand people have seen him bump into me!" Now my mate, who was no match for Lenny, said, "Sorry, Len, I didn't mean it – it was an accident." Lenny was losing it, but laughing the same time with the other doormen. You could see deep down he was worried about his reputation and little things like this got to him.

'Lenny was an absolute lovely man. I thought the world of him, and he had a sense of humour and was very quick-witted, really funny. He also had a very violent side, which came from his childhood, which stayed with him, I presume, but the way he brought his family up with so much love, it's just a heart-warming story, and I still have the utmost love and admiration for Lenny McLean and his family.

Anthony: As I wrapped up talking to Ted, he kept repeating the words 'Oh, lovely'. He then started laughing to himself and said, 'Do you know where I got that saying? That was from Lenny McLean. It was one of his best and favourite sayings. I can hear him saying it now and it's stuck with me to this day. I can see him in my head every time I say it.'

KIMBERLEY ANNE JONES

'I remember Lenny years ago when I was an up-and-coming bodybuilder and I used to see him at Shapes.

THE SHAPE OF GYMS TO COME

I was but a shy little bodybuilder then and he was this massive man with a huge personality, He used to scare the pants off me until I actually met him and he turned out to be a big cuddly bear.

'One lasting memory I have of Lenny was when they used to hold Strongman competitions in this car park. This Strongman was lying on the floor, collapsed after a two-man squat that had gone tragically wrong. They were lifting tons of weights and his ligaments in both his ankles had snapped and all the weight had fell onto their squat partner, who was also collapsed on the floor. It was boiling hot that day and as they waited for an ambulance to arrive, Lenny stood over the top of him, licking an ice-cream cone. All the ice cream was melting and dripping onto his face. Lenny was saying to him, "Get up, and show them you're a man!" Lenny sure was a funny man and his life was important, as is everybody's, only he left his mark to be smiled at forever.'

ANDREA FREATHY

'I knew Lenny in the late eighties, he used to visit 21st Century gym in Crystal Palace, where I worked as a beauty therapist. He used to come in to see his mate, John Huntley, who used to train there and the boss, the late Steve Zetolofsky.

My main memory of the big man himself was the day I met him. He took my hand, kissed it and then started to sing to me – just wish I could remember what song! To me, a fresh-faced eighteen-year-old who had never heard of Lenny's reputation, he was nothing but an utter gent, with a great presence and impeccable manners. (I do remember, however, that he always seemed to have split knuckles!) I also remember the day he had Steve in hysterics, telling him the story of how he got the scar on his backside from where he got shot.

'It was only in later years that I saw one of Lenny's fight videos – I couldn't believe it was the same gent that kissed my hand.'

CHAPTER 12

IT'S ALL RELATIVE

W hile writing this book, we managed to line up interviews with a few of Len's close relatives but for one reason or another in the eleventh hour, they pulled their interviews with us. Whether they thought we were just journalists with the sole aim of digging up some dirt, we unfortunately do not know. You see, the two of us only ever wanted to document Lenny McLean's life, and keep his legacy alive. We did, however, manage to track down two very close family members, who agreed to give us a little of their time, and for this we cannot thank them enough and we are eternally grateful.

LAURA WALL

Anthony: A name you've read about in this book and others concerning Lenny is that of another East End legend, the late Johnny Wall, also known to many as 'Bootnose'.

THE GUV'NOR REVEALED

Johnny was Lenny's first cousin and they were inseparable from a young age and right through their adult lives. He was also a well-respected pro boxer himself, and had gone on to have twenty-four fights at light heavyweight level. Johnny also lost his battle to cancer a few months before Lenny was taken away by the bastard of a disease in 1998. It's a shame that he is no longer with us as you can imagine the stories he could share about himself and Lenny. Their stories will go on forever and will be passed down through generations, which takes us to the next person you are about to read about: Laura Wall, the daughter of 'Bootnose'. I've known Laura for quite a few years on social media and she'd always comment about her Uncle Lenny on pages I run. We then arranged to speak on the phone for an hour and here's what she had to say about Lenny and her dear father, Johnny.

'My dad's mother was Rosie McLean before she married my grandad, who was a Wall. Lenny was named after his father, who was also called Leonard McLean, and Rosie was his sister, making my dad Johnny and Lenny first cousins. So basically me and Lenny were second cousins, but Lenny wouldn't have none of that and I had to call him "Uncle Lenny" and he'd tell everyone I was his niece.

'I remember Lenny from a young age. I had been close to him all of my life growing up, as he was always around my house, going training with my dad or at family parties and stuff. Also, me and Dad were inseparable, and would go everywhere with Lenny. We would jump in the car and go around to see Lenny and Val, and they'd just sit there drinking tea for hours and talking. Growing up, I had a good sporting career and played volleyball for England, and also done karate for eight years. Lenny would come and watch me train and help out with sponsorships from people he knew. He started to become a big part of my life in my teens and then a bit later when I started going to the clubs.

'In the early nineties Lenny and my dad worked together on the doors at the Hippodrome nightclub. I was just under the legal drinking age and me and my dad's brother's kid, my cousin Claire Wall, would pop in there and Dad would show us around. We weren't allowed to drink and the bar staff knew us from my dad telling them who we were. We then started drinking there a few months later as Lenny preferred us there because he knew we were safe. Lenny and Dad would be on the door and sometimes Lenny would sit in the other room called the Star Bar. Lenny would always say to me and my cousins, laughing, "Go in there and enjoy yourself, and if anyone looks at you, come and tell Uncle Lenny and Lenny will go and bite their noses off." The Star Bar was a part of the Hippodrome, like a chill-out bar where you could sit and talk. He would walk back and forth from the door, checking we were alright. If my dad wasn't working, he would always make sure I was alright and that we got into a cab at the end of the night and were safe.

I couldn't move in there, as you can imagine, with all eyes on me from Dad and Lenny. I remember this one particular night we walked in and my dad and Lenny are standing there, and Lenny points to these two massive black blokes who were bouncers and says,

"See these two here, if there's any trouble, tell these two and they will jump from floor-to-floor for you. Now go on, little bums, off you go and have a nice night," but we were safe: in the end every doorman knew who we were, every member of staff knew who we were.

'After a while if we got bored in the Hippodrome and moved on to the Buzz Bar or Emporium, Lenny would always make sure we were put in cabs or escorted by one of his doormen to make sure we got in for free. I was never one to use their names to get in places as I'd rather pay my money but this one night we wanted to go over to the Emporium nightclub and Lenny had said in the day, "Go over there and my mate John is on the door and tell him I sent you over." I don't think Lenny was working that night for some reason.

'So, I've gone up to the front of this massive queue and told the doorman I was Lenny's niece and he said, "Yeah, alright, babe, I've heard that before." It was pouring down with rain and now we had been fucked off from going in. So, I rung my dad up and told him, and he said, "Ring Lenny up and he'll sort it." I told Lenny about it, and he was not happy and said, "Right, leave this to me, I'll sort this out." Within minutes the doorman came back to the door with his face to the floor and said, "Sorry, babe, I'm so sorry. I get it all the time, I hope you understand." He then grabbed me and my cousin and he took us inside. God knows what Lenny had said to him. Like I said, I never had to put up their names because all the doormen knew me. Same when I went to other venues like the Camden Palace and Cairo Jacks, and I knew most of the doormen, like Richard Turkish, Robert Lopez and

Johnny Madden. All of the doormen moved around so they knew us all wherever we were.

'Johnny Madden, my dad and Lenny were all pretty close and all worked together for years. They were a good little team, and were always around the Chinese together. My dad and Lenny were hardly on the doors as they'd be around at a Chinese restaurant called Canton in Soho. If I ever went to the door and they weren't there, I'd know where they would be straight away. The club days were the good old days, because everyone knew us.

'My dad had a video camera way before most people in the early eighties. They used to call him "the gadget man" as he was into everything. It's lucky in a way as all of that sparring footage going around with Lenny and my dad at Kenny Mac's yard, my dad had got filmed for him by one of his pals. Dad used to tape everything in them days, including all of our family events and sport events of ours growing up. It's good now, looking back, that he had recorded all of those memories for everyone to see.

'I remember when Lenny got shot and this particular time I think he got shot in the elbow, although I could be wrong. My mam and dad had gone up to see him at Barts Hospital and he's sitting there up straight, happy as Larry as he always was, eating fish and chips, leaning on his injury. Nothing could hurt him, bullet or nothing. Now my mam was quite squeamish and Lenny starts telling them about the fella in the opposite bed – the bloke was really ill and couldn't breathe tidy – and Len said, "He doesn't stop fucking talking, he keeps coming over to my bed, he's doing my nut in."

So, after a while Dad says to Lenny, "How's the elbow, Len?", Lenny says, "Yeah, it's alright, look." My mam was then telling me the next thing Len's done is pull the sheet off covering it on the bed and stuck his elbow out, ripped the plaster off and shown them the gash in his elbow, which was the size of a fist and had turned gangrenous. My mother's face was a picture and she then said, "Ah, fuck me, Len, what's that?" She nearly passed out. I'm sure they said he could have lost his arm if it had got worse."

Anthony: I then said to Laura, 'I know he got shot in the arse cos he shows it in an interview.' Laura then replied, laughing, 'It might have been there, Anthony, it wouldn't have bothered him anyway, as he would have shown his arse too. He just didn't care, but I'm sure it was his elbow or arm.' She takes up the story again...

'Anyway, Lenny started telling my mam and dad again about the fella opposite him. He said, "He's driving me up the fucking wall, he can't move or get out and he's driving the nurses wild." Lenny then calls the bloke over to ask him something and says to Dad, "Watch this now, see he takes his fucking time!" The bloke almost crawls over and it must have taken him at least a half-hour with his drip in his hand. Gasping for breath, he says to Lenny, "What's a matter, son?" Lenny replies, "I don't know, I forgot now." The bloke turns around as Lenny's crying laughing with my mam and dad. He just used to love winding people up.

'We went on a family holiday once down the caravan. Mam, Dad, my brother and me followed

Lenny down to the caravan. Lenny was driving this Granada car and stopped off at a petrol station. He's got some sweets for me and my brother and he's got about ten quid's worth of chocolate in his hands, including Mars Bars and Kit Kats. So, as he's driving in front of us, he's opened his window eating chocolate, but as he's eating it with his arm out of the window, he's eating it with his little finger up in the air, like he's drinking a posh cup of tea. Well, he drops one wrapper out onto the floor of the motorway. My dad then turned and said, "That's the second wrapper he's dropped." Well, this went on and on – he must have dropped over ten wrappers out by the time we arrived at the caravan. Dad then said to him, laughing, "You fucking hungry then, Len, are you? We thought you were stocking up for the fucking week!"

'Lenny and Dad then took me and my brother around to the arcades and there was this punch ball machine there. All these kids were there, saying, "Alright, Len, alright Len? Len, Len, go on this! How hard can you hit this?" Half hour later, Len and Dad had spent loads of money on it and by now we had a big crowd of people around us. There I was, standing there holding all their jewellery – I've got my dad's watch, rings, I've got Len's rings and they are hitting it and there's noises coming off it, but the kids loved it. Lenny and Dad just loved entertaining kids. They were proper family men, and so funny too.

'Later in life we had moved house and were living in Cyprus Street in Bethnal Green. This one day a friend of my dad's, Raymond Murrel, was round the house. Now he was another character that you very rarely come across today. Lenny had just popped round as well, like he does, for a cup of tea at the same time.

'Lenny had been training in the day and had his top off, flexing, and my dad had his video camera out, recording him. Lenny was then saying he had a pain in his shoulder and Raymond offered to give him a back massage. Lenny's lying down on my front room floor and Raymond's got these oils on him, rubbing them in, and Lenny's going, "Ah yes, that's it, Ray! That's lovely, Ray." Lenny then jumps up at the end and shakes it all off. Dad kept the cameras rolling and caught this rare footage (which now appears in *The Guv'nor* documentary film). Lenny then got up and says to me, "Pop down the fish shop and get me four large spring rolls, good girl." You wouldn't think he was in training, Lenny looked absolutely massive that day in my house.

'We brought this Boston terrier once and we called him Bugsy, at the time he was expensive at £450. My dad always loved dogs and he always kept Staffordshire bull terriers. We had this one called Rocky and the mother of him was Lenny's dog, Lady. Rocky used to go over the park training with Dad and Lenny. Lady used to go too but she was fat and lazy and a lot older. Lady could hardly move and my dad used to say to Lenny, laughing, "That fucking dog's like you, Len." Dad played hell with him.

'Now my mam wasn't an animal lover, she liked looking after her home and Dad would come home sometimes with these dogs and Mam would go, "What's that, why have you brought another fucking dog home?" After a while my mum would then fall for the dog, and it would always end up with Mum cleaning up all the mess from them. I think later on we got rid of Rocky cos my mum fell pregnant with my brother. Dad was heartbroken but the new baby came first. My dad gave Rocky to one of his mates down the meat market, who was also called Johnny Wall.

'Anyway, Dad then went and got another Boston terrier as a bit of company for Mugsie, which we then called Bugsie. Now Mugsie wasn't a full pedigree and my dad used to call him "The Demic". [A demic was a word for something that didn't work properly, hence the floppy ears, unlike Bugsie's, which would stand up on end at all times.] If I remember right, Lenny's dog, Lady, had died and him and Val didn't want another dog. My dad had taken the terriers round Lenny's a few times and he loved them. We were then moving, my dad was working more, I was travelling around training and my mother was in and out, doing things so the dogs weren't getting the attention they needed. So we gave the dogs to Lenny. I remember crying but we were still allowed around to see them.

'Now Bugsie was a very nervous dog and Mugsie we used to call "Lenny" because he was a tough little bastard. You only had to shout around Bugsie and he would shake in the corner like a leaf. Bugsie was sitting on Lenny's lap one day and Lenny shouted, "Val, make us a cup of tea!" The dog shat himself and just shook. I said Len, "You can't shout like that with him on you," but Lenny loved those dogs.

'Years ago my dad got himself and Lenny Equity cards. My dad once did an advert with Lenny for the NSPCC, with both of them in the boxing ring. Dad came home and said, "That's the most boring fucking thing I've ever done in my life! Lenny loved it though, but it's not my cup of tea." All my dad was doing was making roll-ups for Lenny. Dad's the one taking Lenny on the pads and slapping him around the face. I think the advert only went on TV up North or in the cinemas and wasn't shown around London.

'If my dad was around Lenny, Lenny would say, "Johnny, you got to do it," and he'd give it a go. Dad wasn't shy and he'd give it a go. My dad was more into getting his teeth into things and putting money up for films for other people who were friends of his and Lenny's at that time. He put up money for films like the Bentley Boys and was financing them, but then Dad became ill.

'Lenny wanted to be on the big screen and my dad didn't, although Dad did love the camera – he just couldn't stand the all-day set-up of things, with all the takes and cuts on set. Lenny got me a bit of work on the *Lock, Stock...* film set as a runner. It was only a few days but a good experience for me at the time. Also, he had got me work on the TV series *London's Burning*. I had about two weeks' work on that. Glen Murphy, the star of it, was a mutual friend of my dad and Lenny's, and I was well looked after. I remember speaking to the director one day in his office, and by now my dad was ill and had been diagnosed with cancer, and he showed me black sacks of envelopes of people wanting to work there for nothing for the experience. He told me, "You're a lucky girl to be on here."

'I probably could have taken my career further, but because I was so young and quiet, I would just get on with things. If only I'd been a bit more chopsy, who knows where it could have led? I wish I'd have stuck at it, especially with the experience I have had recently on the film set, where me and my son and other family members starred and played extras on the movie, *My Name is Lenny*, which will have been in cinemas by the time you read this.

'Going back to when Lenny was filming *Lock, Stock...*, he used to come around my house and I used to do his lines with him. Lenny wasn't aware at the beginning that he had cancer so when Dad was having his treatment, Lenny was learning his lines. He didn't come up just to learn his lines, but he'd bring the script with him and he'd also go through things with my dad while I'd be making them hundreds of cups of tea at the same time. I remember Lenny saying to Dad, "Fucking hell, John, I'm struggling here. I'm only doing some takes on set and I'm tired. I've got this cold or something and I can't shake it off, I've had it for fucking weeks." The thing is, both my dad and Lenny were fit as fiddles, smoked like troopers but ran for miles. The weirdest thing about it all is they were both cousins, both very close like best friends, and both died of the same illness a few months apart – quite scary when you look at it like that. They worked together, done everything together and ended up passing away together.

'Now my dad's father they called Big Bill, although I never met him – he fell down the stairs and died. If there was equipment for brain scans like they have today, he may have lived. He died young and was in his early fifties when my dad found him at the bottom of the stairs. Dad used to say to me, "Your granddad would have loved you", and I find myself saying the same to my son. It's a shame my son never got to meet Dad. He lived and died for us kids, we were his oxygen, and my grandad was the same with Dad. It breaks my heart that Dad's not here. My dad was one of six and he was known as "Golden Balls". If he had a fight coming up, no one could do nothing around my nan's house as she was all over him.

'When Dad was in hospital, Lenny was there all the time. Dad then got really ill and it got to the point one day when Lenny turned up, my dad didn't want to see him. Basically the only person he'd see was my mother as he just wasn't with it. From the day my dad was diagnosed until he died took just nine months and it broke my heart. Dad was only forty-seven when he passed away and Lenny turned up for the funeral. His son Jamie brought Lenny with him and was more or less holding Lenny up as he was quite unstable. There was no way that Lenny was going to miss it as him and Dad had been together all their lives. Daddy had a massive funeral and a huge turnout and then a few months later, Lenny had also passed away himself. It was hard times for all of us and something you never really get over.'

Anthony: After this very emotional part of the interview I mentioned that I'd also lost my own dad to cancer. I then asked Laura if she could remember any other little stories before I wrapped the interview up and she had this to say...

'Another story I got told about from Mam and Dad

was when Lenny was younger, he and Val had gone out with my mam and dad to the Talk of the Town, which later became the Hippodrome, and Len had spiked Val's parents with some speed. Now Val's parents were quiet people, but Len had put speed in their drink and they were up dancing and didn't shut up talking all night. They were enjoying themselves and had come out of their shells. They didn't have a clue the state of them and were none the wiser, but Lenny and my dad were crying laughing all night.

'Also, when my mother was pregnant with me she had to have an emergency caesarean and when I was born, Lenny and Val came up to see me. My mam's youngest sister who was fourteen at the time was there, and she's told me this story.

'Well, my mother was stitched up from having me and Lenny was sitting in the cubicle and was holding me, and there was this little boy from next door whose mum had just had a baby and had opened my mum's curtain, and came in and on the bedside cabinet were some grapes. The little boy stretched up and took some grapes. Well, Lenny looked at him and screamed, "What are you doing?" messing about. Well, this kid just shook and couldn't believe Lenny was bollocking him. The kid's face went white, and everyone started laughing. My mam said to me, "I was laughing so badly but the pain I was in where I had just been stitched up was unbearable." She was then saying to Dad, laughing at the time, "John, get him out, get him out! I can't have him here, my stitches are going to burst." She remembers looking at a little sink, trying to take her mind off things and thinking, ain't that a lovely sink, that's a lovely sink. It was all quiet until Lenny came up, but then that was Lenny for you. He then went and gave the kid a bunch of grapes and sweets before he left.'

Anthony: Laura had these final words to say about her dad and her Uncle Lenny:

'They were just funny, family men; beautiful, loving, hilarious... the life and soul at parties. They were like a double act, always joking. They were a big part of all of our lives, and it's such a big loss that they are not here now. They were simply amazing, and it's lucky for us all that we have so many wonderful memories of them both to cherish.'

STEVE 'WOSKAS' COLLIS

Anthony: During research for my first book, *The Guv'nor Through the Eyes of Others*, I had the pleasure of meeting Steve 'Woskas' Collis in a café in Hoxton. I lost touch after that but I knew that I had to get him for this book. After obtaining his number, I passed it on to Lee to have a chat with him and to hear what he had to say about his cousin Lenny.

Lee: If ever I said that I had spoken to someone that reminded me of Lenny, it had to be this fella, Lenny's first cousin, Steve Collis. A brief bit of family history for you: Steve's mum is the sister of Len's late father, Leonard John McLean. 'Moggy', as she is known amongst family and close friends, is eighty-three years old and very much alive and well today, with forty-four grandchildren to keep her on her toes. Talking to Steve, I noticed his turn of phrase is very close to that of his big cousin Lenny. He has that same sort of patter, the same gruff but slightly nasally rasp evident in our man Lenny's voice. Funnily enough, Steve was telling me that he knew Len's wife, Valerie McLean, way before Lenny even knew her. You see, as kids they grew up in the same block of flats called Stringer House in Nuttall Street, so Steve knew Val's family years and years ago. Her younger sister was friends with Steve's younger sister, and so on.

Anyway, Steve spoke of his cousin in very high regard and he reeled off a few quick stories and the odd comical anecdote with regard to him. The continuous light chuckle in Steve's voice made it plain to see just how funny his cousin Lenny Boy could be. If you're wondering why I'm referring to Len as 'Lenny Boy' well, it's for the simple fact that this was endearingly how Steve and the rest of the Collis family members referred to him.

Steve told me just how generous and thoughtful Lenny was. He remembers one instance when Len came round to his Aunty Moggy's café that she owned at the time.

'Lenny said, "Right, listen, listen... I want all of you lovely ladies to get yourselves all spruced up for a night out at the White Swan. It's the boozer I'm minding. Anyway, we have a do on there tonight... Now I hope you all like strippers. Right, so I want all you beautiful ladies right up the front. Here, girls, you can leave your purses at home tonight, it's all on Len.'

Lee: Anyway, according to Steve's mum, Moggy, they all had a fantastic night and were lavished with champagne and the works. Lenny Boy wouldn't let them pay for a single thing – 'That's just how he was. He was just like that, was our Len.'

Steve went on to say that this one evening he'd taken his wife down the Barbican for a night out. Lenny was minding the door there at that time. He said that as you walked up, Lenny would make you feel like a celebrity:

'He would shake my hand and give me a massive bear hug, nearly fucking breaking my ribcage. Then he'd even shake my wife's hand. Lenny Boy's hand engulfed my wife's hand and I could see by the expression on her face that Lenny was almost crushing it to bits. Anyway, as we're stood there talking to Len, this big fella walks up with the biggest ears you've ever seen, like fucking car doors they were.

'He's on Lenny Boy's earhole, going, "Oh, come on, Len! You know me, it's me, Lenny, don't you recognise me?", and with that Len turns to him and says, "Yes, son, of course I remember you. I seen you on the fucking telly in that *Snow White* film. Yes, how could I forget you? It's fucking Dopey, isn't it? Now go on, fuck off!" Well, with that the big fella just turned and walked away with his tail between his legs. Len says to me, "That c***'s been up a few times, trying his luck. He fucking knows he ain't allowed in any of my places. Next time I'll unload the c***."'

Lee: Funnily enough, Steve himself nearly got a clump off Lenny one night. He turned up down his pub, The Guv'ners, and as he walks in, he's seen Lenny at the back of the boozer with his back to him. So he sneaks up and knocks him in the back – you know, with his elbow like. Anyway, with that Lenny turns around on a fucking sixpence, his fist clenched. Realising it was Steve, he says, 'Fucking hell, you c***! I thought, do I turn round and knock this geezer spark out or what? Lucky it's you, Woskas!' Steve said, 'Yeah, Len, I'm fucking glad it's me too, you big c***!'

Steve then told me, 'You see, it's different with family, especially with Len. He'd be there for you at the drop of a hat – "Don't you worry about that", he'd say.' He takes up the story again...

'A pal of mine that does a bit of work for me, used to work with Lenny on the windows. Funnily enough, his name is Lenny too. One day the gaffer called Lenny Boy into the office because apparently he wasn't doing the windows properly. Anyway, as they're stood in the office Lenny's got his hands behind his back as if he's sort of stood to attention, but what they didn't know was that he was bending the squeegee thing up a bit in his hands. So when the gaffer said, "Look, Len, you ain't cleaning the windows properly," Lenny pulls this bent-up squeegee out from behind his back and goes to him, "Eh, listen, you wanna try cleaning windows with this! Look at it, son, it's fucked." I think they had to pluck up the courage and let our Len go not long after that. Mind you, I think he got a hefty retirement package...

'I was out at some charity boxing do a couple of years back and who just happens to be there? None other than Roy "Pretty Boy" Shaw. So I went over and tapped him on the shoulder. He turned around immediately and I goes, "Hello Roy, you don't me but you did know my cousin very well." "Go on, boy, who's your cousin?" Roy politely said. So I replied, "Lenny Boy, Lenny McLean." Roy came back very quickly: "Eh, your cousin Lenny was a lot fucking bigger than I thought he was, ya know boy." We had a laugh and a joke about it. To be honest with you, Shawry was a true gent. Let's face it, he didn't have to be – he could quite easily have just told me to fuck off.'

Lee: In closing our conversation, Steve told me that they were a very big and a very close family until sadly many of them started to die young. He reeled off a bunch of people that they had lost early in life – Lenny, for instance, and of course another favourite of the family, Johnny 'Bootnose' Wall. Steve said, 'Many of the men died young in our family,' to which I replied, 'Eh, Steve, let's hope that your generation has ended that sad side of the McLean legacy,' to which Woskas replied, 'Here, I fucking hope you're right, son. Well, I'm fifty-seven now, so we're on the right track!'

I hope he's right too, because Steve or 'Woskas' was a joy to chat with – he spoke to me as if we'd known one another for years.

CHAPTER 13

FRIENDS WILL BE FRIENDS

During Lenny's dark yet exciting journey through life, one group of people that stood by the big man and his precious family with staunch disregard for what the tabloids had to say was Lenny and Val's vast array of loyal friends, who are of course very difficult to find. Here are few of their heart-warming stories.

KAREN LATIMER

Frozen in time are the memories steadfast in Karen Latimer's mind. In a time when music was real and a clump round the ear was seen as a deterrent not a jail sentence, her love and loyalty for all things McLean is as truly heart-warming today as it was from the very first day that she met the family. Like a stick of Blackpool rock, Karen has the skin of a Latimer and the name (McLean) running right through her. No one can tell it like Karen, because no one was closer. So as we near the eleventh hour, with only minutes and seconds left before our publication deadline, we finally meet up, click record on my Dictaphone and listen to what Miss Latimer had to say. So here goes...

'Due to my friendship with Lenny's children, Kelly and Jamie, I became a big part of the McLean family. I must have only been around fourteen years old at the time, it was 1984. In the years to come, Lenny and Val became like second parents to me – they were both so sweet and I will never ever forget them. The McLeans were living in Allen Road near Victoria Park at the time, and life was sweet.

'Now with regard to Lenny as a fighter he was never one to massage his own ego. I mean, let's face it, he never had to! Len's reputation echoed through the streets of London and was the stuff of legends. You see, at home he was a big prankster. He would walk around the house in his pants most of the time, taking the piss and laughing and joking – a very different Lenny McLean to that of The Guv'nor as he obviously was known on the streets.

'This one day we were out kidding around, like kids do, when Jamie had got in a fight with a family down the road. They were a lot older than us and he came off worse. Anyway, as kids do, Jamie said to the dad of the family, "I'm going to get my dad," and the fella goes, "Yeah, well, go and fucking get him!" So we're off. I'm following Jamie like a lost sheep to his house, Jamie runs in and shouts his dad, and with that this monster of a man appears and goes, "Right, come on kids, show me where they are." So Jamie's told his dad and Lenny's off on his way to this fella's house. Lenny only had to growl at this fella and his three big sons and they backed down, they didn't argue for a second – he was just too frightening. So, anyway, that was my first real encounter with Lenny. Let's just say he made an everlasting mark on me from that day.

'Another time we were out larking about and this fella had a go at me and Kelly, so Kel said, "My dad will be coming to see you." Again, this fella also said, "Oh yeah? Go and fucking get him!" Well, this fella's face when Len came walking round the corner was a picture. Len never said a word, he just walked up, picked this fella up by his throat, gave the man a right-hander, and he's landed smack-bang into a bus. "Right, when he wakes up, tell him Lenny said he's never to look at these girls again!" Len shouted. As you can imagine there were so many situations similar to that back then – if I told you them all, we'd be here all day!

'One thing I will tell you is that Lenny never accepted that us girls were growing up. For instance, he would come in my room to wake me up.Lenny's way of doing this was to literally tip me out my bed while saying, "Go on, girl, make your Uncle Len a nice cuppa tea,' before with a clenched fist he would say, 'but don't you dare go and tell my Val though?" You see, big as Lenny was, he didn't want his Val telling him off. Val used to say to him, "Len, you can't just go into Karen's room anymore, you know. How old do you think she is?" And Lenny would say, "Oh, I don't know, Val. What is she, about twelve?' To that Val would reply, "No, Len, she's eighteen for goodness sake!" Lenny still thought we were little kids.

'Funny story, when Lenny had the Guv'ners pub, Kelly and I lived above it and also worked there, but oh my fucking God, he never ever let up! While we were working, he would be on the phone to me or Kel; he'd be going, "Right, how many punters are in?", "What are they drinking?", "How much dough have we taken?" Fucking hell! If you said someone was drinking orange juice, he'd be like, "Fucking orange juice, them kids drinking fucking squash ain't gonna pay the bills. Stick a fucking large whisky in it or something, the tight c***s! Oh, he was relentless, was Len.'

Lee: When Lenny was leaving prison he promised lots of people in there that he'd write to them when he got home, or at least unbeknown to Karen, she would be writing them while Lenny dictated it over to her. She sat for hours writing letter after letter to all of these cons, for Val to simply pull her to one side on her way to the postbox and she would tell Karen to throw the whole lot in the bin. You see, Val didn't want Lenny to keep in touch with all those people from prison, she wanted to put that horrible time behind them. Anyway, weeks after, Lenny would say, ''ere, Val, all them blokes in prison that I wrote to, not one of them shit c***s have replied!' He never knew what had really happened. Karen takes up the story again...

'A little time before the pub days, Lenny had set up an escort agency. Anyway, he asked me if I wanted to work the phones. Well, the wages he was giving me at that time were like three times as much as the average working man's wage so I jumped at it. So everything's going great, until one day this fella is saying dirty stuff to me down the phone and me being naïve, I only went and told Len. Well, fucking hell, Lenny calls this fella up and he's screaming and hollering down the phone at him, "How fucking dare you! You dirty no-good c***, saying filth like that down the phone! She's just a baby, you horrible c***!"

'Well I lost my job after that, and I think the fella took himself off of the agency's client list. I remember Kelly finding out and going to me, "You fucking idiot, Kal, you were on a good earner there! What did you open your fucking mouth for?" I guess I was a bit soft in the head back then.

'Lenny liked to earn a pound note, but he was very generous with it when it was rolling in. I remember on my twenty-first Lenny and Val bought me an amazingly expensive Gucci wristwatch. I was bowled over, I would never expect a gift of that magnitude. But they saw me almost as their third child and would often throw a few bob my way.

'Len's conservatory was his place of sanctuary, he loved that place. He moved his special chair to the opposite side of the room one day as he wanted to watch Val doing the garden. He was so pleased to get his big house with the garden, something he always wanted to achieve. He used to say, laughing, "Look at Val, showing off like a peacock in her garden."

So anyway, it's 1997 and I had sort of lost touch with them for a little while until one day I got a phone call from Kel. She said, "Dad isn't well, Kal. I mean, really unwell." So I've shot round to Avenue Road in Bexleyheath, and there he is in his favourite place, the conservatory, sat there as large as life and as if nothing was wrong. Any other person would be in bed, crippled in pain, but not Lenny – the man simply didn't know what pain was, or at least he didn't show it. So now we're back to normal, chatting as if I'd never been away. Lenny didn't look at all well, but he never once complained. The only thing he ever said was, "'ere, babe, go and get your Uncle Len a couple of tablets, I've got a little baby headache coming on." I used to think to myself "baby headache?" The man had a massive tumour on his brain. He would never let on how bad it was, he was every inch The Guv'nor, simple as that.

'At that time I had my own flat and was living with my boyfriend. Every weekend Lenny would want to be down their caravan in Clacton and he would say, "Right, come on, we're off down Clacton!" He'd say, "Kel, ring Karen and tell her she's coming too." Val would say, "Len, she's got her own life, with her boyfriend and that now, you can't just expect him to let her go off all of the time." Val said that he would say, "Right, well tell him if he don't let her go, I'll bite his fucking nose off!" Well, I always went along with them, because I felt that it was far more important at that time. Lenny wanted us all with him, bless his heart.'

Lee: As I mentioned earlier, Len and Val had a love for Karen like one of their own. Karen helped nurse Lenny and Val to the end. When Lenny was in the last months of his life, Karen would have to read his book to him as he lay in his bed, over and over again. She said that the look of pride on his face as she did so was priceless: 'How could I ever have denied him that? It was, and will always remain an honour to think that just maybe one ounce of what I did may have helped make those last moments of his life just that little bit more bearable. God bless them both, Lenny and Val will remain forever in my heart.'

RACHEL REBECCA HALLIWELL

Lee: Southport-born Rachel comes from a family with, shall we say, 'London Underworld connections', a fact that she is quick to inform me wasn't meant to be a name-dropping start to our conversation. It would simply put me in the picture as to just how she wound up living in the home of Lenny and Valerie McLean, a union with such a bond that very quickly, Val would refer to Lenny in conversation with Rachel simply as 'Daddy'. Rachel informs me that Lenny and Val were more than just friends, they were like second parents to her for many years.

In 1992 Rachel got a job in London and moved down there with the help of one Reggie Kray. Now Reg Kray was a very good friend of her father, which is another story, the detail of which I am not at liberty to divulge at this present time. Rachel was first introduced to a fella called Eddie who had a carpet shop down the Roman Road, East London, and was in turn then introduced to Kelly McLean. At that time Lenny had The Guv'ner's pub and Len's daughter and mutual friend to Rachel and me, Kelly McLean, was running it for her dad and was in need of staff. Well, Rachel visited the pub on a number of occasions and within no time at all she had moved in with Kelly and they became the very best of friends. Now over the next few months, while at the pub, Rachel visited Lenny and Val's house in Bexleyheath with Kelly, and once The Guv'nor's pub came to an end, Rachel moved in to 31 Avenue Road with Len and Val.

Now this is going to seem very odd to readers, but Rachel being a young lady and of course not a London girl, she wasn't really privy at that time to Lenny and his reputation. This of course would soon come to light over the coming months.

At this point I said to Rach, 'But surely, sweetheart, I'm guessing you knew that Lenny was a formidable tough guy?' To which she replied, in that straight-to-the-point scouser tone, 'Oh abso-fucking-lutely!' She went on, 'Without a shadow of a doubt that side of Lenny simply oozed out of him.'

Rachel tells me that in all of her life, and this is one hell of a gee for Lenny given the array of colourful characters she has met over the years through her father's connections, she had never met a man such as him. She said that Lenny was simply a man of his own, with the largest character – the most fearsome-looking of characters too, but the loveliest man she had ever met. Rachel tells me that Lenny used to do some proper comical things. One thing, for example, was that he asked her to cut his toenails. Rachel immediately declined, so while she weren't looking, he flicked fag ash on her head, into her coke can and even into her boots, simply everywhere. She thought to herself, why didn't I just grin and bear it and cut those fucking toenails?

Another time, Lenny and Val were sat in the lounge, Len in his usual chair. Rachel had just walked in from work. No sooner had she taken her coat off than Lenny said to her,

FRIENDS WILL BE FRIENDS

'Rachel, I've got a job for ya! There's two hundred quid in it for ya?' So Rachel's thinking to herself, hey, hey, fuck's sake, this sounds like a nice little few quid. Anyway, so Lenny's going on and on with all of these obscure lines and it suddenly dawned on her. She said to me, 'Lee, do you know what, kid?' 'Go on, Rach, what?' I asked her. She said, 'He was only practising his fucking lines for that TV series he was in at the time called *The Knock*!' So I said to Rachel, 'Now that is funny, Rachel. I bet you were already spending that money that you were going to earn in your head as he was saying it, weren't you, sweetheart?' 'I was, Lee, I fucking was!' she told me.

Rachel told me that every Saturday night she and Kelly went out on the town, up West, and Lenny always used to drive them there. Len would make the pair of them sit in the back because they were always fucking around and giggling like a couple of silly schoolkids. She said Lenny probably made them sit in the back because the pair of them had always had tons to drink before they left the house. She'd always had more, and by the time they were on the move in Lenny's car, she would be bursting for a wee. Laughing hysterically, she said 'he wouldn't stop, you just had to hold it in! I'm telling ya, Kelly would be squeezing my hand to almost the breaking of bones' point, but I couldn't say, "Len, pull over," he would've done his fucking nut! Ha, ha, ha, done his nut in a joking way, of course, Lee.'

One night Kelly and Rachel were on a night out and they happened to be up The Hippodrome. Anyway, Kel being Kel romping around on the dance floor has got them in a bit of bother, because this fella seizes the opportunity to take advantage of the situation. So anyway, Rachel's stepped in and ends up punching this big fella. Word obviously got to Len because all of a sudden he appeared, and you could hear a pin drop: everybody, suddenly, is on their very best behaviour. The fella and his gang of pals make a hasty retreat and there's no sign of them anywhere. Rach said, 'Let me tell ya, the mere idea of Lenny coming down with the hump was enough to frighten off any-fucking-body.'

Rachel recalled that Lenny was such a funny man. One night when they were sat in the lounge, Len was watching *This is Your Life*. Rachel said to Lenny, 'Here, Len, you ought to go on this programme,' and Lenny replied, 'Oh yeah, I can just see it now... That Eamonn Andrews fella would go, "Well, Lenny McLean, here's a fella you haven't seen for a great number of years, but he still remembers the day when you smashed his fucking head in! Lenny, would you please welcome onto the stage..." as Lenny is giggling he carried on with, 'Oh yes, babe, I can just see it now! Ha, ha, ha,' and he and Rachel laughed like schoolkids.

Rachel said that while Lenny had The Guv'ner's pub and she and Kel were living upstairs, they would come down into the pub every time, no matter what events were going on. Anyway, this one night it was stripper night, so obviously the pair of them were down there, having a laugh. Well, one of these strippers (a well-known celebrity) was all over Rachel like a rash – 'He wouldn't leave me alone, he couldn't get enough of me.' So anyway, Lenny found out about it, and the next day he comes home from the gym (Slim Jim's in Greenwich for the record) and says to Rachel, 'Right, I've had a few words with this stripper fella and he won't be trying any of that shit again. Now I ain't having it, Rachel, a fucking fella like that wrapping himself around the likes of you. Well, it ain't happening!'

FRIENDS WILL BE FRIENDS

Rachel tells me that the very next time she bumped into this fella in a very hangdog manner he said to her, 'Hey Rachel, you live with Lenny McLean, don't you?' to which she replied rather sternly, 'Yes, I do,' and that was the end of that little saga.

I said to Rachel, 'Eh, Rach, I'd have loved to have been a fly on the wall in Slim Jim's that day, wouldn't you?' She said, 'I would have, yeah, but joking apart, and this goes out to the fella that was involved in this little episode, it was all in good fun because as this chap is, I'm sure, aware, Lenny was very fond of him too, that's a fact.'

Rachel had these last few words to say, 'I will never forget Lenny and Valerie McLean. They were there for me every step of the way, and I love and miss them so very dearly.'

SANDRA DAVENPORT

'Lenny McLean was a great personal friend to my late husband, Gerald Anthony Ashby, and obviously through this partnership of course, myself and Lenny's friendship would also blossom. Lenny, Gerald and another dear friend to them called Maurice Hope used to train together over Victoria Park. If I'm honest, I think they spent a great deal of their spare time at that park.

'Lenny was like a knight in shining armour when my Gerald fell ill. He would be around all of the time, him and my dear friend Lindsey Fairbrass's brother Craig, who as I'm sure you're all aware was set to play Lenny in a film of Lenny's life. The film of course never came to fruition, but those three spent hours and hours together between my house and "Vicky Park" as they referred to it, and of course with Lenny around they would drink enough tea to sink the *Bismarck*.

'On many occasions they would also come and pick my Gerald up and take him along to boxing shows that Lenny was involved with, in whatever capacity it was at that time. Lenny, like my husband, was a true gentleman, a proper old-school gent – the kind of man that opened doors for ladies and gave them his seat, values of which I'm afraid are somewhat lost in today's society. It is sad really, but unfortunately chivalry is somewhat a thing of the past.

'When my husband sadly passed away, Lenny was there to give a helping hand. Not taking Lenny for granted of course, but I always knew he would be.

'Where I lived in the Roman Road, there was this fella that lived across the way. He was a busybody, you know the type. I used to say, "All you need is a policeman's helmet and you have the full package." Anyway, I arrived home one day only to find a threatening letter on my doormat. I was mortified because I thought it was going to read how sorry he was to hear about my husband, but no, it was some silly hang-up that he seemed to have about some leaflets I had put in the bin. Anyway, I was very upset, especially being as I had just that week lost my soulmate. So as it turned out, the next day Lenny turned up to see how I was and I happened to mention it to him. I didn't think any more of it, but as Lenny left my place he headed over to this man's house, and oh, he didn't half give this man a shaking! It sounds a little funny now, but as I turned away and looked back, Lenny had picked this man up almost above his head and he's shouting at him, "You'll do what I tell you, no second chances! I'm warning you, are you fucking listening to me?" Goodness me, I mean this fella was by no means small, he was quite a size himself. I do remember all of my neighbours out on the front, watching this unfold. They were all probably chuffed to bits, because I bet at one time or another, he had probably bullied everyone in the street.

'Anyway, I think Lenny had scared the man witless, because the next day, the man knocked at my door and left a note of apology, saying, "I am truly sorry for misjudging your character, this will never happen again". Let's face it, that busybody man was a bully, but in Lenny McLean he had certainly met a great deal more than just his match – I think he gave up his role as local busybody from that day forward.

'Sometimes when we were up West at the movies, we would run into Lenny because he was working at the Hippodrome. He would take us over to his pal, who was the head doorman at Stringfellows, and get the staff to all look after us. We never paid for anything, Lenny would of course see to that! We would be in there having a lovely time, while he was obviously outside talking shop with his bouncer pal. Lenny was just that way inclined: if you were in his company, then you were treated like royalty. What a lovely sweet man he was! I just wish there were more men like him around today, I really do.

'My husband never really spoke a great deal about it, but I know that in the past, on a few occasions Gerald had gone to watch Lenny fighting bare-knuckle as they call it. The only thing he ever did say on his return was how Lenny had took them to the cleaners again – "The man was a machine," my Gerald would say. I never asked any more about it, as I feel that sort of thing is men's business.'

Lee: Sandra goes on to say how Lenny was a great big bear of a man who was very funny and gentle – unless of course you happened to get on the wrong side of him, then you were bang in trouble. She also said that Len's wife, Valerie McLean, was a very sweet, homely lady, and quite different to Lenny. She finished with these few words, 'I miss my Gerald and of course Lenny McLean with all of my heart.'

Now in closing this piece, and for the record, I would also like to add this: Sandra Davenport was one of the sweetest and most sincere ladies I have ever had the pleasure to have met.

GARY DENNIS

'Lenny was a good friend of the late Arthur Thompson, the Scottish gangster known as "The Godfather". My dad, Edward Dennis or 'Teddy' to those privileged enough to know him, was also best pals with Arthur Thompson, and due to the aforementioned friendship, it would only be a matter of time before I would myself meet Lenny. Most of the time I would see him over at Ritchie Anderson's house, Ritchie and his wife, Val, were like parents to Lenny – well, at least that's how I saw it, and I think to be honest that Lenny did too. He would always be over at their house, drinking their house dry of tea.

'Now I'm about fourteen years younger than

Lenny, so during the time in which he was minding the clubs in the West End, etc., I would be out on the town on the piss and what have you. Now because of the obvious link-up with Lenny and my father, the mere mention that Teddy's son was in the club meant that he would come and sniff me out. It was as if I had a fucking Sat Nav strapped about my person! Anyway, he would always find me – I mean, how the fuck do you hide from Lenny McLean? So once he'd tracked me down and sorted me out with free drinks for the time I was there, he'd start with the old, "Right, boy, does your dad know you're up West with your pals, up to no good?" He would even go off and give my dad a call and say, "Do you know Gary's up one of my clubs, Ted?" Obviously, after Lenny had gone away, my pals are all ripping the piss and all that, with "Who's he, your Minder?", etc., etc. He did, however, this one night give one of my mates a swift backhander. Unfortunately for my pal, I wasn't with him at the time, but by the stories I'd heard, he was at that time getting a bit leery and Lenny just gave him a quick slap. To be fair, that lad would have deserved it, cos he was a right little cocky c***. Lenny never smashed someone up for no good reason, that I do know.

'Another time we were in the Hippodrome, me, my dad and Arthur Thompson. Now as per usual and at the instruction of the main man, Lenny, we're all sat in the VIP area, so I'm up the bar, getting us drinks, then my dad's up, and so on and so forth. Now Lenny's walked back in and he's clocked us paying for our drinks. Oh, for fuck's sake! With that he's flown over and picked this Chinese head waiter up off of his fucking feet by the neck – I swear to God this fella is dangling four feet off the ground. He's given him a muggy slap in quick succession across both sides of his face and then he's screaming and shouting at him. He's going, "I told you not to take any fucking money off these fellas, they're my best fucking friends in life, you no-good c***!"

'Honestly the poor fella never dared even look at us again, let alone charge us for drinks. You see Lenny was old school, he was just that way. The way Len saw it was that if you were his very close friends, then you were looked after royally by whoever is at your service on that particular night. I don't believe we ever spent a tanner in that gaff, or for that matter, any other clubs that Lenny looked after: it was an unwritten law, set by Lenny.

'I would often drive up to Scotland for bits of business on behalf of my father. On one particular occasion Lenny was coming on the drive up with us – I think it was young Arthur Thompson's funeral, the son of Arthur Senior. Well, between you and me, and the rest of the 'millions' of people reading this book, I think it was possibly the worst fucking thing to ever happen.

'Now everyone knows, or they should do by now, that Lenny loved his cuppas. I swear to God, we ain't even got out of London and on to the motorway yet and Lenny's demanding we stop for a cup of tea. For fuck's sake, I'm thinking, I'd better stop because I don't want Lenny sat in the back of my motor, getting all fucking agitated, not for one minute.

FRIENDS WILL BE FRIENDS

Honestly I could see another pal of mine cursing to himself every time Len got out of the motor for a pit stop. I'm thinking to myself, well, as long as Lenny don't see you moaning, everything will be alright. Well, let me tell you this, a journey that I took many times took about fucking double the usual time, with Len and his fucking love for a drop of the old "Rosy Lee" as he would call it. I'm driving up to Glasgow, gritting my teeth, thinking, never again, Gary, never a-fucking-gain, boy.

'At this one event for young Richard, we were all sitting there and Lenny was sitting next to my dad when Roy Shaw came in and sat the other side for ten minutes. You could cut the tension with a knife. The old man looked at them both and said, "Why don't you two big lumps kiss and make up?"

'Over the years I was privileged enough to be in Lenny's company hundreds of times. He was always a one hundred per cent gent to me, and treated me and everyone that he knew with the utmost respect. I know one thing, and I can say this without reproach, at any given time, or at any given moment, if I or indeed my father ever needed to call on Lenny for any trouble, or simply anything for that matter, then he would've been there for us. See, Lenny McLean was there and had the backs of many people up until the day that he passed away. Lenny was a fantastic man to be around, and an honour to have known. I will never forget the man, God rest his soul.'

ANN BECK

'I knew Lenny and Val from years ago as I grew up by them. I went to the same school as Val, but she was a bit older than me, but I remember she was dating Lenny from an early age. I was also in the same class as Lenny's cousin, Johnny Wall, a very good-looking guy who could hold his own as well as Lenny.

'I lived on the Cranston Estate in the same block as Ron Norris. Lenny and Ron were very good friends and for some time Ron ran the Green Man pub in Hoxton, which Lenny would frequent, and I would help out behind the bar. Ronnie was my son's godfather and Lenny always watched out for me as he did a lot of other people in that area. He was a good friend. He had a lot of respect and for people that knew him, he was a great guy who had it very hard when he was growing up.

'When Roy Shaw took over the London Apprentice in Hoxton, Lenny wasn't too happy. This was when he told him to leave as there was only room for one Guv'nor in Hoxton. This is when the first fight came about and the rest is history.

'I accompanied Ronnie and his wife, Pat, to the fights as Ronnie was very ill. Ronnie said if he knocked Roy Shaw out then he would give Len his Dunhill lighter. He stuck to his word when Len won the second fight. Not long after, Ronnie passed away: he was only forty-four years old. It was a very sad time. He left behind his devoted wife Pat and five children.

'I moved out of Hoxton not long after that. Then a few years later, my dad, who worked in the film industry, told me that he was working on the film *Lock, Stock...* and that Lenny was in it. Dad saw another side to Lenny and said he was totally different to what he had heard, saying what a lovely guy he was, a true gent. There was a softer side to Lenny that not everyone got to see, but if you crossed him or his family or friends you would know all about it. He thought the world of his family and his friends, and for me it was a pleasure and an honour to have known him. There was only one true Guv'nor and that was Lenny McLean. I am yet to meet anyone that could take his place. Sadly missed, God bless him. Thank you for giving me the opportunity of sharing just a little bit about a great guy.'

RALPH FORBES

'The first time I met Lenny McLean was down the Camden Palace, I must have been about twenty-two at the time. Both of my parents were Irish but I grew up in North London. My dad came to London in the sixties and was a bouncer in the Camden Palace when it was called The Buffalo. He used to know the Nashes and various other names. Dad ended up passing [away] young with a heart attack. He was a big bloke, he was the same size as Lenny; I used to look at Lenny and see my dad all the time.

'After that first meeting at the Palace I didn't see Lenny for a while as I moved away to Germany but when I came back, he had become good mates and business partners with my brother, Eric. Eric met Lenny in '96 when they were starting filming of

Lock, Stock.... He was good friends with this bloke called Scouse Jimmy, who introduced my brother to Lenny. Lenny ended up loving my brother, because my brother was such a character like himself and they became very close.

'Basically what happened was my brother had a car showroom and a pub called Taffy Bradys, which were really close to each other. Taffy's was a proper pub, every six months a new manager would come and go, and they just couldn't handle it. My brother bought the pub but it got taken over by a load of foreign drug dealers and gypsies, and Lenny came in and straightened it out for him. What we done was put a big picture at the end of the bar of Lenny and overnight everyone started behaving their selves.'

Lee: I then ask Ralph, could this be the same car showroom which was also used in the 1994 documentary *The Ring - A South London Tale*, the one that Lenny did for BBC2 with Paul Lynch? He replies, 'Yeah, I'm sure it's the same one.' Ralph goes on to say that his brother used to have this little bloke named Jeremy working for him in the car lot. Jeremy would collect Lenny and drive him around, collecting money from places. Basically what Lenny would do was put his name to places if he liked them – he had his fingers in a lot of stuff. There was a lot of cash flying round in them days; people used to get involved with business and rip the life out of each other – 'as soon as you had Lenny on your firm nobody took any money off you. There used to be cars parked at the showroom with money which was Lenny's and my brother's'. He continues:

FRIENDS WILL BE FRIENDS

'I used to go down to my brother's car lot and Lenny would be there. He always drank lemonade, so I'd have to go to my brother's pub and get glasses and ice, and bring them back and give him a drink. Like I said, the pub cleared up overnight but there was still problems now and then.

'Back to the car salesroom, I've seen Lenny throw people out of there – it was a rough area and had problems with gypsies. They would smash my brother's cars up and threaten him for money so he would say, "Come and meet The Guv'nor Friday." Lenny would be waiting and when they see him, they'd run off.

'This one day I was just about to go down the pub and get Lenny a drink as he'd gone with my brother somewhere. These two big gypsies came in and asked for my brother. I said, "He'll be back in ten minutes." Lenny then pulled up in this Mercedes with this other bloke and these gypsies said, "Who are those two? They think they're a bit tasty, don't they?" I said, "That's Lenny McLean, lads." They then said, "We'll come back in the week and don't worry about the motor." They were so frightened of Lenny – he was like the last of that breed.

'This one day Peter Stringfellow was advertising for electricians for the Hippodrome to work nights doing safety and stuff while the club was going. So I've applied for the interview and told my brother about it, and he said, "What you should do is when you're up there, ring me and I'll ring Lenny to tell Peter to give you the job." So I'm in the queue for the interview and I've rung my brother to tell him, and next thing you know, Lenny's ringing and told him to give me the job as I was a lovely bloke. Peter said, "The job's yours, Ralph. You know Lenny, don't you?" I replied, "Yeah, he's my uncle, Peter." Obviously Lenny wasn't my uncle but I used to call him 'Uncle Lenny' – he used to say, "Anyone say something, tell them Uncle Lenny come and see them."

'The thing is with Lenny some people would be so scared when they knew he was involved. Take, for example, 'The Fake Sheikh' Mazher Mahmood, who actually wrote about it in his book. Mazher used to stitch people up and he knew my brother and all that lot and they were doing business. Now, Mazher had tried to set up my brother and rip the life out of him and stitch him up, but my brother had turned up with Lenny and he didn't have the bottle to go through with it. He must have seen Lenny and thought, fuck that, I'm not going to stitch this fellow up, and backed out. That's how fearsome Lenny comes across.

'My brother had gone round Len's one day and when he was parking, Len told him to be careful of the pier because one of the cars was at a bit of an angle. So, Eric said, "No problem, Len," and jumped back in the motor and reversed back and straight into the pier. Lenny's come flying over to the driver's door and Eric just managed to climb over to the passenger door and get away. Lenny chased him around the car and then Eric ran down the road and waited for three hours then cautiously went back and called through the letterbox, "Is it safe to come back, Len?" Lenny shouted out laughing, "Come in, you fucking idiot! Of course it's safe."

'This one day this man had stitched this bloke up

and my brother's gone down to get the money back. These four fellows from South London come out mob-handed. Now these were really big fellas and one says, "You're not getting the money but you're more or less welcome to fight for it." My brother replied, "To be completely honest, lads, I'm not really a fighting man, I've just come down to get the money. You better talk to my boss, The Guv'nor." He then passed them the phone and Lenny said, "Do yourself a favour, son, give that fellow the money." The bloke then says, "Who the fuck's that?" and Lenny says, "It's Lenny McLean here, now give him the fucking money!" Next thing you know he says, "No problem, Lenny. Sorry, didn't realise it was to do with you." So my brother had the money just on one phone call from Lenny.

'The thing with Lenny, he didn't just work in London, he worked all over the country. Whenever Lenny was called in, they had to give him three grand first before he put his name to it and done any business with them.

'When Lenny wrote his book, he was very careful what he wrote. If there was one thing he hated most in the world, it was grasses so he had to watch even if telling a story that he didn't grass anyone himself. So all the stuff in the book was laid right down and was far more exciting in real life, as you can imagine.

'Basically, Lenny used to say he was retired: what he meant was from fighting; he wasn't using his fists anymore, he was using his head. Basically, he was a businessman. Then he got into the acting and he was good at it.

'I was only young at the time compared to my

brother and Lenny roped me in on a bit of business he was doing. Anyway, to cut it short I got caught and locked up in the police station for twelve hours. They were trying to get me grass people up but there was no way I was doing that. Then I had to go and tell everyone involved, and then Lenny found out and he went berserk and called a meet, and told everyone I wasn't allowed in anything like that in future. I remember Lenny pulling me up [on it] as he always wanted people to make the best of their selves. He told me straight I'd be far better off living a proper straight life than going down the wrong path.

'I only knew Lenny for a few years and then he passed away. Once he had passed the pub went downhill and my brothers let it go in the end. He was a very funny man and a gentleman if you knew him; I have nothing but good memories of the man.

'Lenny's story will always go on forever. He was so clever with his humour, and he was a true legend.'

RENO AMBROSIA

'I will start by saying that I am somewhat of a country boy, or at least I was until I came into direct contact with Lenny McLean one evening. From that day forward, my eyes had been well and truly opened. I had started to date this girl, and she worked at a club in the West End called Legends. The fella she had been in a relationship with just a few weeks before we met was a lowlife wife beater and had been slapping her around for some time, hence the reason for their immediate breakup.

FRIENDS WILL BE FRIENDS

'So like I say, I had been seeing her for a week or so, and this one evening she asked me if I would pick her up from her place of work, that being Legends nightclub. Ronda, the girl I was seeing, had said to me earlier that day, "Just go round the back and the bouncer will let you in." Right, that sounds easy enough, I thought to myself. How fucking wrong could I be?

'So anyway, I rock up at the Club and make my way around the back, to the tradesman's entrance, shall we say. I bang on the door and this enormous fucking gorilla in a black leather coat allows me in. Right, so I've no sooner stepped across the threshold when I felt these huge fucking hands on me. With that he's spun me around and lifted me about four fucking feet off of the ground, and he's screaming into my face, "You fucking lowlife c***! You're in trouble, boy. Think you can lay a fucking hand on this poor little girl?" I'm fucking shitting myself at this point, I can hardly breathe. In an attempt to stop him killing me, I was trying to lay my fists on him, but who the fuck am I kidding? He's like the fucking Hulk! With that, and just as I'm turning purple, Ronda comes running through and she's shouting, "Len, Len, it's not him, Len! He's my new fella." As if nothing had happened this gorilla just let go of me and I landed in a heap on the floor. I'm coughing and choking, the lot, trying to catch my breath – I honestly thought I was on my way out.

'In a mood change quicker than Usain Bolt's feet, this bouncer fella is picking me up off of the floor and he's going, "Here, boy, on your feet son. Sorry, did I rough you up a bit?" He's joking and jesting, while I'm still fucking dying. I laugh about it now, but fuck me, I thought I was a goner – I'm just pleased as punch that I hadn't actually done something to really upset him.

'Anyway, Lenny starts messing with me then and he's and throwing shots at me, going, "Here, boy, good job I never done this, or this, or giving you a proper belt like this." As he's throwing his fists in my direction, I'm thinking, "yes it certainly is, you big fucker". I never actually let those words leave my lips, mind. So that was my first meet with the big man and believe me, it was also the very last time I inadvertently upset him. Talk about mistaken identity!

'From that day forward I became quite close to Lenny. Not best pals, I don't mean, just every time I went to pick Ronda up, I would park myself up with Lenny and he'd tell me little stories. He was one hell of a storyteller, and an awesome fella to be around. Let me tell you this, he fucking hated drugs, loathed and detested them – a point he lamented on many occasions. But worse than that, he hated gropey, sleazy, leery blokes. He would watch them as we were sat there, and he'd be saying to me, "Look at that cheeky c*** over there, grabbing that bird's arse! If he does it one more time, he's getting a backhander,' and with that Lenny flies into action. Most of the time he would steam over and the look of sheer terror on the face of the fella was enough; Lenny knew that he wouldn't act so flash in one of his clubs again. Other times though, the fella may require a "little tug" as Len would refer to it, and that was a little bit more hands-on. Len would grab the top of their head like they were a doll and shove them with some force towards his other bouncers, saying, "Get this no-good c*** out of my club!", or other times he'd simply grab them around the throat and sling them through the doors.

'He hated dirty fuckers around women taking liberties. I can hear him now growling, "No-good c***s, taking a liberty in my club." I was there, week in week out, and I saw those same faces come back into the club, and let me tell you, they were as good as fucking gold. Mark my words, they didn't want the wrath of Lenny again.

'I have seen Lenny lose it on many occasions; he was frightening to watch. A few times I'd sneakily followed him out the back, just to see how tasty he was. I know that sounds a bit wrong, but it was like watching an animated character from a movie when he blew up in a rage. This one time these two big fuckers were coming it a bit leery with the bar staff and Len's got the hump. In the blink of an eye he's grown ten times in size and he's over there; one of them has turned around and gone to plant one on Len. With that, he clumps the pair of them. They're immediately dazed as Lenny drags them out through the back to his office. Oh my fucking God, that was the worst mistake that fella done, trying to belt Len! He's gone to town on the pair of them. All I could hear outside was these two fellas screaming. Len steps out of the office about two minutes later and goes to his other door staff: "Get fucking rid of 'em!" and "I don't wanna see 'em round here no more". Put it this way, after what I'd seen when I peeked through that office door, they wouldn't be rushing back to one of Len's gaffs any time soon, I'm positive of that.

'Lenny used to sit in his office watching the CCTV cameras for any trouble and on the odd occasion I used to sit in there with him. The first few times I was in there, he said to me, "Here, boy, go down the road for Lenny and get me a kebab. Listen, boy, just tell 'em it's for Len and they won't ask you for any dough, and if they do, I'll go and sort 'em out." So I make my way down there and I have to be honest, the first time I went, I felt a bit silly, so I paid for it myself. What a mistake that was! Lenny went off his nut. He's gone to me, "You what, those cheeky c***s took money off of you? How fucking dare they when they know it's for Lenny?" Well, with that he flew out of the office and obviously went down to the kebab place and gave the fellas there hell. When he came back, he said, "They won't take any dough off of you next time, boy."

'Funnily enough, a few days later I went in to get myself some food and he was bang-on right: they never charged me a penny and treated me like royalty too. For years I don't think I ever paid for a kebab from that place.

'Lenny told me a great deal of stories over the times spent in that office, but I will finish with this. Back in the eighties and nineties, if you were out up West and on a night out, it would definitely pay you to be careful just how you acted. You know, make sure you didn't come over a bit too leery, just in case you weren't quite sure exactly which clubs were minded by "Big Len".'

KEN AT WHISTLES BOUTIQUE

'My name is Ken and I am the proprietor of Whistles Boutique. We are, and have been, a top end retailer of men's and women's fashion for the past forty years on the Roman Road in the East End of London. One of the first times Lenny paid our little establishment a visit was in the late seventies – I think Len was in his late twenties. What I'm about to tell you is so funny, I will never forget it for as long as I live.

'Lenny pulled up across the road from the shop, and as he was sat there a fella walked up and got straight into the back of Lenny's car. With that, Lenny jumped out of the motor and made his way across the street to my shop. As he walks in, he goes, "Fucking cheeky c***, he thought I was a cab driver parked up there!" He then went on to say, "I'll give him fucking cab driver!"

'So of course everyone in our shop is wondering why the fella is still in Len's car, so I said to him, "Here, Len, you do know that the fella is still in your car, don't you?" and Len replied, "I know he's still in there, Ken. I've locked the c*** in, that'll teach him to jump in the back of my motor." Lenny left that poor fella locked in his motor for at least half an hour while I sorted him out with some new attire.

'Now as you're all aware Lenny was a hell of a size. I measured him for his last suit in the mid-nineties and he weighed in with a massive sixty-two-inch chest with a forty-four-inch waist and a colossal twenty-inch neck. Len was longer in the body than in the leg: at six foot two inches tall, his leg was a regular size thirty-one inches. As I cast my mind back, I remember him being at his largest size back in the nineties. He was so big that I remember having to order his shirts in special.

'From the first day that I met Lenny, he had always been a proper gentleman. There was the odd time that he would come in the shop and he was a little aggy – not to us, just in his demeanour. We obviously all trod a little lightly around him on occasions like this, because let's be honest, from the stories we had heard with regard to Lenny and those giant fists, neither I nor any of my colleagues would've fancied ever upsetting the man. Not that he ever made me or any of my staff feel uncomfortable and just to reiterate on my previous words, Lenny McLean acted with the utmost decorum and was an old-school gent through and through. It was a pleasure to have served him.'

ROBERT HAYES

'My dad, the late Alfie Hayes, grew up and was best friends with Lenny when they were kids. I met Lenny numerous times when I was with my dad later on in life. Obviously the most memorable occasion was in 1993 at the fantastic party he threw for us at his pub, The Guv'ners. The first thing that struck me was his deep voice and obviously his size, but also his ability to make you feel instantly at ease.

'I had heard all of the stories, but I never, ever felt anything other than welcome in his company. I remember my dad meeting Len one Saturday at midday after one of my youth football games; I must have only been around thirteen years old at the time.

FRIENDS WILL BE FRIENDS

It was in this office-style building, not in a pub or a bar. As my dad and Lenny greeted each other with a hug, Lenny lightly patted my not-too-clever head, and asked how I'd got on. Although I can't remember the exact result I mentioned that I had scored and he responded with "Good boy" and then we all went for food and had a good laugh, with the pair of them joking. Lenny was immaculately dressed, crisp white shirt, suit and looked like he was going to a meeting. They sat down to talk about Lenny's new book, which he was hoping to get a publisher for. He then showed Dad the written extract about my family – I think that he simply wanted to make sure that my dad was pleased and not upset by anything he had written with regard to our family.

'We all met again the following month. It wasn't a long get together as Len had a meeting that day, but I think they still managed to polish off about twenty mugs of tea between them. On this occasion, I remember that Lenny had handed my dad a draft of his book, which would eventually become his bestseller, *The Guv'nor*. Lenny also did something that will be etched into my mind forever. He took out a framed picture of himself and wrote on it, "To my old pal" before handing it to Dad. On the way home I asked why he didn't sign it and Dad's reply was quite simple: "He never needed to, son."'

'A week later, my dad had a picture done of himself and signed it "Paul Newman", which he sent to Len for a wind-up. That's how close they once were, and the respect they showed each other was genuine and true. From what I could see in the times that I spent with my dad and Lenny, there was a deep bond, a mutual respect. They were the greatest of friends.'

JON WARWAY

Another person who had been at the party in The Guv'nor pub was Patsy Hayes' son, Jon. We spoke with Jon and he had this to say about the night.

'I remember Lenny held a party at his pub called The Guv'ner's for one of my family members – I was about seventeen at the time and thought I could handle myself, but that was until I met big Lenny. He was talking to my mum at the time, who then introduced me to him, and he shook my hand with a firm grip and then gave me a little tour of the pub. Lenny was talking me through some of the many pictures he had up on the walls of the pub, and I paid particular attention to the Page Three girls, as most seventeen-year-old boys would. Lenny then said, "Do you like them, son?" I said, "Yeah, Lenny", half-expecting him to set me up with one, but he just gave me a pat on the back and walked away, laughing. He was a great man and a true East Ender and I'm proud to say that I met him.'

CHAPTER 14

THE CHAUFFEUR

Lee: Eddie David. Take a look at the name that heads this section, remove the 'd' at the end of 'David' and add an 'ES'. There you have it, and as a fan of the man this book is in dedication to, you should by now have the name of the popular character Lenny played in the nineties TV series, *The Knock*.

Lenny's driver is sat outside LWT Television Studios waiting for Lenny to return from his audition. He walks back to the car, the driver winds down the window and the big man says to him: 'There you go, my son, your name's gonna be up in lights.' He is of course bewildered at this time, but in the months that follow it will all come to light. As it turns out, Lenny tossed up his driver's name as a suggested name for his character on *The Knock*, but in the mix-up and probably due to that booming bucket of nuts'n'bolts voice that he had, it became Eddie Davies instead of the driver's name, which is of course Eddie *David*. Very similar, although not quite right – oh well, there goes Eddie's chance of his fifteen minutes of fame, yet another party talk-up piece cast asunder for another day. So anyway, I'll let Eddie David take it from here and go back to the very beginning.

EDDIE DAVID

'I'm a London cabbie; I worked out of a very busy cab office on the Roman Road called Ace Cars. I worked out of that gaff for many years and on into the mid-nineties, which marks my first proper meeting with the man himself, Lenny 'The Guv'nor' McLean. I never realised it at that time, but this meeting was about to change my life forever. The changes were very subtle at first. I mean, I can have a row myself to a certain extent, of course not in Lenny's league, but I can hold my own. But once I got teamed up with Lenny, I never needed to because once everyone knew that I worked for Len, I was immediately shown a certain amount of respect. Even in the local Chinese takeaways and the barbers and that, these people would never charge me a tanner, simply because I was pals with Lenny McLean. You see, Lenny's name carried so much weight across London, even up until the day that he died. But also, because of this, a lot of people were fucking jealous of Lenny; so obviously due to my involvement with him, they were jealous of me too.

'Before you read my story, if you would like to get an image in your head of the real Lenny McLean, watch him in *The Knock* and on the *Richard Littlejohn Show*, and you have him, because that there was the real Lenny McLean. Now being a Londoner myself, I had obviously on numerous occasions heard the name Lenny McLean in and around the East End, and to be honest, all around London for many years. Even going so far back as the late seventies, I would see him. You see, Lenny was a very well-known and well-respected figure as a fixer and a fighter, even back in those days. Let's face it, in Gangland Britain, back in the seventies, you had to be somebody of value to be known amongst the faces, especially at Len's young age of just twenty-one or so.

'Now in the seventies, I was in my late teens and back then Lenny was somewhat of a drinker. I often used to see him leaving a certain boozer, getting into his motor, which believe it or not used to be a fucking little Mini that he used to drive around in. Can you imagine that, the size of Lenny! Even back in his mid-twenties he was a fucking size, and watching him trying to get into a poxy little Mini... Well, you can picture it yourself now, can't you? To be honest, on a few occasions I almost thought about stopping to see if he wanted a lift, although something inside advised me that this wasn't the best of moves, so for that reason I never acted upon it. Apparently, Lee informed me while we chatted with regard to this one day, Lenny actually smashed that little Mini into a load of big council bins on his way home one night, writing the motor off by all accounts.

'Right, before I get any further into this, I'll tell you a little bit about the firm I worked for. As I mentioned, I worked for Ace Cars in the Roman Road, not too far from Lenny's house. It was a very busy office that had a great number of drivers, many of which on various occasions had the odd run-in with Lenny. You see, Lenny didn't suffer fools very well, and if he hired you to drive him and you weren't up to the job, he'd get the right raving hump, this being the case with many of the fellas at our office.

'A bunch of the cabbie lads at our place didn't have time for Lenny, simply because he'd lose his rag with them, and let's face it, they weren't going to argue back with him, now were they? But he probably only ever got the hump with them because most of them didn't even know their way out of the Roman Road, let alone anywhere else.

'My first job came about when Lenny wanted me to take him over to Limehouse Police Station. There was a problem with regard to someone to do with Lenny's film who had been pulled in to Limehouse nick and he had on his person eighteen grand of Len's money, and I was the driver that was taking Lenny to get it. Believe you me, he was doing his absolute nut in my cab; he was going crazy cos they had hold of his money. Lesson one learned in my early days teaming up with Len: don't get in between that man and a pound note, cos let me tell you, that must have been the longest ten-minute drive I had taken in my many years as a cab driver.

'I was always on call for Lenny: it was important to him to have a motor readily available. You never know what could arise at any given moment with him. Anyway, this one evening, my phone goes and it must have been around half past two in the morning. Oh no, I think to myself, it's Jamie – you know, Len's son – so I pick up the phone, and he's ranting and raving about these bouncers that have had a go at him up a West End nightclub.

'Anyway, so I shoot over to Len's, he jumps in the motor and we're off up West. I'm not even thinking about asking if he's OK, I can feel the violence oozing from the back seat. So we pull up at the club; they're at the door and inside the foyer, this bunch of clowns. Anyway, Len jumps out of the car, steams over and he's into the pair of them. I must say I hardly saw any blows; Len was so quick that it was over in seconds. He turns and walks back to the motor and jumps in. These two big lumps are stretched out across the pavement. So anyway, not a word is mentioned on our drive back. Lenny was the sort of fella that could have a row with five fellas, smash them to bits, and then never say another word about it. Not like all these other plastic gangsters that have one little row and then talk about it and gee it up for weeks. No, not Len, he would just be sat in the back of my car, singing away to himself.

'Lenny was a doer, not a talker, and by far the fucking best I've ever seen. Another thing about him was that when he went into a row, he fucking grew in size. I don't know how he done it, but he fucking did, he actually got bigger! A very scary sight was Lenny with the hump. He was a giant – if Lenny put his arm around me, as we were driving along, I could not fucking move, I have never felt so much power, so you can imagine the power he wielded in a tear up.

'I was parked outside another club that Lenny minded called Cairo's one night, and Lenny has come flying out of the front door with this fella by the scruff of the neck. Anyway, Lenny's slung him in the street. With that, he comes walking back, this fella, and tries to do Len over the nut with a bottle – big fucking mistake. Lenny's just swung round, I swear to God it was like something from a film. Lenny's done him with a shot so powerful that he's lifted this fella off the fucking floor. It was surreal, the man was just a fighting machine. There will never be another like him.

'It's funny, you know, you could see Lenny do this sort of thing on the street and have a big tear up, then I'd drive him home and go in for a coffee. His Val's there waiting like the amazing wife she was, and Len would go, "Alright, babe, sort us a cuppa out for the boy." He was a completely different person, cracking jokes, acting the fool. It was weird in a way, just how quick he could switch it on and off. I mean, it was as if he was playing a part in a film, and to be honest, in a way he was. Everybody knew that when Len stepped out from his front door, he meant business, and Lenny's line of business just happened to be violence. And he was the fucking Guv'nor, make no mistake about that. All of these stories that surfaced in books after Len had died, saying I done this to Lenny, Lenny didn't want to take us on and whatever else was all a load of absolute bollocks. Listen, not one of them ever said it while Lenny was on the manor, not naming any names, but not fucking one of them, and you know who you are. I simply say that you should allow him the same respect now that he's gone that you did when he was alive.

'The amount of people I had had over the years frightened half to death because they had upset Lenny! You see, he would sling them in the back seat of my motor and give them a bit of a growl and a talking to. I remember this big fella that worked at the Hippodrome. Well anyway, he was harassing the gaffer's wife. Oh my fucking God, he wasn't a small geezer himself, and well, Lenny had him in the back of my cab in tears, he was begging and pleading with him. He was going, "I won't do it again, Len. Please Lenny, I didn't realise what I was doing", and all that sort of thing. Well anyway, he was a good boy from that day on, and the gaffer's wife was happy again.

THE CHAUFFEUR

'It's funny, you know, Lenny being the big and powerful fella that he was, he was never a fan of big loud booming noises. I mean, I don't know why, cos his voice sounded like a tank rolling down the cobbles anyway if he was shouting. But if we were in the car stuck in traffic, and a bus would fly by, like they often do in the centre of London, Lenny would jump out of his skin. Every time I can hear him now going, "Oh, you fucking bastard".

'This one particular time we're driving along, going to Cairo Jacks to pick Len's wages up. Anyway, as we've pulled up these three big fucking scaffolders are walking across the road and they've bumped into my motor. Well, Len's jumped out of the passenger seat and he's got these three mugs up against the wall in a fucking rage at them. I think the busyness of the loud London traffic had given Len the hump, and these three just tipped him over the edge. Because, on the other side to that coin, when Lenny was minding a club, if there was some trouble, he would go over and be very polite with them at first. He would always give them the benefit of the doubt at first and say, "Now, now, come on, boys, behave yourselves!" Now if they played up a second time, well, that was it, he would just do his nut, and let me tell you, you didn't wanna see Lenny doing his nut. I have never seen a man so big that was so fast, Lenny could do multiple headbutts; I've never seen anyone else anywhere that had the speed and ability that this man had. I mean, no wonder he became The Guv'nor. How many bouncers can put their name on a venue, I mean, just their name, and it was protected, nobody dare fuck about?

'Something I would like to talk about and to sort of set the record straight is the time Lenny done eighteen months for the murder that he was cleared of. Lenny was in Fuerteventura just before this happened. I remember picking him and Val up from Gatwick, I think it was the night before this incident happened. At that time I used to drive another fella that worked at the Hilton – he was a concierge in the casino, if I remember right. So anyway, Lenny's banged up and maybe looking at a possible twenty stretch, I'm running Val about to Wandsworth Prison to see him and then back and forth to the solicitors, etc. Anyway, I picks this fella up – you know, the fella I mentioned that works at the Hilton – and he goes to me, "That's a shame, about that Lenny McLean who got nicked for that murder, isn't it?" I nodded in agreement, and he goes, "Yeah, that fella that Lenny supposed to have bashed up got slung out of our casino, and I saw the Old Bill bundle this naked fella into the back of a hurry-up wagon, and from what I could see, they were giving him a right good going over, because the van was parked up and rocking about all over the place." He goes on with "Apparently the police were having a hell of a lot of trouble with him." Anyway, at that time, nobody could find anyone that would come forward and say anything in defence of Lenny. So with this new information, I shoot straight round to Val's in Bexleyheath to give her this bit of news, which she relays immediately on to her solicitors. With this new evidence coming to light, Lenny gets a reprieve.

'I must just say for the record, I'm not saying I was the fella that got Lenny out of prison, but maybe with a lucky little twist of fate with me picking this fella up from the Hilton, Lenny was back home with his family, that's all. It's just nice to think that I might have played some small part in his release. I mean, he'd already done eighteen months for fuck's sake, what a travesty!

THE CHAUFFEUR

'I will say this though, at the time that this evidence came to light, Lenny was doing his nut in the nick. I think he was at breaking point because even I felt the wrath of it. You see, at this time I was spending a hell of a lot of time around Len's house till all hours of the morning, as Val and I were going through the case and trying to find loopholes. Well, this one night, two big fucking lumps turned up at my door and gave me a stiff talking to in respect of spending too much time at his house. I told Val at the time and she said, "Oh, fucking ignore it, Eddie, I'll have a word with him." It was nothing to do with that really, Lenny knew I was trustworthy and solid, he was just in a bad place mentally and anyway, did he think I was on a fucking death wish? After Lenny got out of prison, he couldn't apologise enough to me, and also he got the other two fellas to do the same. Everything was sweet, I knew that Lenny didn't mean anything by it.

'Funny too because when I look back on it, those few months trying to help Val with Lenny and all that actually cost me my own marriage because my wife gave me an ultimatum: either I stop working for Lenny McLean because I'm out at all hours and hardly ever at home, or say goodbye to her.

'So I'm sat round Len's one afternoon and I'm a bit down, and he goes to me, "What's up with you, son? I said, "Nothing, Len, honest." He said, "Come on, son, I know you, what's wrong?" So I says, "OK, it's Donna, Len. I think she's playing away." With that he goes, "Where is she now? At work, is she? Take me there, come on." Well, it was probably a mistake, but I took him. When we get there, I go in to get her and when she comes out, Lenny goes, "Alright, Don?" She says, "Yes, I'm fine, Len. What's wrong?" and Lenny growls at her, "Tell me his fucking name! Don't fuck me about, what's his fucking name?" Anyway, she tells him – she wasn't scared of Len, she just knew that he would find out in the end, and this way she possibly had time to warn the fella. Anyway, I persuaded Lenny to leave it because I wanted to get back with Donna, and that was sort of the end of my dealings with him. It was the only way, and I do believe with my missus telling this other fella that Lenny McLean had the hump and was after him, this made him back off and eventually paved the way for me and Donna to start again.

'It was only about eight months after this that I found out about Lenny's illness. I couldn't believe it. I didn't honestly know what to do – should I go round? Should I ring Val? I was in turmoil, and then a bit later that week, I bumps into Jamie, and Jamie says, "Oh yeah, Dad's unwell, Eddie, but he's on the mend," so I thought to myself, Fantastic, Len's beat it; he's come out the other end and won his battle. I was, however, wrong, and later found out that people often get a bit better before it finally gets worse. Next thing I find out is that Lenny has passed away. I was shocked to say the least, devastated if the truth be known. So when the time came, I went along to the funeral. I saw Val and the kids and family, etc., but I kept myself out of the way. I have always believed that it's a time for the family mainly and Val was so busy with that many people that I never got the chance to talk to her that day, but I did what I wanted to do, which was say goodbye to a very dear friend.

'As I mentioned, I used to take Len all over, picking up money for this, money for that, picking up scripts and taking him down the gym, etc. So we're driving over Hoxton way, close to where Lenny was born, and he says, "Here, boy, pull over at that pub over there," so I did, and he goes, "Right, stick your nut in the door, and give me the SP on how lively it is, where people are, and how many, that sort of thing." So I did, and then I jump back in the motor to report what I've seen to Lenny. So next thing, Lenny goes in the boozer. I can see a bit of a melee going on through the frosted window and I can hear a lot of shouting and that, then after about five minutes, Len walks out, straightening his tie. Not a single mark on him and he's whistling to himself. He jumps back in the motor and goes, "Away you go, boy," and that's it, it's never to be mentioned again. Funny though cos as we're driving along through Hoxton, the area must have stirred up some old memories, cos all of a sudden he goes to me, "Here, son, you must hear a lot of stuff being said about me." I goes, "Well, yeah, not half, Len. It's hard not to, mate. Look, every fucker knows you and I drive a cab, so it sort of goes with the job." With that Len goes, "Go on, son, what do people say about me?", so I goes, "Well, people seem to respect you, Len. They don't really say anything other than good things about you."

'I remember running a few people to Joe Pyle Senior's beneficiary. Funny too, because Roy Shaw was obviously there, due to the fact that he and Joe were big pals. Lenny and Roy as usual were just glaring at one another the whole night – Lenny would always speak highly of Shawry as a fighter.'

Lee: I would like to finish Eddie's piece off with this final thought. I asked him, did Lenny ever mention people that used him, done him down or wrong done him? To which he said this:

THE GUV'NOR REVEALED

'Lenny was never a man to talk anybody down behind their back. I am obviously aware of the odd few people that fell out with him in the last few years of Lenny's life. But let me just say this, and for the record, Lenny always spoke very highly of all of his friends and acquaintances, he never ran anyone's name down in any capacity. If Lenny McLean had a bee in his bonnet, you would know about it as he would deal with it head-on, like everything else in his life. Lenny put himself on offer for a great number of people through his traumatic and eventful life, and for that alone I feel that the man deserves the utmost respect.'

CHAPTER 15

ON A MEET WITH THE GUV'NOR

In our many years of research into Lenny McLean, the two of us have shared one resounding regret, which is that neither of us ever met the man himself. Fortunately, though, as we have seen, in Len's short yet remarkable and mildly nefarious life, there were many people who did. The many stories they had to share with us, both on and off the record, ooze with a charismatic notoriety that only a man as notable as Lenny McLean could ever truly command. The chapter that follows will give you an insight into meeting and spending time with the one and only Leonard John McLean or simply 'The Guv'nor'...

DAVE RUDD

Lee: I spoke with Dave and it turned out that his late dad (also named Dave) knew Lenny as he was a cab driver in

London and was often parked up in the fleet of cabs that always lay in wait outside the Hippodrome. Dave said that his dad often mentioned Lenny to him and many times he recalled little stories with regard to the odd skirmish that he'd been witness to way back then.

'It's funny, I've seen Lenny give the odd clump, and dish out a bit of violence on numerous occasions, and each time I saw such a thing he'd always been alone and sometimes he'd dealt with a bunch of three- or four-handed troublemakers without even breaking into a sweat. This one time I heard a commotion coming from inside the Hippodrome and all of a sudden I see Lenny come flying through the main doors with this big lump of a fella by his throat. Now Lenny's almost lifting this bloke off of his feet, he's screaming at the top of his lungs to him. All of a sudden he's slung him in the road – almost hitting my cab, as it turned out. This happened to be quite useful to my father because as Dad's looked up from behind his newspaper, he's recognised the fella, known to everyone around as one of the North-East London lot. Yes, my dad would ponder this time and again. Yes, son, I'm almost positive it was one of them. So anyway, with that my dad said Lenny's just shouted to him, "Now fuck off, cos next time I'm gonna hurt you!" Anyway, the fella obviously thought better about retaliating and had it away on his toes. Now my dad did say he couldn't swear to it being one of them, but he said if it wasn't, then the fella must have a doppelgänger.

'So anyway, it's settled back down, my dad's nerves

have settled and he jumps out of his cab to have a smoke. With that, he said, Big Lenny comes over for smoke and a chat, and Dad's thinking, he's probably still fuming a bit and he'll tell him all about it, but no, not Len, he never mentions a thing about it, not a single solitary word. According to my dad he just asked him how his night was going, had another roll-up, bid Dad a good night and made his way back into the Hippodrome.

'Dad recalls that in all of the time he'd known Lenny and seen him having a row, he never once mentioned it to him. Now this alone simply proves the sheer strength and character of the man because, let's be honest, my dad always said other fellas would be talking a row like that up for years.'

Lee: As I'm chatting with Dave, I happen to mention another fella that he had remarked on in past phone messages: 'So, this fella from your gym called Larry, did you say he had worked with Lenny?' Dave recalled the following...

'This fella, now well into his sixties, who's a regular down my gym in Uxbridge, worked with Lenny in the early nineties. This Larry fella is a really big chap too – not as big as Len, but still, a very big and powerful geezer. After years of training alongside Larry, it's plain to see that he was, and probably still is, a fearless and formidable character himself in his own right. But I sense that his past life seems to have left him a little untrustworthy, shall we say?'

THE GUV'NOR REVEALED

Lee: The man said that although he would feel uneasy conversing with us as a contribution to the book, he doesn't mind sending the odd story our way, so back to Dave again...

'While working in Soho, Larry's been sent to mind the odd high-stakes card game involving many notable faces from the Underworld. Anyway, this one night everything's going smoothly at the table until he shouts to Len that it's going off downstairs with three paratrooper fellas. He knew they were paratroopers because they'd stated they were, using this as a point of entitlement to enter the club. With that, Lenny comes flying down the stairs and as he nears closer, he seems to leap into them and smashes the three of them to pieces. He simply then straddles over them and says, "Listen, you fucking muggy c***s, it's only due to the respect I have for the military that I haven't gone into you boys proper. Now fuck off before I lose my temper!" For fuck's sake, he's just smashed three military soldiers without breaking a sweat! The man was a force of nature.'

Lee: On numerous occasions Larry had expressed to Dave just how much Lenny's family meant to him. He said that unlike most fellas who would be talking about violence the whole time, Lenny obviously never thought that he needed to talk himself up in that manner. Good old Len would be talking about his wife and kids the whole time.

This one time they were passing a well-known gypsy site over in Langley called Mansion Estate, and Lenny spots these two teenage boys, crying and looking frightened and upset. Len being Len, he marches over and says, 'What's the matter, boys? Has somebody upset you?' The boys said, 'Yes, some people from that gypsy camp over there stole our bikes.' With that, Lenny walks on to the site and just as he does, all of the gypsy fellas came out of their caravans. So, Lenny's gone, 'Some lowlife mugs on here have gone and pinched these boys' bikes. Lenny then says 'listen, I ain't fucking going away until someone gives me the bikes back!' With that, there's a bit of mumbling going on amongst the gypsies and within half a minute, one of the fellas is walking over to Len with these boys' bikes. Len takes the bikes and says, 'Right, let's go then, boys,' to the two young lads, and walks off the site without so much as a raised voice. According to Larry, most of the adults on that site knew exactly who Lenny McLean was and obviously thought better about starting a row that they weren't ever going to win. Larry was witness to Lenny doing stuff like that almost on a weekly basis.

So, as my conversation with Dave is almost over, he tells me that Larry said Lenny McLean was always very good to him, although he was aware that Lenny could, and would, turn it on in a split second, turning into an absolute animal if riled. 'Lucky for me,' Larry said, 'I was always on the right side of the man.' He finished off by saying that in the short time that he spent around Lenny, it was clear as day that if anyone had trouble and needed muscle, Lenny's was always the name that was thrown up. As far as he was concerned Lenny was the best at what he did, and in all of his life, thinking of the things he had been involved in, Lenny McLean was, quite simply, a one-off.

THE GUV'NOR REVEALED

EDDIE LUCAS

'With me being a doorman myself, another name I had read and heard about growing up was a fella many people referred to as the world's toughest doorman, a bouncer that in many ways was held in a similar league to Lenny. This fella's name was Gary Spiers from Liverpool.

'Now Gary, like Lenny, was no stranger to violence. In regard to reputation and size he himself was a giant and a hardman but also a man like Lenny with legendary charisma.'

Anthony: The question now was, had Gary and Lenny ever met or heard of one another? After years of research my question was finally answered after I caught up with one of Gary Spiers's closest mates, a fella that had even been a pall-bearer at his funeral service.

'I first met Gary Spiers in the seventies when he'd just come back to England from doing karate in Japan. My brother (who was a professional wrestler) put Gary up so I more or less grew up with him, training and doing the doors together in Liverpool's roughest pubs and clubs.

'We were out after work one night and Gary had just had a bit of trouble, which he sorted in seconds, so we moved to a different corner and he says, "We better call it a night. I got an early one in the morning. Lenny McLean's just rung me and I've got to shoot down to London to sort some stuff out." I remember Lenny and Gary going on a few debt collections together. Can you imagine it, with them pair knocking on your door? They were both over six foot, weighing twenty stone, with big moustaches at that time and looked as if they'd been separated at birth. Just their look alone would scare most people. I can guarantee you one thing, wherever they went, people paid up straight away.

'A few people tried to get a fight on between Gary Spiers and Lenny but both men had so much respect for each other, they agreed not to fight.

'This one time Gary and I were on our way to London for a couple of days to do some close protection for a golfer who was staying in Park Lane. On the way down to the job, Gary said, "We'll nip and see Lenny McLean." Now I'd heard of Lenny and the stories that surrounded him, but I'd never met him. We ends up in the East End of London in this car showroom, there was a Rottweiler tied up at the side. Gary had some business to do with Lenny. I fucked off to get a cup of tea and leave them to it. Basically, if he had problems in our neck of the woods we would sort it out for him and vice versa. Both men then came back and Gary introduced me to Lenny. Straight away, we hit it off, and Lenny started to tell me stories. He and Gary were talking about old debts they'd collected. So there we are in this showroom and Lenny's now telling me about some of the fights he's had, acting them out in the process. His hand speed for his size was astonishing.

'Lenny then said, "You hungry, lads, fancy a bit of food?" Gary and I were both hungry after the travelling, so we didn't turn it down. Lenny took us to this café. Well, I say a café, but I think it was a pie'n'mash shop run by a little family. He ordered us some food and we sat down and chatted. I was only a young lad in my twenties at the time, but Gary had known him for a long time. He started talking about the fight business again as well as other stuff, like the doors. I remember him saying to me, "Always get stuck into people when it goes off and always be super aggressive." This has always stuck in my memory to this day.

'This was the only time I ever met Lenny, and I found him to be a complete gentleman. It was a shame to hear that he had passed away so young and only a few years later, Gary had passed too. The two of them were one-offs taken too soon.'

LEE 'CHUNK' NIGHTINGALE

'I'd known a lot of faces from an early age and they all spoke of this man called Lenny McLean. Lenny's status was legendary between London doormen, and he was a beast of a man on the doors, as you had to be back then. You see, there was no coming second best in that game.

'I spent over ten years myself on the doors with the likes of these beasts. I first started at the age of seventeen at the same club that Lenny used to work, called Camden's in Bethnal Green. Lenny wasn't there when I started but he did come down once to have a word as a doorman had refused his mate entry to the venue. When I say "have a word", what I mean is he shouted so loud, I winced. Lenny grabbed the doorman around the throat and growled at him. Now remember, this was my first night on the door and my first ever meeting with Lenny, and if I'm honest my arsehole twitched a little bit. I was only a pup at the time, I was new to all of this, but I also liked the power he had and the way he put himself forward. I was now seeing the real Lenny as I had only heard stories regarding his reputation up until that day. I even had the pleasure of him coming after me once but that's a different story, and I can laugh about now.

'So anyway, what happened Ant was this, and you've probably had the same yourself working the doors but you always get some plastic gangster you've given a backhander to who's been causing murders, and they would always throw in the "I know so and so, I'll get him down to do you, and so on". Well, in this case I called it the "Lenny card" – he must have had so many fucking people saying that all over London and Essex, and I bet most of them never even knew him.

'Anyway, this one time I was working at a club and I'd been doing the doors for a few years by now, so this bloke came in who was a mate of Lenny's. The bloke was drunk and chinned this other man. So I jumped in to break it up and the bloke threw a punch at me, so I put him on his arse in self-defence. Then this bloke's mates were all standing there, shouting, "You're in trouble now," and yet again the Lenny cards were thrown at me. Like I said, I'd heard it a thousand times.

'We then managed to throw them all out of the club. One of the doormen working with me said, "Lee,

I don't want to scare you but that is one of Lenny's mates." I started having flashbacks to the time when Lenny had the doorman by the throat, but at the end of the day, I was only doing my job and I wasn't being hit by anyone, no matter who they knew.

'Next day I received a call from a mate of mine asking if I knew who had chinned this bloke. My mate was also good mates with Lenny, and Lenny now knew where I worked and was asking questions, so now I knew it was the real deal. I told my mate it was me and the bloke was out of order and had taken a liberty or two. He said he'd go back and explain and have a word with Lenny. The next weekend I was at a family party and my mate was there. All night he kept coming up to me, saying, "Look, Lee, I can't do nothing, mate. He's fuming, and he's coming to see you at the club. Sorry, mate, I can't help you anymore."

'So now I'm thinking, what the fuck do I do? I'm thinking, shit, I'm going to have to have a rumble with The Guv'nor, and to be honest, I don't fancy my chances, and I haven't got a tank at hand to stop him. This was the early nineties and I was probably around twenty-two-ish. At the end of the night I collared my mate and said to him, "Do me a favour, mate. Just have one more word with him and tell him he would have done exactly the same in my shoes." My mate starts laughing loudly and says, "Look, I've spoken to Lenny and he isn't very happy, but he did say that the bloke probably deserved it." I didn't know what to say to my mate, he was a proper wind-up merchant. I can tell you now I nearly fucking danced all the way home!

ON A MEET WITH THE GUV'NOR

'I was at the British bodybuilding championships at Wembley in 1992. Hippodrome doorman Mick Theo, who was competing, wasn't happy with his third place, so he launched his trophy and kicked off. I could hear heavy stamping and shouting, so I looked around and saw this huge lump with a moustache stamping up the stairs, with a blue T-shirt with Mick Theo's name on. I clocked it was Lenny and he was furious. I never saw so many big fellas in one place shrivel so quickly at the sight of Len – Lenny had the ability to adjust some people's sense of their own "toughness" simply by growling at them. It was a good day and something that will always stick in my memories.

'The thing is, if you count the number of people across the country, there was only a few in Lenny's league. There are hardmen everywhere, but I look at Lenny as a different kind of hard. His voice, his face, his hands... just everything about him, he was born to be scary. He was the stuff of legends amongst the fellas on the doors. All I'd add is that he was the last of a dying breed. He knew the streets from the bottom to the top. He was a gentleman when needed, and a machine while going to work. He demanded respect but also gave it. I'm not saying he was a saint, but he had values and he righted a lot of wrongs for people. His name travelled far further than his body could take it. His name will never be forgotten in London, and amongst the circles that still tread the cobbles they will no doubt carry it on for many years to come. I for sure will remember him forever.'

MARK BOWMAN

'I have always indirectly been somehow involved in Britain's gangland, and years ago while corresponding with Peter Gerrard, he had mentioned to me that there were to be two book signings coming up. The first of the book signings was to be held at Dillons on Oxford Street, London, and the second, I was told later, was going to be held at WH Smiths, situated in Liverpool Street Station.

'So, it's the day of the signing. My pal and I have made our way to Dillons and are now waiting in a queue. After a while Lenny arrived on sticks. Listen, Lenny still looked very big, strong and powerful, and he had two pals with him. Now, I wouldn't particularly say that these fellas were Len's minders because why on earth would a man in the late stages of Len's illness require minders, but, in any case, what I will say is they were big fuckers with an air of menace. [Lee has just informed me that they are friends of him and Anthony, called John Houchin, known simply as "The Neck", and Al Crossley, a Britain's Strongest Man competitor.] It was plain to see by the sheer determination on Lenny's face that there was no way on earth that he was ever going to miss a book signing for his fans. So, Lenny got himself sat down, as he staunchly soldiered on through the signings, but you could clearly see how tired he was looking. When it came to mine and my pal's turn, we took the opportunity of having a quick photograph.

'I will never forget Lenny McLean, and even though

I met him in not the best of circumstances, I met him all the same. The man was a solid gold gentleman, even during the pain he must have been going through in the last few days of his life.'

BIG JOE EGAN (TOUGHEST WHITE MAN ON THE PLANET)

Lee: A well-respected name from the boxing scene is Dublin's finest export, actor and speaker 'Big Joe Egan', or as the King of the Ring, Iron Mike Tyson, once nicknamed him after sparring, 'The Toughest White Man on the Planet'. With increasing trepidation I tracked our man down, who was on set, filming with another boxer, Julius Francis.

Joe then goes on to tell me that he had heard the name Lenny McLean and a plethora of tales and stories surrounding this fearsome protagonist for years and years, and of course being Irish, it's par for the course for the likes of 'Big Joe' to be privy to the dark and murky world of bare-knuckle fighting. Anyway, initially, to my dismay Joe informed me that he had only met Lenny the once, in 1982, when Joe was just sixteen years of age and had recently won his fight at The Porter Tun Rooms, Whitbread Brewery in London.

As Joe is stood, being congratulated by friends and family alike, he spots a giant of a man making his way over to him, and to his delight it's none other than The Guv'nor of The Cobbles himself, the man, the legend Lenny McLean. Joe went on to say, 'Lenny put his massive hand out to shake mine, as my hand is engulfed by his giant mitt, and let's face it, even at the tender age of sixteen I was no small fella myself, so much so for that matter I was of such a size that they were pitting me against men at least ten years my senior. Anyway, Lenny said to me in his booming nuts and bolts voice, "You done well there, my son. Keep up the good work, boy," and with that he simply left me to stare in awe as this Hulk-sized figure stepped through the crowd and back to his awaiting entourage of other well-known fighters.'

Joe goes on: 'This meant the world to me, that a fella from that world and stature would take the time out to come over and give me a Lenny The Guv'nor McLean gee-up, as he himself would put it.' He went on to say, 'I am sad to say that I never got the chance to meet Lenny again over the following years, as I had always wished I could have thanked him for giving me those words of encouragement that stayed with me my whole life. Not so much the words, just simply the fact that it was Lenny "Boy" McLean.'

He was also called in to present a show for a successful YouTube channel known as 'Top Boys', featuring Lenny fighting Dave 'Man Mountain' York.

In closing our phone interview, Joe had this to say: 'Lenny "Boy" McLean was a born fighter from undoubted fighting stock, and a man that put himself on offer every waking moment of his fraught and somewhat tortured life to come to the aid of people that didn't have the tools nor wherewithal to keep the not so nice people at bay. Lenny McLean did, and for that reason alone, to me and many of my dear and close friends, he will always be "The Guv'nor". RIP, Legend, from "Big Joe".'

ON A MEET WITH THE GUV'NOR

SAMMY REESON

Former British boxer Sammy Reeson was the first to hold both the British and European cruiserweight titles, and in the May of 1989 he went on to fight for the WBC world title against Puerto Rican Carlos De Leon. This turned out to be only his second defeat in a twenty-six-fight career and his final fight too. Afterwards he turned to collecting scrap metal for a living and dropped out of the boxing world completely.

'The first time I seen Lenny was when I was seventeen at Freddie Hill's gym in Battersea. Lenny came there with his cousin, Johnny Wall. I watched him spar with quite a few people there, including the British and European Middleweight champion, Kevin Finnegan. Lenny never took it lightly and I witnessed some wars there.

'This one day, this geezer got a bit lairy with Lenny and it kicked off big time. Let me tell you this, it took about eight people to get him off that man. A few years later, Lenny went on to fight a good mate of mine named Johnny Clarke, who was a good heavyweight back in the day, and Lenny beat him in the second round with a magnificent uppercut.

'A few times I went up to the Camden Palace I said to my mates, "Let me see if my mate's on the door." Lenny would then spot me and shout, "C'mon, boy, come on through." The last time I saw him was in a café in West Hill, we had a good chat. Len was apparently on his way to Pinewood Studios at the time on some project. A while later I heard that he had passed away and I was gutted. I always found him a very nice fella and he was always good to me.'

DAVE ANDREWS

'Lenny was one awesome man and the nicest and the scariest guy I have ever met. I knew him from Woody's club in South Woodford, back in 1984 – I was about eighteen at the time. He had such a presence but when you spoke to him, he was a good laugh as well.

'One Sunday in Woody's me and three other friends were having a late afternoon drink in there because it was open until 4pm. We were the last ones there and Lenny asked us to drink up as he wanted to go home because his shift was over. He then asked again, and my friend, who was a big chunky six-foot four inch cocky eighteen-year-old, said, "In a minute." Lenny then shouted at the top of his voice, "In a minute, in a fucking minute!" With that, he grabbed the back of his neck and launched the mouthy doughnut out of the place. He then came back to the three of us remaining and said, "You lads are alright, but that fucker gets on my nerves! But drink up now as I do want to go home." So we gracefully downed our drinks, thanked him and got ourselves off double-lively.'

ROBBIE MARTIN

'I first met Lenny when I was a young lad of about thirteen. I was boxing at this local gym one day and my dad and a few of his mates came in. I was getting ready to spar with my mate when my dad introduced me to this one guy who was huge; my dad said, "This is Lenny McLean." I was trying to put some lace-up gloves on by myself when Lenny said, "What the fuck are you doing?" in a very quiet Cockney accent, and being a cheeky little sod, I said, "Piss off, I'm fighting my mate in the ring when I get these on."

'Lenny then got hold of the back of my neck with the world's biggest hand. At the time I must have been about five stone soaking wet and his other hand then held the arse of my tracksuit pants, and he threw me over the top rope into the ring and said, "I'll fucking fight you, you little fucker." So I thought, I better do a good job. When I got out of the ring he just jabbed me on the jaw and smiled. I felt so proud at this. I'm now forty-six years old and live in New Zealand, where I run a gym. The thoughts of the big guy that day have stayed with me forever.'

TONY CAREY

'The first time I met Lenny McLean was around about 1995. I lived in a place called Erith, which is not far from Bexleyheath, where Lenny was living at the time on Avenue Road.

'I used to have a very big cleaning round and had a couple of lads working for me. I remember Lenny's house was derelict and had just been done up. I was near his house, doing some windows, and two of my lads turned up and said that Lenny had moved in and he wants us to clean his windows.

'I walked in and there was this fella who I didn't know from Adam – he was chatting to the two lads who worked for me. Lenny sees me walking through into his conservatory and turns to me and says, "Alright?", and before I know it, he's taken me out into his garden and he wants to show me what he can do. I'm thinking, what's this fella up to? So he starts demonstrating how he fights and mimicking how he would do it. Now I'm six foot five and a big lump, but he's talking to me like a normal man. I was thinking, who is this lunatic? as I laughed to myself. My mate then brought me a cup of tea outside as we continued to chat. Just by looking at him you could see he was a fighter, his size and strength and the way he could turn it on with the snap of a finger.

'After that first meeting I went on to clean his windows once a month. I got to know his wife, Val – I can't begin to tell you how lovely Val was, and she was such a lady too. The house was immaculate; they would have you clean the inside windows as well as the outside. You could see the magic between Val and Lenny; she worshipped him, as of course he did her too.

'Basically, I went there once a month for more than three years and you get chained to people. Every time I went to the house I'd be there for over an hour, drinking tea with Lenny and sometimes Val as well. Lenny took an interest in the window cleaning as he had done it himself when he was young. He would tell me about how he got sacked from cleaning windows and that the bosses were too scared to sack him, and on one occasion they sent the police to tell him instead.

'When we were in his house me and the other lads

would say, "Why don't you come out for a drink with us, Lenny, come and have a few beers?" Cos he was always a good crack and was up for having a laugh. But he told us that he never went out as every time he went out there was always some idiot who would start trouble, that he couldn't even take Val out as he didn't need the nonsense.

'I remember this one time he was well chuffed with himself and said to me, "Did you see me on TV last night?" He had been on *The Knock* and I was gutted that I had missed it. I remember him telling me about the time he went to New York after the Mafia had put up twenty thousand for him to fight, and Lenny had beaten the Mafia's top bareknuckle fighter senseless.

'We were sat in his conservatory one day and Lenny was making us a cup of tea, like he always did. He's then on the phone talking to someone and getting really vicious, then he'd put the phone away and say, "Biscuit, lads?" as if nothing had ever happened.'

CORAL BLACK

'I was born in Hoxton, the same as Lenny. My dad and all my family knew him. When I was little, he was just this big guy to us who everyone knew.

'Growing up, we heard all the stories, like the one when he'd been collecting money around the doors, and he was on the Tube with his mate, Terry Myring, counting out his money. And this guy is watching them, at which point Lenny looks up and clocks this guy watching him. Lenny's then said, "Is there something you want? If you can take it off me, it's yours." The next thing you know, this geezer gets up and walks towards Lenny, Lenny's laid him out and as the doors opened at the next Tube station, Lenny has lifted him up and put him out on the platform and sat back down counting the money as if nothing's happened.

'Lenny used to have a sweet shop in Cherbury Street; I lived opposite in the flats. I used to work there for a few hours on a Sunday for Len's wife, Val, when I was thirteen. Lenny worked there a few times himself; they didn't have it very long. Lenny was lovely to me. He loved kids, and he was a bit of a teddy bear to us – he would spoil us all of the time, giving us free sweets.

'When he worked the door of the Camden, I was a lot older and Lenny would say, "Get in there, come on, quick," as he moved us to the front of the queue and we'd get in for free. He looked out for us in there and always made a fuss of us. He was a big, larger-than-life character.'

RAYMOND LYONS

'My pal Timmy Castles and I are DJs, and in the eighties and nineties we worked in and around London Town. One time, around about 1985, we got a call from a place called Cairo Jacks, up West. The manager wanted the two of us for a private function that had been arranged at his place. We accepted and added it to our diary.

'Anyway, a few nights later, we turn up at this place and starts setting our gear up. The gaffer had said on the phone that as part of our duties we would need to keep anybody out of the place, because of course it was a private function. So with that information, me and Teddy (which was Timmy's nickname) and I are just having a look around when, all of a sudden, from the top of the stairs appears this giant of a fella and he's walking down towards the door of the function. I turns to my pal and goes, "Fucking have a look, Teddy. Look at the size of this c***, he looks like some fucking heavyweight boxer or something!" Then no sooner had I finished my sentence and this massive fucking geezer is parked up right in front of Teddy and myself, and let me tell you, he's that fucking big, he's almost blocking out the light.

'With that, he says to me and my pal, "Here, boys, have you got any change for the fag machine?" So of course, out of sheer fear, both of us are scrambling in our pockets to sort him out with the right change. All done, he's got what he needs, he says, "Cheers, fellas" and walks straight through the function room doors. At this point we're peering through the door, watching nervously as he goes over to the fag machine; he gets his fags and then comes straight back out and goes on his way. But no, it ain't that fucking easy. He does do all of that, but then to mine and Teddy's fear and dread, he just sits himself down in the room that he ain't supposed to be in.

'"Oh for fuck's sake," I says to Teddy, "that c*** ain't allowed in there! You're gonna have to go in and tell him." To which Ted replied, "I'm gonna have to tell him, am I, Ray? Are you fucking mental? What do you think I am, soft in the fucking head or something? He'll fucking murder me, you soft silly c***."

'Ray says, "Well, what the fuck we gonna do? The gaffer will do his fucking nut if we don't ask the fella to leave, but if we do approach this fella, he'll swing us around like a couple of rag dolls. He'll smash us to fucking pieces.'

'Anyway, just as we're about to venture into this suicide mission, the gaffer himself walks down the stairs and says, "Alright, fellas, everything OK?" so I says to him, "No, not really, mate. There's this big fella that's just walked in the function room and we're just about to tell him that he has to leave."

'I points at this fella through the door, showing the gaffer who it is we're referring to, and with that, he's laughing his fucking head off, and he goes, "No, fellas, that's Lenny, he works here. Are you pair fucking mental or what?" I'm thinking to myself, thank fuck for that, I wasn't looking forward to upsetting him one bit. At this point the gaffer calls Lenny over and introduces Ted and I to him. Lenny had a bit of a laugh and a joke with us about the mix-up, and then shook our hands – obviously the size of those huge mitts of his engulfed mine, almost crushing my hand.

'Lenny at that time was limping a little. Lee informs me that he'd been shot prior to this and he hadn't long been out of hospital, having suffered a gangrene infection. I remember someone carelessly knocking into him and Lenny going, "Oh, for fuck's sake, son, watch where you're going!" I also remember Lenny was carrying a magazine of some kind. Anyway, with that he whips it out, flicks through to one of the pages and says to Teddy and I, "Here, my son, who's that?" As he's pointing to a photo of a big fella in the magazine, with a fucking massive moustache, anyway I goes, "I don't know, Lenny, who is it?", and Lenny goes to me, "It's fucking me, you plum! Can't you tell?" Lenny's laughing like fuck at this point, what a diamond of a fella.

'So, a few weeks later, I'm working back at Cairos again at some do, and I'm at the decks, playing some soul, funk and a bit of Motown and that sort of thing. Anyway, when I came offstage, Lenny pulls me over to one side and says, "Here, son, you're the best fucking DJ I've ever heard." I was buzzing with this; it was my claim to fame. Lenny McLean reckons I'm the best DJ around, I was thinking to myself, that'll look good on my posters from now on. I have to be honest, when Lenny's book came out years later, I scanned through it first to see if I'd had even the slightest of mentions from him. Well, I wasn't in Lenny's book as it turns out, but with thanks to Lee and Anthony and this book of theirs, I sort of got my wish in the end.'

MIKE CASEY

'I will start by saying this, I never would profess to my being great pals with Lenny McLean as I only met the man a handful of times. Lenny and his family chose to holiday down Clacton in the mid-eighties, where my mum worked in the camp's reception. I was in the forces at the time, so while on leave from army duties I would spend my time at the camp, keeping my mum company.

'So I'm in the office, chatting to my mum when the door opens and this booming voice from this giant colossus says, "Alright, my son?" to me, and then continues of course with all of the usual McLean patter to my mum: "Hello Doll and how's things for you this fine morning?"

'I never really heard much more as I was still mesmerised by the size of this man. I did, however, catch a little sweet young lady peeking her head round from behind her dad. This, I came to realise later, was his daughter, Kelly. Anyway, Lenny sorted what he needed to sort and then turned and said, "Ta-ta, sweetheart, be lucky" to my mum and left. Anyway, I followed them outside, still in awe at the size of him, and as we got outside there's this fella out there. He's the camp security – Darren, I'm sure he was called. Anyway, he stood there prancing around with his gigantic snarling Rottweiler. We're all in a line and this dog jumps forward, growling. Every one of us jumps back – well, all except our man Lenny. With that, Lenny goes into, like, an Incredible Hulk type of pose, a similar pose I've come to recognise years later while watching him on YouTube before he tore into that gypsy fella. With that, Lenny growls back at this dog like a madman, the dog squirms, whimpers and runs with its tail between its legs and cowers behind its owner. So I guess we know who The Guv'nor is here now, don't we? And I think by now so does this Darren fella, who's gone whiter than driven snow. With that, Lenny walks off as large as life, laughing to himself and singing that song from the Monty Python gang, you know the one, 'Always Look On The Bright Side Of Life'. I'm still laughing thirty years later as I recall this story.

ON A MEET WITH THE GUV'NOR

'Lenny, Val and the kids came down the clubhouse on the odd evening. Kelly followed her dad round like she was attached to him, it was clear to see from afar just how close those two were. Anyway, this one night the bouncers were acting up a bit, a little firm of them, three- or four-handed. I watched as Lenny kept glancing over at them. Remember, these are big powerful fellas too, but of course this means nothing to Lenny, he'd eat them for breakfast without batting an eyelid. Also, you have to understand Lenny is on holiday with his wife and kids, and they don't need to hear all of that sort of profanity, now do they? So all of a sudden, and as cool as a cucumber, Lenny put down his lemonade, walked over to them, whispered a few words in the mouthiest one's ear, tapped him on the head like he was a naughty little schoolboy and walked back to his family, smiling. What Lenny had said to that fella, well, I can only imagine, but believe me whatever it was, it certainly did the trick because they never once raised their voices above a whisper while Len was on camp, not so much as a murmur.

'I spent some time in the small gym down the camp with Lenny. We would just stand in amazement as he put almost every weight in that gym onto the bar and benched it like it was two sticks of fucking candy floss. I still cannot believe it to this day, the man was like King Kong. Also, when he pulled that screwed-up face and started throwing a bunch of combination punches – "Flip, Flip, Flip" he would go with each blow. My arse went like a proper good 'un, like it never had before, or to this day, like it did in that moment. Luckily for us boys, he was just educating us a little as to the speed and power he had in his artillery. To this day I have never seen anyone quicker or more powerful. Listen, the man was a six-foot three-inch, twenty-one-stone powerhouse, with hands like dustbin lids.

As I grew up without a father figure, I like to think those precious times spent in Lenny's company and those educating worldly words that he could just reel off at any given moment were in truth the exact things that I feel I'd missed out on. Well, thanks to Lenny McLean and those sunny days down Clacton Camp, God bless that man, I never did miss out! Because Lenny, you taught me how to be a man amongst men, honourable, loyal and respectful, and for that I am eternally in your debt. Oh, but please don't come to collect it!

'Just to finish, what I would like to say is that on those few occasions, Lenny McLean was one true gentleman and it was an honour to have known him.'

JIMMY BURNS

'I lived in Hackney, East London, and Lenny came out of Hoxton so we lived about a mile apart. I'd always heard his name when I was young and growing up.

'The first time I ever met Lenny was down in his cousin Billy Walls' shop in Kingsland Road. Billy was a proper character, a funny geezer, and the brother of Johnny 'Bootnose' Wall, who used to train and spar with Lenny.

'Anyway, we were into the furniture game at the

time and this other bloke we knocked about with owed Lenny money. So, one day Lenny walks in and smacked the bloke straight across the face, not a punch but a slap. Lenny soon had his money and then Billy introduced me to Lenny, who turned out to be a very funny bloke.

'Another day I was outside Billy's shop and Lenny's walked up to this parking warden, pointing and said, "Listen, son, you can give that car a ticket, this van a ticket, that car a ticket, but see that blue Mercedes? You can't give that a ticket as it's mine, alright?" The warden says, "Alright, mate, no problem, I won't give that one a ticket. Stay as long as you like." Lenny was right in his face, very intimidating but funny.

'Billy was a second-hand furniture dealer but also sold other stuff too. This one day we had sold Lenny this multi-gym, but Billy had lost all the nuts and bolts to it. Well anyway, we had to deliver it over to his house in Bexleyheath and Lenny's said, "Put it in the garage for me, boys," so I've said to Billy, "None of the nuts and bolts are with this, Billy." Billy then replied, laughing, "Don't worry about it, Jimmy, he'll never put it together, it will just gather dust in here." I was thinking, if he goes to put it together and sees stuff is missing, there'll be fucking murders, but thankfully we never heard another word.

'I got talking to Lenny, who also knew my uncle, Tony Burns, who was a top trainer at Repton Boys Club boxing gym. Tony used to bump into Lenny, running around Victoria Park. Lenny would have his little Staff with him training and Tony had a big Alsatian dog. Now Lenny was huge and Tony was a tiny guy but everyone respected Tony because of his Krays' connection – Tony was Reggie Kray's best man at his wedding. So, Tony says to Lenny, "Stop your dog barking at my dog, Len, cos if your dog bites my dog, you know I'll kill it, don't you?" Lenny then bent over and whacked his Staff and said, "Don't bite Tony's dog." Both men were laughing and had total respect for each other.

'Lenny once offered to get my mate out of Wandsworth Prison. He said, "I'll have him out of Wandsworth and into Ford Open Prison." My mate was a huge Greek man, but he just cracked up in Wandsworth. So I said, "Lenny, do us a favour. Can you go and visit him?" Lenny said, "I'll go and see him, son. Better still, how good a mate is he?" I said, "He's a pal, he's a good mate, Len." Lenny said, "If he's that good a mate, give me two grand and I'll have him out of Wandsworth and into Ford in two weeks."

'A few weeks later, he was moved to Ford Open Prison. Lenny also went to visit this geezer at this open prison and the bloke was telling him that this big screw was a bit of a fighter, so Lenny says to the screw, "You're a fighter, are you?" Lenny then went over, messing about, and took a swing and it just missed this screw's face. The speed of the punches going past his face was amazing and the screw's face was a picture.

'I'd taken this bloke over to Pinewood Studios this one time to clear the film set from the *Mission Impossible* film. When we turned up, we didn't have anything on us like paperwork to get in there. We got to the barrier and said, "It's OK, Lenny McLean sent us over, mate." Next thing you know, the barrier went straight up – Lenny's name had a lot of sway.

'Every time I seen Lenny around he would say, "Do you want to borrow any money, son?" all the time – you could rely on him for things like that.

'Another time, Billy and I have gone round Lenny's house and his wife, Val, has let us in. As we were talking, Lenny says, "When I was in prison, I had a really bad toothache." He then starts pointing at his mouth and he says, "Yeah, it was really bad but there was something playing on my mind at the time. The tooth was bad, but I didn't realise how much the pain was because I had that on my mind. Now I've got rid of that thing on my mind I want my toothache back to see how bad it hurt." I looked at him and thought, what the fuck. I said, "Give me a pair of pliers, Len, and I'll pull your tooth out." He leant forward and said, "You go near it, Jimmy, and I'll punch both your fucking lungs in!" I looked at him and he went from being serious to saying, "I'm only joking, son." That's how he was, and every time I saw him, we had a laugh.

'This one time, my father-in-law had a row with this big geezer on his doorstep. The geezer had sprayed my father-in-law in the face with gas. My father-in-law had picked up a wooden elephant from his passage and smashed him over the head with it and he's backed off. Anyway, he's rung me and said I'm having some aggro on the door, so I've flown round there, tooled up, and said, "What the fuck's going on?" Now this bloke was huge and I says to him, "What the fuck's going on? I'll tell you what, mate, hold up, I'll give Lenny a call." He replied, "What, you know

Lenny McLean?" I replied, "Yes, I got his number in my phone." I tell you what, I've never seen a big geezer melt like a snowman in the sun – he fucking shat himself. He said, "Please, mate, don't ring Lenny. Someone sent me round here. Whatever you do, don't ring Lenny, he'll fucking kill me." I told him I was going to ring him and he soon fucked off from there and was never seen again. Everybody knew you didn't fuck about with Lenny. He was a hardman and you knew not to tangle with him.

'It's a shame he passed away so young as he had gone through his life being an East End boy, and fighting and having it hard, and he was such a natural actor. Lenny didn't need to go to stage school. Just look at him in *The Knock*, he was a natural and could have made it big. The man was a true gentleman, who sadly passed away before his time.'

LEON CLARKE

'I only met Lenny the once, in 1980. My brother had a pub called the White Hart in Old Kent Road. This one evening, I was out with my girlfriend and we get up to my brother's pub, but he had popped out. The bar girl then says to me, "Your brother has asked, will you watch his pub until he comes back?" Now I'd never worked in a pub in my life but my girlfriend had some experience and jumped straight into it.

'An hour later, these three fellas walk in and one of them is a fucking giant. I didn't know who they were, I didn't have a clue, but I went up to serve them. I said to them, "Good evening, gents, how can I help you?"

ON A MEET WITH THE GUV'NOR

The big one, who I would find out later was Lenny, says to me, "You must be Leon, you're Les's little brother, aren't you?" I replied, "Yes, I am." I think Lenny had heard about me from my brother and the Scottish accent may have given it away.

'Len then asked me, was my brother about, and I replied, "He's nipped across to see Michael in the Five Bells, but he said he won't be long, although I've been here an hour and there's no sign of him." I then asked them, did they want to wait and did they want a drink?

'I poured them a pint of light and bitter and they had quite a few of them. They were joking and laughing, and chatting up my girlfriend. Lenny was very interested in what Saudi Arabia was like as I'd mentioned that I hadn't long come back from there. All three men were proper gentlemen and were there for a few hours until my brother turned up. None of them looked for any favours and paid their own way. Everyone in the pub knew who Lenny was except for me and my girlfriend. It was then pointed out to me who he was when he left. I was still a bit naïve and asked, "Who is he?", and this bloke said, "That's The Guv'nor." I could see why – he was a big bloke and dressed very smart – the same as his mates – but he had something about him.

'Lenny had gone on to either a nightclub or gambling den with my brother as they ran about in the same circles. We were asked to go with them, but turned it down as we were tired and had been working all day. I found out later in life just who Lenny really was after reading his book, *The Guv'nor*, and I had met him once and witnessed why he had that title.'

THE GUV'NOR REVEALED

JOHN CATHERALL

'I remember Lenny from a young age as I used to live in Cherbury Court in Hoxton and basically, Lenny and Val had a sweet shop near my house. We were kids at the time and I remember him weighing the sweets and effing and blinding. Sometimes if a few of us went in there, messing about, he'd chuck us out.

'I would always get Lenny to serve me as he had these big fuck-off hands, like shovels. Now in them days a scoop would usually get you a quarter, but Lenny would put his hands and you'd get nearly twice as much. Val would be effing and blinding at him, shouting, "Lenny, don't put your hands in, use a scoop." It was like a comedy sketch you'd see off the TV, thinking back to it now.

'This one night, my mate Ray and I went to the Barbican Jovi's nightclub. This was around about 1980. We walked in and Lenny was on the door, he said, "Alright, boys, how's it going? Pay the woman and be good lads." So we pay our money and just as we're going down the stairs, there was this massive bang and the windows have gone in and there's glass everywhere. A few seconds later, Lenny comes flying down the stairs holding his back and knocks the pair of us out of the way. We then went down inside the club. There were a few people in there and we just didn't know what was going on, it was just pandemonium. We then found out when Lenny had his back to the door, two men had showed up on a moped and fired shots, and Lenny had got shot up his arse.

ON A MEET WITH THE GUV'NOR

'I don't think anyone got caught for the shooting and I suppose being a doorman and a fighter in that line of work, Lenny could have upset anyone. Whether he caught up with them or found out who it was, I do not know. He was such a great character and a very hard man and someone you didn't mess with.'

DARREN HUTSON

'I used to box on a Sunday at the Kings Hotel in Seven Kings. They were easy bouts because most of my opponents were drinking lager all day. I remember this one particular fight where I just danced around for about a minute then hit my opponent three times in the gut, sending him down. After I had finished I was at the bar, drinking my orange juice when this big hand slapped down on my shoulder and it was the size of a shovel. I looked up and it was Lenny, and he turned to me and said with a cheeky smile, "You're a clever fucker, aren't you?" He must have been impressed with my performance and it was a precious memory given by a legend.'

PAUL GRANT

Lee: Paul met Lenny McLean in the nineties when he was sixteen and working for a damp proofing company, who were on a job in Lenny's house at 31 Avenue Road, Bexleyheath. He said he was greeted by Val and made to feel welcome; there was a short, older fella there, and after describing him to me, I came to the conclusion that it was probably Lenny's favourite uncle, Fred. This man said to him, 'Here, son, do you know whose house this is?', to which Paul replied, quite puzzled, 'No, I don't, sorry.' Anyway, the man said, 'It's Lenny McLean's house, do you know who Lenny is?', and Paul replied in the same puzzled manner, 'No, sorry, I can't say that I do.' With that, this man gave Paul a quick-fire class in who Lenny was and what he did.

'So, I'm outside round the back of this place, drilling the bottom of the house walls ready for some injecting, and this huge shadow appeared and I turned my head and looked up at this geezer, and this man was bigger than the Hulk. He then said, "Alright, my son? I'm Lenny McLean, this is my house."

'I almost wet myself, I ain't fucking kidding. He was fucking huge; he shook my hand, and his hand was about the size of my head. Val then came out and went, "Here, Len, leave the boy alone," and Lenny goes in that menacing, growling voice, "Don't worry, babe, I'm just making sure he does a proper job." Lenny then just burst out laughing, and goes, "You're alright, boy, I'm only joking with you." With that he walks off into the house, shouting to Valerie, "Do us one of your lovely teas, babe."

'I was chatting to my uncle a little while after working at Lenny and Val's, and I asked him if he knew of Lenny, and my uncle said, "Of course I do, Paul. Everyone knows Lenny McLean, and I'm telling you, the man is a fucking legend."

'My uncle went on to tell me that I had already met Lenny about ten years ago when I was a small boy of about six or seven. I said, "How come?" and my uncle said, "Remember when I used to take you down the Thomas A Becket boxing gym?" and I said, "Yes," and my uncle said, "Yes, well you were shadow boxing in the ring one day, and you shouted Lenny out for a fight." I said to my uncle, 'For fuck's sake, I'm glad I was just a little kid saying that to him! Fucking hell, can you imagine? By the way, what did Lenny say?" My uncle said, "Nothing, Paul, he was too busy laughing."

'I spent about a week at the McLean residence and they were the nicest people you could ever wish to meet. By the end of my time there, I almost felt like one of the family, they were just so nice and welcoming.'

NORMAN BUCKLAND

Norman is another well-respected hardman, who has also earned the name 'Guv'nor', in and out of the ring. He's another doorman and ex-boxer like Lenny, who picked the 'Guv'nor' title up in the ring and is now trying his hand in the movie world – the same as our Lenny would have done. Norman took some time out of his busy schedule to say these few kind words.

'Lenny McLean was one big, strong, powerful man. I bumped into him a few times while working. I was once working for Star guard security, minding this man called Vic. It was at one of the rock star Prince's concerts at Wembley Arena and we had access to all areas but the security started to large up to me, so I gave them a good telling-off. The next night the security got Lenny in; he didn't speak to me but just stared. That stare alone was enough to turn most men into concrete – I was nice to them after that.

'It's hard, being a doorman – I've done it all of my life – and especially where Lenny worked in the West End. He was one hard bastard and very intimidating, the man could win most fights with a simple look. I used his look a few times, and it fucking worked as well, so let's say that I learnt off the master. I have only good things to say about him.'

To wrap the conversation up, we asked Norman what it felt like to be known as The Guv'nor, to which he replied, 'Listen, boys, I'd fight anyone, anytime, anywhere. I could be sitting on a toilet and someone kicks the door in, and I would still fight them. I was The Guv'nor and it was the best feeling in the world. It was a good feeling, knowing people as respected as Lenny had held that title, and I am honoured to have followed in The Guv'nors' footsteps.'

CHAPTER 16

THE NEXT GENERATION

Three well- respected men from the unlicensed game and other walks of life who crossed paths with Lenny McLean were Roy Shaw, Joey Pyle and Jimmy Tippett. With the three men no longer with us, we managed to get hold of the next generation, their sons, and here's what they had to say about the times they spent with Lenny.

JOEY PYLE JNR

Joey is a very well-known figure in the London area today; he followed in his dad's footsteps and has become a successful promoter of unlicensed boxing shows. Joey Sr's interview with Anthony is featured in his debut book entitled, *The Guv'nor Through the Eyes of Others*. Lee finally managed to track down young Joey, and over many hours of chats, this is what he had to say.

'I first met Lenny at the Camden Palace, back when I was just a young fella of about nineteen. I was out for the night, parked up at the Pally, when Lenny comes over to say hello. So, now me being a cocky little fucker back then, I says to Len, "You do know that I'm with Roy's corner for your fight with him, don't you, Len?" Lenny just laughed, patted me on the head and said, "Right, come in, son, get yourself a drink," and from that day forward, Lenny and I got on fantastic.

'As well you all know, Lenny was a giant of a man, 'is hands were bigger than my fucking head. Lenny just oozed charisma from every pore, and when you were in his company, it sort of brushed off onto you too.

'So, myself and Lenny, we're walking along Trafalgar Square one afternoon, and you know how busy that fucking place is. Anyway, we're just about to cross the busy road and I'm stood over by the traffic lights, waiting to press the button. Len shouts, "Here, Joey, what you fucking about at? Get yourself over here, son!"

'So, I've ran over to Len, and with that he just sticks his massive arm in the air with one finger up – you know like he used to go "Bosh" as he pointed up towards the sky. So, with that, he's stepped out in front of the fleet of buses, and in that terrifying, booming fucking voice of his, he's shouting to the traffic, "Fucking hold up, you c***s, Lenny's crossing!" and he walks right across the middle of the busy road. The cabbies and buses and every fucker have stopped in their tracks, nobody dares move. I swear, as true as you see me sitting here right now, it was like Moses, and the parting of the Red fucking Sea, and when you think about that for a second, it was too: Lenny's parted a Red Sea of fucking London buses. I mean, let's face it, it wasn't just down to the sheer size of the man, it was that fucking gruesome scowling face of his: one little growl and you done as you were told. I mean, who's gonna fucking argue, for fuck's sake? The man was a law unto himself; he was an absolute legend, he really was.

'Len's collected many a debt for me over the years, so many I've lost count, and let me put it this way, there was no one on any planet as intimidating as Lenny paying you a visit. Now that's a fucking scary thought, as I'm sure you'd agree.

'This one time we've hit the pavement to pick up some of my debts, and I have Len behind me in case it goes a little bit boss-eyed. So, I've knocked on this fella's door, the door's open, this fella is a lot bigger than I am. Anyway, he doesn't even see me, he just sees this figure stood growling at the back of me, blocking out the sun. The fella thinks it's a fucking solar eclipse, so anyway, he's gone as pale as you can imagine and he's stuttering and spluttering. If I'm honest, I think he's actually pissed himself, poor fella, but anyway, he owes what he owes, so I've gone to him, "Right, my good man, pay what you owe, and I'm off your plot in seconds. Otherwise, I'll have it away on my toes and this fella behind me will be having a chat with you." Suffice to say, this geezer's ran back into his house, and within seconds, he's back at the door with a roll of fifties in his mitt to pay me. At that point I've simply bid him a good day, and left him to his daily business. By this time, Lenny's back in the room and he's Mr Nice again, whistling as we leave this fella's mansion.

'You see, in my experience, most of the time, Lenny just had to show his presence. It was worth paying his wages for the day just to have him stand over at my motor while I squared off a bit of business with some client. It simply saved me the hassle of the slight chance of any aggro.

So, Len and I are out one sunny afternoon, picking up a few debts as usual, and we turn up at this one fella's place, on a gypsy camp. Anyway, this gypsy fella is at the back of his static caravan, with his hose in his hand, cleaning down his little rockery. Now this fella has given me the runaround the previous week, and Lenny, of course, is aware of this. So anyway, Len wants to put the frighteners on him a bit for fucking me around.

'So, he's walked straight through the back way to him, picks the geezer up with one hand and the hose pipe up in the other. Len's given the fella a backhander and decided to stick the hose pipe down the bloke's throat. With that, the fella is choking – he's laid on his back, his fucking belly is filling up with water, and Len's now trying to pump the poor fella's stomach – it was like something from a cartoon. Len's knocked him spark out, with a Lenny-style backhander, and he's now stretched across the geezer like a paramedic, trying to revive the poor c***. Christ, it was like something from a fucking cartoon!

'It's funny, you know, I've often thought to myself, you imagine yourself sat in your cell in the nick and the door opens, and the screw goes, "Right, here, mate, this is your new cellmate"… Oh, for fuck's sake, I'd be plotting my escape from that point on!'

Lee: Obviously, I asked Joe his honest opinion with regard to Lenny and Roy Shaw – you know, with Joe and his dad being great pals with both men. Joe said he remembers his dad having trouble with those two, especially at social events, where both Lenny and Roy were required to attend.

'My dad used to have Lenny sat on one side of him and Roy sat on the other, and Lenny's going to Roy, "Here, look at this bullet hole in my arse! I bet you ain't got a fucking scar like that," and Roy would retaliate with, "Yeah, I notice it's a scar on the back of you, probably a scar from when you were running away." Dad said he used to be saying to the pair of them, "Oh, for fuck's sake, you two, turn it in and sit the fuck down!" You see, as my dad always said, "It's silly, all of this. I mean, they're both awesome fighters in whatever capacity, just leave it alone." In my opinion, on any given day the result between Lenny and Roy could have gone either way, it would all just depend on which one of them was on top form at that given moment.'

Lee: Funnily enough and for quite some time, there was always talk of a fourth fight for Lenny and Roy. You'd have Len and Roy over Streatham in South London, there would be the press there and a whole bunch of well-known figures and celebs and all that, and there's Roy and Lenny posing for photographs, trying to outdo one another, while all of the time the hype is getting bigger and bigger. Then over the next few weeks, like water to a flame, it's just another piece of history to add to the Lenny and Roy archives. It was never going to happen, we all knew it deep down.

I asked Joe, did he see Lenny at work, minding the Hippodrome and that?

'Oh yeah, on many occasions I would be round the corner, collecting a bit of dough from a few people, and I would pop in the Hippodrome and see Lenny. Lenny and his cousin Johnny "Bootnose" Wall would always be sat in Len's office. I would drop in there and see Len and have a lager or two with him. The place always seemed quite peaceful when I went in, Lenny would see to that. This one night, though, I was stood waiting to chat to Lenny outside the Hippodrome and this fella's giving Len a bit of earache. With that, Lenny's just gone "bosh" and clumped the geezer just with, like, an open-handed slap, sending the fella flying over the bonnet of a car, and the fella's obviously thought to himself, fuck that, I'm off, and he's legged it up the Charing Cross Road. Obviously, the fella simply thought to himself, if that was just a slap, fuck getting a proper smack off the big c***!

'Another time, while we were on a debt, I just stepped from the car and Lenny's give this fella a fucking blinder of a belt to his stomach, and the geezer's projectile vomited all over my fucking brand new suit and shoes, and all inside my new motor! To be honest, I think that Lenny had it in for this fella as soon as he's seen him, cos he was a "sovereign boy" as Lenny used to call them. He fucking hated those sorts of fellas, he'd say, "Look at these fucking lot of sovereign boys, all fucking harry dash! They don't know fuck all about real life, the no-value c***s!" Yeah, he wasn't one to suffer fools, old Lenny.'

Lee: Joe would often pop in Len's house, either to pick Lenny up for a bit of work or just to visit for a chat. He dropped in one particular day and Len does the usual and shouts to Val to make him a cuppa. With that, Val shouts, "Do you want any biscuits, Joe?" and Joe says he shouted back, "Yeah, you got any ginger nuts, Val?" and as he's turned around, there's Kelly, the sweet little carrot top, stood with her hands on her hips, staring at him, sort of going, "Fucking gingers, you taking the fucking piss?"

'Everyone just starts laughing. Me and my fucking big gob! Glad I didn't ask for garibaldi fucking biscuits, especially with Lenny going a bit thin on top at that time.

'Jokes aside, Lenny was one diamond of a geezer. Obviously, I'm aware of all of the charity stuff Lenny organised for quite a number of unfortunate people. I had shares in Lenny's pub, The Guv'ners, along with Charlie Kray, and Len would often be running charity nights for this and that. You see, Lenny would never see you go short. I mean, when my dad was away, doing his long stretch on a cat A, Lenny would often pop round to see us and he never left the house without bunging my mum a few hundred quid. He was just like that, Lenny. People are so quick to dig the man out, and it's very refreshing that the likes of you and Anthony are around to document the honest, kind and generous side of the man. I will add this for the record, Lenny was never a bully. The only people that ever threw that bullshit around about Lenny were people that he'd had to give a clump to, or maybe a telling-off and a quick growl for doing something that required him to step in. Let's face it, no one said anything bad about him when he was alive. That says it all in my eyes.'

JIMMY TIPPETT JNR

Anthony: I first met young Jimmy over thirteen years ago when he told me various stories about Lenny. I lost touch with him and then through Facebook we were back in touch. An interview was arranged but due to certain circumstances, Jimmy ended up in jail. I was then contacted by a woman named Susan Walsh, saying Jimmy was in HMP High Down and wanted my address so he could send a write-up. Jimmy then got out a few months later and finally had his autobiography, *Born Gangster*, released. Here's what he had to say about the times he met Lenny McLean.

'I knew Lenny McLean through my dad, Jimmy Tippett Snr, who was a famous boxer in the forties and fifties, and also a regular up the Thomas A Becket gym in the Old Kent Road. Whenever I saw Lenny he would always make time and rub my head with his massive hands and say, "Hello little Jim, right, Jimbo, let's do a little shadow boxing. We all work out up here, no slouching around. Now come and put some gloves on and come and punch this bag."

He would then turn to my dad and give him a wink and a grin.

'I remember seeing Lenny at a few boxing shows my dad and Eddie Richardson put on at the Yorkshire Grey pub in Eltham. Lenny would always come over and praise me up. I remember him pointing at me one day and telling my dad, "See this one, he's going to be a world champion one day." Lenny would always make you feel a million dollars, even at a young age.

'When I first went up the West End clubbing when I was seventeen, my dad would say, "Pop into Stringfellows or better still, pop in and see Lenny at the Hippodrome," which was London's best club at the time, "and he will sort you out." I then went up there with a few of my pals, Elliot, Marius and Lamy. I remember walking up the steps of the main doors and asking two giant stern-faced doormen in dickie bows, long Crombie overcoats and padded knuckle gloves, "Was Lenny there, please?" The one growls at me and said, "Who wants to know?" I then replied, "Can you tell him it's Jimmy Tippett's boy here." Literally a few seconds later, Lenny comes charging through, dismissing the two big lumps on the door. He looked immaculate as ever, in a Prince of Wales check double-breasted suit. Lenny then said, "Hello Jimbo, come on in." He then gently pulled me in through the crowd to the VIP bar.

'Lenny then said, "How's the old man, did he tell you to pop in and see me?" Larger than life, he then called over to a pretty blonde waitress to bring a bottle of bubbly over for his friend's son and his pals. My friends were all open-mouthed in awe of how I was being treated by the big man. Lenny was a total gentleman and said, "I'll keep an eye on you, Jimbo. Don't pay for nothing, just say you're big Len's guest, alright?" He then gave me a big wink as he left us with the free reins of London's hottest night spot.

'Much later, and a little worse for wear on the bucketloads of champagne we were given free of charge, my friends who were older than me got involved in a heated argument with a group of drunk blokes. Lenny was there like lightning. He then said, "Jimbo, you stay with me, your mates are going to get you in trouble. Imagine what your dad would say." He then starts shouting at my mates, "Right, you lot, now fuck off! You're old enough to know better!" I could have died and I felt so embarrassed as they had come up with me.

'A little while later Lenny said, "Come on, Jimbo, I'll take you home. It will make me feel better, knowing you got home safe." We walked along to Shaftesbury Avenue; all the cars were beeping, people shouting out of the windows, "Alright, Len?" We then walked to the NCP car park in China Town and walked down the sloped circular ramp until we came to the level Len's car was on. As we walked towards a black Ford Granada Scorpion Lenny pushed the button on his key ring, opening the doors and making the interior light come on. He then says, "Posh, aren't I, young Jim?" as he chuckled to himself. Then he made me put my seat belt on. I remember thinking to myself, I wish I hadn't gone to the bloody Hippodrome now, my friends have been thrown out and now I'm being taken home like a naughty schoolboy, but that is what a gentleman he was, proper old school. Lenny also looked after my sister Carrie the same way when she was in town.

'On the way home that night we stopped off for a steak and chips at some late night kebab house he knew of. He then took me back home to my parents' house called Three Gables, which was a huge mock Tudor house in Keston, just outside Bromley (known as the Beverly Hills of Kent). As we drove through the gates into the drive Lenny said, "Look at that Merc and that Jeep, it's the size of a house!" The old man has had it right off, touching his nose, giving me another wink. The lights went on and my dad came out, a bit worse for wear, as he'd been out on his Friday night drink with the chaps. He called Lenny in and said to me, "Put the kettle on, son" as he and Lenny embraced at the door before walking through into the kitchen diner. They then sat down laughing over something or other. Lenny then says, "He came in, Jim, with some scallywags so I brought him home because I couldn't have him getting into aggro." My Rottweiler, Tara, came in and started growling at Lenny. Len then patted her head and said, "Nice little puppy." I thought to myself, laughing, she's ten stone and two years old.

'I once saw Lenny when I was training for an unlicensed fight at his pal Reggie Parker's and he was watching over me with a glint in his eye. Another time I was fighting top of the bill in Ilford. I'd knocked my opponent down and through the ropes in the second round and Lenny jumped up, all excited, punching his hands in the air. I looked at the video a few years back and it looks as if Lenny is in the ring himself and jumping out of his ringside seat as I hit the man down.

'A funny story regarding Lenny I recall was when he was looking after this so-called face in the late eighties and he went to Scotland with him to collect a debt. The guy messed Lenny about and didn't stop putting his name up, so in the end Lenny took two gold Rolex watches encrusted with diamonds on the preference of selling them. The guy was cako bako [red-hot] and thought he was a big-time gangster, and would tell anyone who listened how big Lenny was for taking the watches.

'I happened to be in the face's house one day when I noticed a huge picture in an expensive frame of him and Lenny in matching suits like Danny DeVito and Arnold Schwarzenegger out of the film *Twins*. I said to him, "Why do you say bad things about Lenny but have that photo on display in a huge glass cabinet?" The man went bright red and changed the subject pretty sharpish. The same so-called face had the *Long Good Friday* theme tune taped over and over on the cassette in his car, which he played over and over in his Jaguar XJS convertible.

'When Lenny was dying, he went on the *Richard Littlejohn Show* with a walking stick. Me and my dad were watching it and Dad then says to me, "See Lenny there, son, he's dying and he's walked out and said, 'I came into the world fighting, and I will go out of this world fighting,' that's a real man, Jim," and I couldn't agree more.

'My late dad is very well known and respected in the same game as Lenny although different generations. Lenny had the utmost respect for my dad and Lenny always looked out for me and my sister when we went out.

'A true modern-day warrior who was fearless until the end and that describes Lenny perfectly.'

GARY SHAW

'The first time I met Lenny McLean was just after he had beaten my dad, Roy "Pretty Boy" Shaw, for the first time. As most of you will know, my dad had of course beaten Lenny in their first fight, and this was set to be the first of two re-matches.

'Funny with Lenny because I was only about twelve years old at the time and at that age, older people never seemed to give you the time of day. This wasn't at all true with Lenny, he had all the time in the world for kids and always made a point of talking to me. This for me was very honourable given who my dad was, especially with their greatly documented rivalry.

'Now I'm not saying for one minute that there wasn't a certain amount of angst between the two of them, but let me tell you this, most of it was just a media pantomime. Look, my dad and Len weren't having a love affair, but they had mutual respect, and that's a fact. With regard to those three legendary fights they had, this is basically what my dad said to me, and this would always be my final word on the subject.

'In their first meet at Cinatra's Nightclub in Croydon on 23 May 1977, my dad said he went hammer and tongues at Len, and Lenny was on the backdoor from the first bell. Dad just went into him, smashing him.

Lenny's lack of confidence soon became apparent and he beat him hands down.

'There were some murders going on from both camps in the second fight again at Cinatra's, on 10 April 1978. My dad always claimed that it was down to the "ginseng", as most of you will know. This I couldn't comment on, because it was my dad's word.

'Their third and final fight, held just a few months later at the Rainbow Theatre, Finsbury Park on 11 September 1978, was very straightforward, and my dad was always very frank about this . Dad said that Lenny simply walked straight through him, and beat him fair and square – there was nothing he could do. My dad was a very proud man, as was Lenny, and he was left with a bitter taste in his mouth from his losses with Len.

'In all honesty, if my dad would have been asked to fight Lenny when he was hundred years old, not out of his feelings towards Lenny, just out of pride, then yes, he would have taken on the challenge. That was just my dad's way. Like I said, he was a very proud man. Many people over the years tried to wind my dad up, and despicably, none more than in his last few years on this earth, at a time when he had Alzheimer's. People tried to wind him up all over the place, of which I managed to put a block on most of it, but obviously, I couldn't be there all of the time.

'I went with my dad on a few shoots that he was featuring in for TV and papers and that, and Lenny was there for the same thing. My dad and Len were always quite amicable, no matter what you've read. Now I apologise if that chips away at the media myth, but like I said, a lot of it was just propaganda, and let's face it, it built up an enormous amount of notoriety that done my father and Lenny the world of good.'

Lee: I asked Gary to elaborate a little more on his dad and Lenny's attitudes to each other while in the same company and he had this to say.

'Like I said earlier, a lot of it was for the cameras. One time we were on some shoot for a Danny Baker show and Lenny was there filming too. Anyway, afterwards we all went back to Lenny's pub, The Guv'nors, and had some free drinks and a laugh and joke. I always found this funny, like I said, that we're all there in Len's pub. Anyway, the door flings open and this fella walks in, large as life, with two big fucking minders in tow. Now this place is packed to the rafters with Britain's finest gangsters and villains. Add to that mix that it's Lenny's pub, and Lenny and my dad are there. Two of the most feared fellas on the planet, and Lenny probably had a laugh about that one.'

Lee: Last time Gary happened to see Lenny was in Clacton, Essex. Gary said that he was in a chip shop and he spotted Len, who must've been down there holidaying with his family. Anyway, Gary walks over to Lenny and goes, 'Alright, Lenny?' He says Lenny sort of looked down at him with that growly face he used to do, and said to Gary, 'Sorry, son, do I know you?' And Gary said, 'Yeah, Lenny, I'm Roy Shaw's son, Gary.' With that, Lenny goes to him, 'Fuck sake, boy, you ain't like your dad, are you?'

Anyway, they had a laugh and a joke, and with that,

Lenny invited Gary along to his caravan for a cuppa tea and a chat. Gary couldn't make it, unfortunately, as he was just leaving Clacton to go home. I asked him for his opinion on his father not attending Lenny's funeral and he said the following.

> 'It was more out of respect for the McLean family. Dad had wanted to go, but in chats with the late Joey Pyle, they came to the conclusion that it would be more respectful for him not to attend. Roy did say though that with something as sensitive as a funeral, the choice he made would never have been the right choice in some people's eyes.'

Lee: I finished off by saying to Gary, 'Eh, mate, some people just love to stoke the smouldering fire.' Gary finished off by saying, 'When all's said and done, my dad and Lenny done very well for themselves and made the best of the whole situation.'

That closing statement I could not agree with more.

JAMIE MCLEAN

Last but not least, who better to wrap this chapter up than none other than The Guv'nor's son himself? In what had been a very busy year for him with the release of the documentary, *The Guv'nor*, and the brand new movie, *My Name is Lenny*, on the horizon, we managed to get a few words from him in his busy schedule.

> 'Lenny McLean, what does that name mean to you? Why is he such a fascination to so many people? He

never won the heavyweight championship of the world, or an Oscar and yet he was idolised by millions. I believe the reason for this is quite simple: he was the same as you and I, a man who was never educated but able to achieve great heights in whatever he put his mind to.

'My dad was never given anything, only beatings from his stepfather. However, what he had was the passion and drive to better himself and the strength and determination to fight for everything he ever wanted. Growing up with him wasn't always the easiest because of his conflicted mind, but life in our house was loving and always funny. The love I felt from my mum and dad made me the man I am today.

'My dad loved my mum unconditionally. Though the sad times came after we lost him, we were relieved in a way that he went before her. Because although he was so young, my dad simply couldn't have faced life without his soulmate and my lovely mum, as they really and truly were forever in love.

'I often wonder what he would be like now. His violent life was something he hated and it was like a weight around his neck. As you all know, his acting career was just about to take off and in the next heartbeat, he was taken from us. He would have loved to have been the centre of attention for all of the right reasons, and for the things that he had achieved.

'I'm not sure how he would have coped with social media as he really was an old-school kind of fella, in as much as if you had something to say to someone or to criticise, it should be done face to face. He would have called trolls, as we know them, cowards and slags.

THE GUV'NOR REVEALED

'I've always been pretty silent about my dad over the years as I have nothing to prove. However, I always knew it was his absolute ambition to see a film about himself made. Any archive interview over the last twenty years can testify to that as he talks about it numerous times.

'It has been an honour, as his son, to finally make my dad's dream come true by not only making the documentary, *The Guv'nor*, but the forthcoming British film, *My Name Is Lenny*. The film is a one-off, just like my dad. He died with friends and family who truly loved him then, and still do to this day. I love you, Dad. My dad, Lenny McLean, The Guv'nor.'

CONCLUSION:
A LEGACY SET IN STONE

I t's now January 2017 as we wrap up this manuscript, and between the two of us face the difficult task of downsizing our carefully collected 140,000 words to 100,000, taking into account that we are still being contacted with stories from all paths Lenny crossed in his short but amazingly colourful life.

We have travelled thousands of miles on our journey to meet numerous people who all had a story to share and made countless phone calls to people, some of whom we now class as good friends.

A big thank you must go out to our partners, Anne-Marie Thomas and Julie Gant, and Lee's daughter, Ellie-May Wortley, for putting up with our hours of conversations daily. We have bounced so well off each other in writing this book that we have both agreed to continue our partnership in the future and work on more books down the line, and I think you'll all agree that at some stage there will be another Lenny book from us both. We are both extremely proud that we have kept this going for the past twenty years and will continue to keep spreading the word as the train gathers more steam in this rollercoaster ride.

One person who also needs mentioning is the late Valerie McLean. While writing his first book, Anthony spent numerous hours on the phone to her. Val never held back if she had something to say and had him laughing various times. If it wasn't for this woman we do believe we wouldn't be writing now. In our eyes, she was The Guv'nor, whatever others may think, and we're sure others will say the same, and her giving Anthony her blessing to do his book kept him going when he was close to calling it a day. After that book was published Val passed away, on 18 December 2007, but her children live on, which takes us to Kelly. We both agreed it meant the world to us to have her backing on this book dedicated to her father. With the book now in the can, Anthony continues to run his Facebook page and Lee has also joined forces, running a page with Kelly called Dedicated to My Dad The Guv'nor, as well as helping her with her new book, *My Dad, The Guv'nor*. Lee has been like a father figure to Kelly and has guided her in a way that he feels Lenny might have done, had he not been taken so early in his life.

We believe Lenny's stories will go on forever and his legacy is set in stone. There was nothing more he wanted than to see his name in lights, something he tried so hard to accomplish in his own lifetime, and by the time you're reading this, his son Jamie's new film, *My Name is Lenny*, should be out and hopefully a box-office success.

Just to finish up, it's a 'fucking obsession', of which we

cannot deny. We are, and remain, somewhat obsessed in some degree with the extreme fighting unit that was Leonard John McLean. Lenny was a man with the charismatic edge only ever seen in a Hollywood film star, or maybe the odd pop and rock star. At that time to us he was the God of the Fighting World, not the boxing world, the fighting world, and in our many years of research this myth has become a reality. So, let us take a second to analyse the reasons for this fact.

Lenny McLean was to all intents and purposes simply a 'club bouncer', 'a doorman', so I think you will all agree with us when we say this. For us, a man living in the East End of London as a 'bouncer', working to earn a crust for his family and who built up such a reputation that it spread to the far corners of the globe just had to be something special. And as we researched and interviewed most of the people for this book, it became plain to see why this man, alone and unaided, became the stuff of legends, and without doubt the absolute personification of what is now known as 'The Guv'nor'.